PENGUIN BOOKS
THE CALCUTTA COOKBOOK

Minakshie Das Gupta's flair for cooking and culinary skills were hereditary. Her grandmother and mother are still remembered as great cooks. She had her first cooking lessons in her mother's kitchen in Calcutta when she was knee-high. Her much-acclaimed book, *Bangla Ranna* was the first collection of Bengali and Anglo-Indian recipes presented in a scientific format. She died in 1994 and *The Calcutta Cookbook* was the culmination of a lifetime of interest in food from all over the world, particularly from Calcutta where she was born.

*

Bunny Gupta and Jaya Chaliha are free-lance journalists and writers. Bunny is also a teacher and an innovative cook. Jaya works with craftspersons and underpriviledged women and children. They have been writing together for over a decade. They enjoy and love the cosmopolitan flavour of Calcutta.

The Calcutta Cookbook

A Treasury of over 200 Recipes
from Pavement to Palace

Minakshie Das Gupta
Bunny Gupta
Jaya Chaliha

Illustrations by Utpal Basu

PENGUIN BOOKS

PENGUIN BOOKS
Published by the Penguin Group
Penguin Books India Pvt. Ltd, 11 Community Centre, Panchsheel Park,
New Delhi 110 017, India
Penguin Group (USA) Inc., 375 Hudson Street, New York, New York 10014,
USA
Penguin Group (Canada), 90 Eglinton Avenue East, Suite 700, Toronto,
Ontario, M4P 2Y3, Canada (a division of Pearson Penguin Canada Inc.)
Penguin Books Ltd, 80 Strand, London WC2R 0RL, England
Penguin Ireland, 25 St Stephen's Green, Dublin 2, Ireland (a division of Penguin
Books Ltd)
Penguin Group (Australia), 250 Camberwell Road, Camberwell, Victoria
3124, Australia (a division of Pearson Australia Group Pty Ltd)
Penguin Group (NZ), 67 Apollo Drive, Rosedale, Auckland 0632, New Zealand
(a division of Pearson New Zealand Ltd)
Penguin Group (South Africa) (Pty) Ltd, 24 Sturdee Avenue, Rosebank,
Johannesburg 2196, South Africa

Penguin Books Ltd, Registered Offices: 80 Strand, London WC2R 0RL,
England

First published by Penguin Books India 1995

25 24 23 22 21 20

ISBN 9780140469721

Typeset in New Cenury Schoolbook by Digital Tchnologies and Printing Solutions,
New Delhi
Printed at Shri Krishna Printers, Noida

Contents

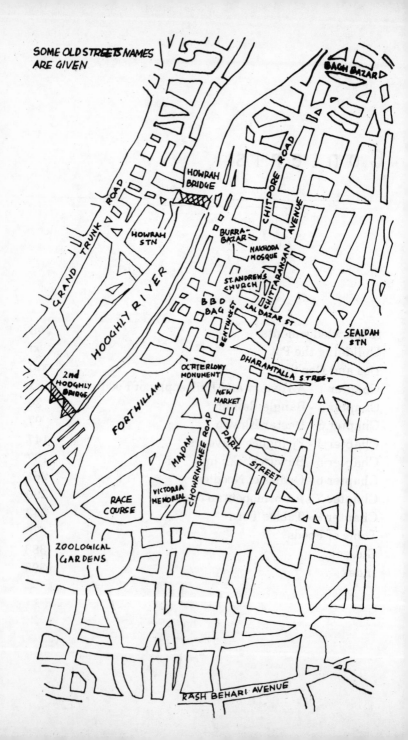

Acknowlegements

We thank the beautiful people of Calcutta who have contributed to much of the contents of our book.

Dr K. T. Achaya
Sheikh Naqbul Ahmed
Mrs M. P. Birla
Mr Anil Banerjee
Mrs Atoshi Barua
Mr Pranab Basu
Mrs Rekha Basu
Dr Natalia Bieck
Ms Joyoti Chaliha
Mr Indrajit Chaliha
Mr Sachin Chaudhuri (late)
Mrs Seeta Chaudhuri
Mrs Reena Chandiramani
Dr Hiralal Chopra (late)
Ms M. Daryani
Mr Naren C. Das (late)
Shri Netai Das
Ms Swarupa Das
Mrs Namita Das Gupta
Mrs Hansa Kumari Dev Burman
Dr Meelie Deb Roy
Mr Tapan Desai

Mrs Manjula Duggar
Dr Geraldine H. Forbes
Mrs Sara Gangjee
Mrs Flora Gubbay
Mrs Arundhati Gupta
Mr Jayaditya Gupta
Mr Rajib Gupta
Mrs Penny Jacob
Sm Gunwati Devi Jain
Mr A. C. Kar
Mrs Krishna Khaitan
Mr Sudesh K. Khullar
Mrs Eunice King
Maharajkumari Karuna Devi of Burdwan
Mrs Gouri Lahiri
Dr D. K. Lahiri Choudhury
Dr Sheila Lahiri Choudhury
Mr Chatu Lalwani
Mrs Kitty Madan
Dr Pranay Chand Mahtab
Begum Naseem Ara Mirza
Mr Humayun Mirza
Mrs Aditi Mukerjea
Mr Norman Nahoum
Mrs Rubee Noor and family
Mrs Zarina Patherya
Mrs Niloo Parshad
Mrs Amita Prasad
Mrs Lalo Puri
Mrs Ann Rodrigues
Mr Abdus Salam
Sm Saraswati
Mr Aditinath Sarkar
Dr Geeti Sen
Mrs Samarpita Sen Gupta
Shri Kanhaiya Lal Sethia
Sahabzada M. M. Alam Shah
Mrs Reshma Shah

Pandit Gaurinath Shastri (late)
Begum Sherbanoo
Mrs Flower Silliman
Mrs Tara Sinha
Mrs Laura Sykes
Mrs Shirin Tata
Mrs Mithoo Vacha
Mrs Paromita Viswanathan
Professor N. Viswanathan

FOR RECIPES

Amber Restaurant, Waterloo Street, Calcutta
Mr Durgapada Barik
Mrs Pia P. Barve
Mrs Yolanda Beale
Ms Mona Benham
Sofia Bibi
Mrs Parul Bose (late)
Renuka Devi Choudhurani (late)
Ms Rakhi Das Gupta
Ms Rosie David
Mr Ananta Charan Das
Mrs Renukana Das Gupta (late)
Mrs Caroline Fernandes
Mrs Lydia Fernandes
Mrs Shantilata Ghosh (late)
Mrs Sohinder Grewal
Mrs Hazel Gupta
Mrs Suraiya Gupta
Lt. Col. Hamilton
Begum Jani of Avadh
Begum Unaiza Khan Chowdhury
Mrs Chandra Lalwani
Mrs Rupa Mitra
Mr S. K. Mitra
Mrs Anisa Naidu and Nathu
Members, Nari Seva Sangha

Mrs Radhika Neelakanthan
Mrs Sita Pasricha (late)
Puniya Devi
Mrs Sudha Ray (late)
Mrs Arati Sengupta
Mr Abdool Shakoor (late)
Mrs Ranjana Shivram
Mr N. A. Siddiqi
Mr Zacharia, Executive Chef, Taj Bengal, Calcutta

Unlidding
the Pot

The Calcutta Cookbook is more
than a cookbook. It is a culinary
chronicle of travellers and traders,
many of whom built the city of
Calcutta and its distinctive
cuisines.

For the first time, recipes
from the Bay of Biscay to the
China Sea and from Central Asia
and Tibet to Sri Lanka, have been
tasted, tried and collected in a
golden treasury for the cook and
the collector.

We have found a wealth of
legends and archival material
that go back to ancient times. We
have returned to the present via
oral history, true life stories and
personal diaries and notebooks.

We have had the privilege of
talking to the elders in different
groups in our city about their food
philosophy and habits. We have

enjoyed their hospitality, savouring an invasion of flavours from Arabia, Afghanistan, Europe, China, Tibet and from nearer home.

Many of the recipes in the book are family secrets from the kitchens of Calcuttans. Armenian, Jewish and Portuguese recipes come with a distinctive Calcutta flavour as do others. Sometimes our attention has been drawn to local substitutes such as crayfish for lobster and molasses for demerara sugar. Often the original ingredient has been forgotten and a new dish created. Prawn temperado is malai curry in some homes.

The manner of presenting these recipes may appear awkward. We request you to bear in mind that these are often experiments by countless men and women whose experiences, in the bazaar and the kitchen, have been recorded as faithfully as practicable for you to try them out in the same spirit. We hope you will be able to cook them without much difficulty. Wherever the cuisine originated, there were limitations of local meats and vegetables, oils and herbs. If you are at a loss for the prescribed ingredient, let your imagination find a substitute and invent a new recipe for the cooking pot.

We have tried to make the book readable from the first page to the last and therefore you will find departures from conventional styles. Another consideration in the difficult task of choosing the recipes has been with a view to preparing a meal with dishes from one chapter or a medley from many. We have planned this menu: Chinese chicken corn soup, bawarchee's smoked fish and the American coleslaw, Jewish mahashash, moghlai shami kebabs ending with the perennial Bengali speciality, mishti doi or mango or tipari (gooseberry) fool in season.

We thank David Davidar, Renuka Chatterjee and Anubha C. Doyle, our publisher and editors for helping us through the teething troubles of this book with infinite patience and understanding.

Calcutta
Poila Baisak, 1401 Bangabda

Dos and Don'ts

There are a few basic ground rules for using the recipes in this book.

- Wash rice and leafy vegetables several times before putting them in the pot.
- For a perfect pot of rice, add half a teaspoon of salt to the water before it comes to the boil and allow to simmer for half an hour. A few drops of lime juice added during the cooking helps to keep the grains firm.
- Remove the scum rising to the top of the pot while boiling rice or dal.
- Heat the oil to smoking before adding the tempering or phoron and immediately lower the heat to prevent

burning. Cover the dish after the phoron has been added to get the full flavour of the spices.

- Add hot water to gravy to enhance the flavour.
- Cook vegetables on low heat and avoid adding water, if possible.
- The cooking medium for all the dishes in this book is refined vegetable oil unless otherwise specified.
- Spices mentioned in recipes, including turmeric, are used powdered unless otherwise specified.
- Use glass or ceramic dishes for marinating.

The cooking pots of Calcutta have a personality and cannot be standardized. Some temper their cooking in the beginning, others reserve it for the end. Some add sugar to their dals, others would not dream of doing so. We have tried to take the middle path to suit every palate.

The measurements used are basic:

1 cup is 250 grams
1 teaspoon (tsp) is 5 grams
1 tablespoon (tbsp) is 10 grams
1 egg cup is ¼ cup or 3 tablespoons
Dessertspoon has been explained in Mona Benham's recipe for Fowl Curry Koormah in Chapter 5. 1 dessertspoon is equal to 1 tablespoon as in the text. Mona Benham uses tablespoon to mean a larger spoon, normally used for serving, equal to 2 dessertspoons.
handhot is 100° F, 36° C

In the modern kitchen, the grinding stone has been replaced by the mixer-grinder.

As with the method, so with the words. Many of the recipes have been collected either verbally or from notebooks. We have tried not to change the wording, so there is a variety of measurements, like 'handful', and temperatures, like 'handhot'.

- Read a recipe twice before you start to cook.

Chapter 1

A History and Philosophy of Food

Calcutta's chronicle began on a hot, wet August afternoon in 1690 when a hungry Job Charnock climbed off his ship on to the steps of a muddy ghat (landing stage). Charnock was a rough and ready East India Company factor and the ghat a common architectural feature of India's river-banks. The river was the Hooghly and the place Sutanati, one of the three principal villages which became Calcutta. Sutanati, already a booming cotton yarn market, is still the commercial centre of Calcutta. Once the capital of British India, Calcutta is at present the first city of the eastern state of West Bengal. Just south of the Tropic of Cancer, the metropolis has spread out on either side of the river.

It is said that Charnock

Myths,
Beliefs
and
Rituals

Sahib was served khichuri, a meal of rice and dal cooked together in a terracotta handi (cooking pot), by a flabbergasted villager. The spontaneous sharing of a meal with an unexpected guest is the hospitality so characteristic of the Indian householder. Little did Charnock know that his lunch of khichuri was the gastronomical link through most of India.

There was a time when Calcutta was part of the great Sunderbans bordering the Bay of Bengal, the largest estuarine delta in the world. The inhabitants of this marshy mangrove swamp lived off a diet of the fruits they gathered and the animals they hunted. In ancient times, the hunter's wife dug the earth for arum root, waded the ponds and marshlands for aquatic plants and caught tiny shrimps and molluscs. She took her gatherings home to complement her husband's shikar of mongoose, wild boar, turtle, iguana, hare and porcupine. If lucky, she would barbecue a haunch of deer.

The Bengalis were amongst the foremost maritime people of the subcontinent. They navigated the rivers and seas and caught vast netfuls of fish and crustaceans, the freshwater variety in particular.

Of the wild grasses that grew in profusion, rice was perhaps the only one that yielded a grain fit to eat and was cultivated. We know that lentils were cooked, that sugar cane and coconut were ingredients and that ginger, long pepper, sesame and turmeric were added for their medicinal properties and to titillate the palate. Sesame oil was the cooking medium. Native fruits like the hog plum, the white, yellow, bitter and ridged gourds and yam were favourites.

Then the Aryans arrived from Central Asia. They had invaded northern India in the second millennium BC and reached Bengal much later, after the sixth century BC. They were attracted to the Gangetic-Brahmaputra delta by the fertility of the soil and the regular and abundant monsoon. The Aryans were now ready for empire-building. Our history books tell us that the first 'imperial' formations were in Magadha (modern Bihar). It was only in eastern India, in the rice growing belt, that populations were large enough to support kingdoms which evolved into 'empires'. The Aryans planted and reaped the natural wealth of the fertile land criss-crossed by rivers rich in fish.

They introduced Vedic rituals in the preparation, serving and eating of food. In turn, they fell in love with the tropical fruits—the mango, the jackfruit, the wood apple, the coconut and the ubiquitous banana. With care and artistry, the bounty of southern Bengal was transformed into delectable dishes—sweet and savoury—fit for the gods.

As in many other religions, the central ritual of the Vedic and Brahmanic period was a sacramental meal. Brahmins and Kshatriyas, kings and princes gathered in a formal assembly around the homa (sacrificial fire). The gods were invoked through chants to join them. Agni, the God of Fire carried the food offerings in their subtler form to the rest of the pantheon.

In Hinduism as is often practised today, fruit and flowers, uncooked and cooked food are offered to the gods. It is believed the gods accept the intention behind the offering which is then transformed into prasada—food blessed by the gods—and is shared by the devotees.

The ancient Indian believed that all natural elements united to create food and that all food was sacred. To illustrate this food philosophy, the discovery of food in all things, the virtue of sharing, the sin of hoarding and the celebration of soma (the nectar of immortality), we quote 'Sadamada', a hymn from the Rig Veda, as given in *India International Quarterly* (Vol. 12, No. 2, 1985) from "The Vedic Experience" by Dr Raimundo Panikkar.

My song shall be of Food, producer of strength, through whom the keeper of nectar smote the demon.

O savoury Food, Food of sweetness, you are our chosen for whom we long. Come, be our strong defender!

Come to us, Food our delight, bringing pleasurable
refreshment.

Your flavours, O Food, are spread through space,
high like the breezes they are scattered.

Those who share your sweetness with others are
truly your friends, those who keep your fine taste
to themselves are stiff-necked wretches.

On you, O Food, is fixed the great Gods' desire.
Great deeds are done under your sign, the Serpent
slain.

If you have proceeded on high to the splendour of
the mountain even from there, sweet Food return
for your enjoyment.

From waters and plants we imbibe the choicest
portion. Therefore, O body, thrive, attain full
stature.

We drink you, Soma, brew of milk and barley,
there. Therefore, O body, thrive, attain full
stature.

You herbs and wheaten cakes, be wholesome and
strengthening. Therefore, O body, thrive, attain
full stature.

We sing your praises, O Food. From you we obtain
as butter from a cow, our sacrificial offerings. O
you, convivial feast of gods and men.

Just as man is said to be made up of the three gunas or
qualities which are reflected in his appearance and his
appetites, food too is divided into three kinds. Satvic food is
light, bland, usually vegetarian and white and gold in

colour. The finest rice mixed with ghee (clarified butter), milk and milk products, honey and fruits—fresh and sun-dried—are the foods for ascetics. Rajasic food is gold and red in colour, consists of meat, fish, eggs, wines and beer (in moderation) and are passion-arousing foods suited to kings and warriors. Tamasic food is red and black in colour, consists of flesh of small animals, pork and beef, scaleless fish and food cooked the day before.

The Brahmins at the apex of the socio-religious order are largely vegetarian and eat satvic foods. But the Bengali Brahmin found the flavour of Bengal's sweet water fish irresistible and fell to temptation. To save his position at the top of the ladder, he manipulated the Shastras (book of religious rituals) and 'vegetarianized' the denizens of the deep, calling fish the 'fruit of the ocean'.

Food is also classified into kancha (uncooked and unripe) and paka (cooked and ripe). Anna is the Sanskrit word for rice which when cooked is bhaat in Bengali and is a central fact of Bengali cultural existence.

Dairy products became increasingly a part of the trapper's and gatherer's diet. Paramanna, the first among foods, was the name given to rice and milk boiled together and has been the traditional offering to the gods for thousands of years. Sweetened with iksu (sugar cane), the strength-giving properties of paramanna makes it the auspicious food on important occasions. Popularly called payesh, it is the first solid food a child is offered at the Annaprasanna, the weaning ceremony, celebrating this momentous step from the mother's breast into the arms of a wider world.

We get a vivid picture of the kitchens in medieval Bengali literature collected in the *Mangal Kavyas*. The author, a sixteenth-century poet, Mukundaram Chakravarty's ballads narrate a social history peopled by real and legendary men and women. The woman prepares the anna and therefore a bride is accepted by her new family when they eat the rice prepared and served by her. Chand Saudagar, one of the great gandhabaniks (spice merchants) in *Manasa Mangal*, was looking for a daughter-in-law. The rigorous test to find the perfect match for his son, Lakhindar, is allegorical. The task set for the bride was to render edible lohar kalai (lohar—iron, kalai—lentils) and illustrates the importance of the strength of the woman as much as that of the man as the sustainer and contributor to the moral and material well-being of the clan. Behula, who passed the test, has become the ideal of a good Bengali wife. A woman's culinary activity makes her a participant in the sacrificial aspect in which cooking is closely connected to religion. Preparation of a meal is also linked to the knowledge of kama (desire). A young woman must study the rules of culinary erotica and develop them into an art to win over and keep her husband's attention—a universal feminine strategy. We read somewhere that a wily wife often threw in some dwarf beans, the traditional tonic recommended for potency.

The best compliment paid to a woman who is a good cook is to compare her with Draupadi, wife of the Pandava brothers in the *Mahabharata*. In Bengal, she is the role model for wives and cooks. For, after all, did she not satisfy five husbands and no one was turned away hungry from her kitchen.

The food chain goes on to connect the living with the dead. It is believed that the pindo (food and water) offered by the descendants sustains the spirits of dead ancestors.

The rules of dos and don'ts governing personal cleansliness, pollution of food and when to eat what and in what company were effectively enforced by religious sanctions and celestial occurrences. For example, bathing and changing into clean clothes dried in the wind were prerequisites for the daily puja (worship). Women did not enter the kitchen at all times and before doing so, a head bath was mandatory. Before a solar or lunar eclipse, visible in India, all cooked food is disposed of. During an eclipse, the hearth is not lit. Food, cooked or uncooked, is not eaten. After an eclipse, the kitchen (and its contents), is washed before the cook goes back to work. The reasons given are that in the absence of the main illuminating celestial bodies—the sun and the moon—it is believed that contamination by insects and other harmful bodies may go undetected. The pace of modern city life does not always warrant this practice in Hindu households. But in villages, it is still observed.

In India there has always been an active awareness of the environment. Conservation and preservation was a way of life. Water being the primary need, a king was required to dig dighis (ponds) as one of his claims to fame. The ponds provided potable water, employment, storage in times of drought and a source for irrigation of the paddy fields. The mud extracted in the process was used as building material for the houses.

Food was freshly cooked and served. What was not consumed was given away or fed to the birds. The eating of different kinds of fish was governed by their breeding times. Fruits were allowed to ripen and here again there are many Bengali jingles which children still learn at their mothers' knees, warning of the consequences of eating narkeli kool (Indian plum) before Saraswati Puja (feast of the goddess of learning). The puja marks the coming of spring and the ripening of the fruit.

Calcutta is in the rice bowl that stretches eastwards to China and Japan. The major festivals centre around rice. The goddess Durga's annual visit is the city's biggest festival. She comes riding on a lion with weapons in her ten hands as the protector against evil. Another popular manifestation of Durga is Annapurna or Annada, the giver of food, and is represented with a bowl of rice in her hand. Quite understandably these are two favourite names for the girl child.

There are two kinds of rice depending on the method of dehusking the paddy—aatap or sun-dried and siddha or parboiled rice. Each kind has many varieties known by different names and used for different occasions. Among the sun-dried varieties grown mainly in the adjoining district of Burdwan, are the small-grained scented Kamini, the fragrant Gopalbhog and Gobindobhog. Gopal and Gobindo are affectionate appellations of the god Krishna. Most people are familiar with the long-grained Basmati rice from northern Indian which is used for the best polau. The ancient process of parboiling rice obtained by soaking and steaming the paddy retains the vitamins and micronutrients in the outer layers which are lost in the milling and polishing of sun-dried rice. Among the parboiled varieties, Chamarmoni is prescribed for a weak constitution and Dudhershar is so named because of its creamy colour. Through research a number of hybrid varieties of rice have been developed which are disease resistant, grow fast and are high-yielding. These are unimaginatively given code numbers like IR 5 but the more successful ones have names of girls like Ratna and Padma.

Cooking rice is not as easy as it appears. You do not just add water and boil the mixture. Unless each grain is soft and separate, you have failed the test of a cook in West Bengal.

In Vedic times, dal is mentioned and identified by the word supa, similar to the English word soup. The cook was called supakar which can be taken as an indication of the importance of dal in the diet. Dal is the main source of vegetable protein and can be called the main fringe food or the second staple in the Indian diet. Dal is cooked in many ways and eaten as an accompaniment to rice or breads. Each preparation demands a different sambhar, a combination of whole spices fried in mustard oil or ghee giving this otherwise bland liquid a delicious individuality. Recipes are handed down from mother to daughter giving every bowl of dal its own special flavour.

That food and health are related was a feature in the early civilizations of Egypt, Mesopotamia, Greece, India and China. Dietotherapy was highly developed in the Ayurvedic tradition of healing and came second only to religious observances in the treatment of the sick. Taste sensations were leading indicators in the diagnosis of disease. The ready availability of bottled vitamins and tonics has taken over and become a dietary supplement. In recent times, however, we see a return to naturopathy and herbal treatments in medicines and cosmetics.

It is common sense that foods are prescribed according to the seasons. Cooling foods in the hot summer like the bottle gourd, green mango and yoghurt. Blood purifying bitters like the fried neem leaf and the bitter gourd in spring to prevent skin eruptions. Heating foods in the cold winter such as richly cooked meats and deep fried foods, nuts and dried fruits.

Similarly, foods are prescribed according to their cooling and heating properties depending on the nature of the disease and certain physiological conditions. During pregnancy and lactation cooling foods are avoided whereas someone suffering from fever is given cooling foods.

Everyday foods were also prophylactic and antiseptic. Kalai or biuli dal was used as a contraceptive, and dumurer dalna (fig stew) was given to diabetics. Turmeric was used as an antiseptic and honey with ghee proved to be a throat soother and a laxative. There was practically no disease for which ghee was not rubbed on, swallowed or offered to the gods and the older the vintage, the better. Its intrinsic long shelf life conferred an even longer span of life upon the user.

Pepper, garlic, cloves and other spices were known and used as medicines in the Ayurvedic system, supported by the accompanying correct foods. Hippocrates attributed the anise and dill mouthwash to India and Charaka, the Indian medicine man, is said by some to have been the inventor. Potions of herbs and mushrooms were used as specifics for different diseases and have stood the test of modern science. A list of hundreds of kitchen garden herbs handed down by the medicine men, Sushruta and Charaka, have increased many-fold in the contemporary Ayurvedic system.

Until medieval times, spices in the Bengali kitchen were minimal: turmeric, green ginger, mustard, long pepper and jamila (sour citrus) being the main flavouring agents. Long pepper was first replaced by black peppercorns and later by the cheaper chilli. The Bengali learnt to season his food with many more spices that became available and he readily devised their own particular order, proportions and combinations in using the aromatic imports of asafoetida, cumin and saffron. One of the combinations that the reader will meet many times is panch phoron made up of cumin, nigella, fenugreek, aniseed and mustard seed. It was the spice trader of Bengal who brought the three Cs—cinnamon, cardamom and cloves—the trio of garam masala into West Bengal cooking.

Writing about the chilli, Dr K. T. Achaya, a well-known food specialist and the author of *Indian Food: A Historical Companion*, says that 'perhaps the single fact about food history that most Indians find difficult to accept is that chillis have not always been with us.' The Central American import is called hara mirich (green pepper) generally as opposed to kala mirich (black pepper). In Calcutta this now indispensable ingredient is called lanka because it reached here by way of Sri Lanka. It grows profusely almost everywhere and the red variety is dried and ground into chilli powder. The connoisseur looks for the chilli of his choice among the red, green and purple heaps in the fresh herb stalls in Calcutta's vegetable markets. The tiny deadly pungent dhani lanka is grown close to Calcutta. If shoppers had to open their bags for a spot inspection, at least half a rupee's worth of chilli is sure to be found.

The manner of eating food has remained more or less the same all over India. Food is eaten with the fingers of the right hand from a platter which to begin with was probably a large leaf—like the banana leaf—cut to size, or dried sal leaves pinned together with twigs. Later, disposable terracotta plates, stone or metal platters were used. Each dish is spooned into individual bowls placed around each platter. The platter is called a thala or thali and the bowl, bati or katori. Chinaware has largely displaced the thala bati everywhere.

The order of eating the various dishes has not changed since the days of Khullana, whose love story is evergreen. Dhanapati, a spice merchant and a pigeon fancier, lost his favourite bird. The beautiful Khullana found it and stole his heart when he came to claim it. He brought her home as his bride and she cooked the bou bhaat (bou—bride, bhaat—rice) for her husband's clan according to the custom. Invitations were sent out for the bou bhaat. Durbala, her maidservant, then went to the haat (weekly market) with fifty kilograms of cowrie currency. Ten strong men carried home her purchases. The first item on her shopping list was ghee, then a variety of vegetables—bottle gourds, spinach, brinjal, arum, yam, beans, banana flower—and fruits— jackfruit, mangoes, coconut, water chestnut and banana. She bought the freshest carp and live shrimps. Meat included hare, goat and venison. The dry groceries included cane sugar, bay leaves, wheat flour, turmeric, lime, camphor and oil. And the spices were cumin, fenugreek, asafoetida and aniseed. For dessert, she purchased yoghurt, thickened milk; for utensils, mud vessels; for serving, mud plates and cups. She rested a while and refreshed herself before returning home to render her accounts. Khullana and Durbala then bathed and entered the kitchen to cut, chop and dice the vegetables according to the shapes prescribed for individual dishes. We hasten to add that the chicken has outrun the hare and the deer on the shopping list.

   This balanced and nutritious meal has become the standard in Bengali homes today with variations depending on circumstance and occasion.

To begin at the beginning, we bring recipes to our readers of a time before Charnock landed in Calcutta, made up of what there was to eat within easy reach. The recipes follow the order of eating and we include more than one version of khichuri, the meal that changed history for us here.

» This is a summer special, easy to cook, good for health.

Neem Begoon

Crisp Fried Neem with Brinjal

Serves 4 - 6

Ingredients:
- **100 gms brinjals**
- **a handful of baby neem leaves**
- **1 cup oil**
- **turmeric**
- **salt**

Method:
Dice the brinjals and coat them lightly with salt and turmeric. Heat the oil to smoking in a wok. Reduce heat and put in the brinjals. When they start to soften, add the baby neem leaves and fry till the leaves are crisp.

Care must be taken to see that the leaves are really young, they should be pink. Old leaves make this dish bitter and unpalatable.

» Kalmi saag is a water spinach used widely in China and called kylan. We have taken the liberty to include this dish in this chapter, although some of the spices are introduced later. The spinach and shrimps were the hunter's wife's morning gathering.

Kalmi Saag, Kucho Chingri Diye

Shrimps with Water Spinach

Serves 4 - 6

Ingredients:
- **500 gms kalmi saag**
- **250 gms shrimps**
- **1 tbsp mustard oil**
- **¼ tsp ground nigella seeds**
- **¼ tsp ground aniseed**
- **2 cloves garlic (crushed)**
- **salt**

Method:
Chop the kalmi saag and steam it with salt till just tender in a shallow pan. Heat the mustard oil in a wok till it is smoking; reduce heat and sauté the peeled and cleaned shrimps for 1 minute. Add the ground nigella seeds, ground aniseed and the crushed garlic. Add the steamed saag. Stir, cover and cook for 2 minutes. No water is added to this dish. The dish is no less tasty even if the shrimps are omitted.

» We have said in Chapter 1 that the hunter's wife dug
for arum. Her ways of cooking it have been modified
with the changing times, but the basic methods
remain the same. The stalks and roots are
particularly tasty and the large leaf could be used as
a sunshade. The arum is part of monsoon eating (see
Arandhan, Chapter 2, pg 41).

Kochu Bata

Mashed Arum Root

Serves 4 - 6

Ingredients:
* 1 tender arum root
* lime water
* ½ cup coconut
* 1 tsp black mustard seeds
* 2 green chillies
* 1 tsp sugar
* salt
* 1 tsp mustard oil

Method:
Peel and cut the arum root into thin slices and soak them
in lime water, as it may otherwise make the throat itch.
Crush it on a grinding stone, wash it again and grind it fine.
Grate and grind the coconut very fine. Grind the black
mustard seeds with the green chillies, add the sugar and
salt to taste and mix with the arum root. A teaspoonful of
good mustard oil mixed before serving adds zest to the dish.

» This recipe for kalaier dal (split black lentils) is very
old and almost forgotten.

Kalaier Dal, Chingri Maachh Diye

Split Black Lentils with Prawns or Shrimps

Serves 6

Ingredients:
- **200 gms kalaier dal (split black lentils)**
- **250 gms prawns or shrimps (cleaned and shelled)**
- **3 cups water**
- **2 tbsp oil**
- **2 bay leaves**
- **½ tsp aniseed**
- **6 - 8 peppercorns (slightly crushed)**
- **2 tsp ginger (minced)**
- **1 tbsp ginger paste**
- **1 tsp sugar**
- **salt**

Method:
Heat a griddle well, reduce heat and roast the split black lentils (kalai dal) until they just turn colour. Do not over-brown. Bring the water to the boil in a deep pan. Add the dal, remove scum and reduce heat. Cover and simmer until done. The dal should be quite thick. Heat the oil in a small wok to smoking. Reduce heat and add bay leaves, aniseed and peppercorns. Stir fry for 1 minute, add minced ginger and the prawns or shrimps. Stir fry until there is an aroma from the spices. Pour over dal. Add the sugar and salt to taste. Let the dal come to the boil and simmer for 5–7 minutes. Before removing from fire add the ginger paste. Mix well, cover and remove from fire.

» The literal translation of shada tarkari is 'white vegetables' which would mean no spices at all. No ground spices are used, and all the difference comes from the phoron, the small amount of whole spices used to 'finish' a dish. The combination of vegetables can be changed according to taste and availability. Coconut is optional.

Shada Tarkari

Mixed Sautéed Vegetables

Serves 6

Ingredients:
- 100 gms potatoes
- 100 gms red pumpkin
- 100 gms wax gourd (potol)
- 100 gms ridged gourd (jhingey)
- 100 gms brinjals
- 50 gms string beans (barboti)
- 2 tbsp oil
- 2 bay leaves
- 1 tsp panch phoron
- 4 tbsp coconut (grated)
- salt to taste
- 1½ tsp sugar

Method:
Peel and dice the potatoes, red pumpkin, wax gourd (potol), ridged gourd (jhingey). Dice without peeling the brinjal, top and tail the string beans (barboti) and cut into inch-long pieces. Heat the oil till smoking in a wok. Reduce heat and add bay leaves and panch phoron. When the panch phoron stops sputtering, add the potatoes. Stir fry for 5 minutes then add the wax gourd and the brinjal. Stir fry for another 3–4 minutes and add the other vegetables. Add the salt and sugar. Cover and cook on gentle heat after stirring well.

When the vegetables are nearly done, add the grated coconut. The mixture should be just moist. Stir fry over high heat until the coconut is lightly browned and the vegetables are tender but not slushy. Remove from fire and keep covered.

» We give you three recipes for khichuri—from the blandest version to the party dish. The first was probably cooked in a mud pot by the pre-Aryan Bengali in what was to become Calcutta. The second, which is common in many households today, was perhaps offered to Job Charnock in Sutanati. The third we know was cooked by Basanti Devi, wife of C. R. Das, a Bengali Nationalist leader, and was a favourite of Netaji Subhas Chandra Bose.

Moong Daler Khichuri

Khichuri with Split Moong Beans

Serves 6

Ingredients:
- ½ cup rice
- ½ cup split moong beans
- 1 tbsp ginger paste
- 2 tsp aniseed paste
- 3 cups water
- 2 tsp ghee
- 1 tsp whole aniseed
- 2 bay leaves
- salt to taste

Optional: (to be cut into 1-inch pieces)
- 6 inch piece bottle gourd
- 1 medium ridged gourd
- 1 medium brinjal

- **1 medium sweet potato**

Method:
Boil together in a deep pan the rice and split moong beans with the ginger paste, aniseed paste, in the water with salt until it has absorbed the water and reached a soft thick consistency. Heat the ghee to smoking in a ladle (hatha), reduce heat and fry the whole aniseed and bay leaves until the bay leaves turn colour. Pour over khichuri and cover.

Optional:
When the khichuri is half-cooked, bottle gourd, ridged gourd, brinjal and sweet potato may be added it.

Bhaja Moong Daler Khichuri

Roasted Moong Dal Khichuri

Serves 6

Ingredients:
- ½ cup rice
- 1 cup moong beans (roasted)
- 1 tbsp ghee
- 1 tbsp mustard oil
- 2 bay leaves
- 2 green cardamoms
- 4 cloves
- 1-inch stick cinnamon
- 1 tsp cumin
- 3 cups water
- 1 tsp turmeric
- 1-inch piece ginger (sliced)
- ½ cup peas (shelled)
- 1 tsp sugar
- salt to taste

Method:
Heat the ghee and the mustard oil together to smoking in

a deep pan. Reduce heat and fry the bay leaves, green cardamoms, cloves, cinnamon and cumin for 2 minutes. Add the roasted moong beans (available in grocery stores) and rice. Stir fry for 3 minutes, add the water, the turmeric and the sliced ginger. Let it come to the boil, take off the scum and add the sugar and salt to taste and the shelled peas. Cook until the water has been absorbed and the khichuri is soft but not thin.

Fried wax gourd (potol), brinjal and potatoes cut in thick discs and fried in ghee are good accompaniments to this khichuri on a rainy day.

Char Daler Khichuri

Khichuri with Four Dals

Serves 6

Ingredients:
- **75 gms rice**
- **¼ cup arhar dal (split dried red gram)**
- **¼ cup matar dal (split dried peas)**
- **¼ cup chholar dal (split dried Bengal gram)**
- **¼ cup moong dal (roasted)**
- **½ cup coconut (grated)**
- **2 tbsp mustard oil**
- **2 tbsp ghee**
- **4 cloves**
- **4 green cardamoms**
- **1-inch stick cinnamon**
- **2 bay leaves**
- **1 tsp whole cumin seeds**
- **2 or 3 red chillies**
- **1-inch piece ginger (sliced)**
- **4 green chillies (slit)**
- **water**
- **sugar to taste**
- **salt to taste**

Method:

Boil the arhar, matar and chholar dal together till they are cooked and quite dry, with the grated coconut in a pan. Heat the mustard oil and ghee to smoking in a large pan. Fry the cloves, green cardamoms, cinnamon, bay leaves, whole cumin seeds and the red chillies. Add the rice and the roasted moong dal and fry for 5 minutes. Add the ginger and green chillies and water enough to cover the mixture. When the rice and dal are cooked, add salt and sugar to taste and the previously boiled dals. Mix well. This khichuri should be dry and the consistency more like that of polau.

» Gota siddho is the traditional food eaten the day after Saraswati Puja when mothers keep a fast for their children and honour the goddess Shashti.

Gota Siddho

Casserole of Whole Moong Beans and Vegetables

Serves 8

Ingredients:
- **500 gms whole dried moong beans**
- water
- **8 small new potatoes**
- **8 peas in their pods**
- **8 broad beans (sheem)**
- **2 sweet potatoes (quartered lengthwise)**
- **1 white radish (cut to match the sweet potatoes)**
- **10 whole peppercorns**
- **4 cloves**
- **2-inch stick cinnamon**
- **4 green cardamoms**
- **1-inch piece ginger (sliced)**
- **a bunch of spinach leaves with shoots and roots**
- **1 tbsp ghee**

- **4 tbsp milk**
- **salt to taste**

Method:

Roast the whole dried moong beans on a hot griddle and pressure cook them with 2½ cups of water for 15 minutes. Reduce pressure with cold water, uncover cooker and add the new potatoes, peas in the pod, broad beans, sweet potatoes, white radish, peppercorns, cloves, cinnamon, green cardamoms, sliced ginger.

Add ½ cup more water and salt to taste. Cover and cook until vegetables are done and the dal is thick. Add a small bunch of spinach leaves with roots and shoots if possible as these give a special taste to the siddho. Cook for another 5 minutes. Add the ghee and the milk just before taking off the fire. Do not reheat. Serve with steaming rice.

» In Bengal, we say that the flesh of the young goat and that of the old sheep are the most palatable. For our next recipe, the meat should be that of a kochi pantha (young goat).

Panthar Jhole

Goat Stew

Serves 4

Ingredients:
- **500 gms goat's meat**
- **2 tsp turmeric**
- **1½ tbsp mustard oil**
- **1 tsp chilli powder**
- **1 tsp coriander powder**
- **2 tsp cumin powder**
- **1 tbsp ginger paste**
- **6 cups water**

- **6 green chillies**
- **250 gms potatoes**
- **1½ tbsp ghee**
- **¼ of a fresh coconut (diced)**
- **1 tsp whole cumin seeds**
- **1 tsp sugar**
- **salt to taste**

Method:

Cut the meat into 1-inch cubes. Marinate for at least half an hour in a little turmeric and ½ tablespoon of mustard oil. Mix 1 teaspoon of turmeric, chilli powder, coriander powder, cumin powder and ginger paste in the water. Heat 1 tablespoon of mustard oil to smoking in a pan and pour in the water with the spices. Let the oil come to the surface. Add the green chillies, cover, reduce heat and simmer for 10–12 minutes. Add marinated meat, cover and simmer until it is three-quarters done.

Peel and quarter the potatoes crosswise and fry separately. Add to the meat with the sugar and salt to taste. Cover and cook till done.

Heat the ghee in a small frying pan and fry the fresh diced coconut till golden brown. Now add the whole cumin seeds and when they sputter, pour the ghee with the coconut and the cumin seeds on to the panthar jhole. Cover and remove from fire.

» The standard ambole is made of a variety of fruit, vegetables and even fish, soured with tamarind water and sweetened with molasses. The one given here was called sambole by Minakshie's grandmother.

Sambole

Sweet and Sour Vegetables with Shrimps

Serves 4 - 6

Ingredients:
- **100 gms shrimps**
- **turmeric**
- **1 small brinjal**
- **50 gms red pumpkin**
- **2 medium sized sweet potatoes**
- **2 tsp mustard oil**
- **1½ cups water**
- **2 strands fresh tamarind**
- **2 tbsp molasses**

Method:
Clean and peel the shrimps and coat them with turmeric. Dice the brinjal into 1-inch pieces, peel the red pumpkin and the sweet potatoes. Sauté them in the mustard oil in a small pan. Add the water and the fresh tamarind. Cook over gentle fire until done. Add the sugar cane molasses. Remove the tamarind strands. Pour into a stone or glass bowl, cover and serve at room temperature.

Ashkay Pitha

Rice Flour Pancake

Serves 10

Ingredients:
- **300–400 gms rice powder**
- **hot water**
- **salt**

Method:
Soak the rice powder in hot water and stir into a thick pancake-like mix. Heat a non-stick pan or a lightly greased griddle on a low fire and heat a little salt on it until the salt pops. Brush the grains of salt off the pan and spread a little batter. Cover with a damp cloth and cook till done. The pancake will look dry and bubbly on top when it is cooked.

This bland pancake is delicate and quite delicious if eaten with date palm molasses (gur) or fresh moong beans and salt.

» Paramanna or payesh, the first among foods, can range from a pristine dish of rice and milk sweetened with sugar cane to a rich sweet dish full of nuts and raisins and flavoured with rose water and camphor. We give the basic with suggested embellishments.

Paramanna or Payesh

Sweetened Rice and Milk

Serves 4

Ingredients:
- **4 cups milk**

- **1 large tbsp small grained sun-dried rice (aatap)**
- **75 gms sugar**
- **green cardamom (ground) to taste**

Method:

Bring the milk to the boil in a deep pan and add the rice. Cook, stirring frequently until it has reduced by half and the rice is almost blended with the milk.

Take it off the fire and add the sugar. Stir well and put back on a gentle fire for 5 minutes, taking care that the payesh does not boil. Sprinkle with ground green cardamom.

Variations:

- To sweeten add 4 tablespoons of liquid date palm molasses (nolen gur). Let the payesh cool a little before you do this as it curdles easily.
- Fry the rice in 2 teaspoons of ghee before boiling, and add a one-inch stick of cinnamon and a bay leaf during the cooking. Sweeten with sugar and add a tablespoon of raisins and chopped almonds before you take it off the fire. Decorate with chopped pistachios and sprinkle with rose water.

Chapter 2

Bangla Ranna

Jhal,
Jhole
and
Ambole

The train approaches Calcutta.
Winter is round the corner. The
skies are a pure blue brushed by
wisps of white clouds. Looking out
of the window, a land of green and
gold rolls out to the horizon.
Yellow mustard flowers and
purple brinjals punctuate the
green of the paddy fields. Here
and there a cabbage patch lends a
sombre tinge. Now and again a
huddle of huts crowd round a
duck pond fringed with stately
palms, lanky papaya trees and
untidy clumps of banana. This is
Sonar Bangla.

The banana is one of the most
important tropical fruits available
all year round and the plant is a
symbol of prosperity in Hindu
religious ceremonies and social
events. Mocha (banana spadix),
kala (the ripened banana fruit),
and thor (the tender white inner

sheath of the stem) are eaten for their flavour and food
value. Kanch kala (plantain), is always eaten cooked. Kala
pata (banana leaves) cut into rectangles are environment
friendly plates. The outer sheath of the stem is also cut and
made into artistic boat-shaped receptacles in which fruits
and flowers are offered to the gods. Thor and mocha are
Bengali delicacies. There are many recipes the preparation
of which epitomizes the subtlety of Bengali cooking.

Calcutta's piscophiles have a permanent love affair
with fresh water or estuarine fish and crustaceans. They
know that the smaller varieties add taste to a vegetable
charchari or ghonto whereas vegetables are added to the
larger fish to enhance their flavour. The Bengali reluctantly
accepts the headless jumbo prawn's flight from the market's
cement platforms to international tables. At least, coral
filled heads which are the 'real thing' to a connoisseur are
sometimes sold to discerning customers. These are fried
with chilli and turmeric powder for Sunday lunch. Shoppers
look on with mixed feelings as the claws of a wriggling crab
are snipped off before they are taken away for a sizzling jhal
in a light spicy gravy or a devastatingly laboursome kankrar
jhuri (stir fried crab meat).

Sunday morning bazaar for Mr Mukherjee is as
important as a round of golf at the Royal Calcutta Golf Club.
He examines the gills of Calcutta's fish of fishes, bhetki, or
lifts a tiger prawn from its bed of crushed ice to verify if the
crustacean can hold up its head, a sign of freshness. The
deal is clinched. The purchase safe in a green plastic bag is
put into the portable ice box in the boot of his little white
Maruti. In a few hours the prawns reappear in coconut milk
as bagda chingrir malai curry. The seasoned shopper waits
for the greenhorn to move off before he settles down to
haggle over hilsa, strikes a better bargain and leaves with
the pick of the catch peeping out of a hole in his well-worn
shopping bag.

Visitors enjoy a tour of the city's fish markets and are
fascinated by the lively koi (climbing perch), the wriggling
catfish family of tangra, magur, shingi and the pink-bellied

Calcutta

JODHPUR CLUB

L U N C H

Becty Norwegienne

—

Steak & Kidney Pie

—

Cold Turkey & Ham

—

Pressed Beef

—

Pressed Tongue

—

Spiced Hump
Salade

—

Apple & Black Currants Pie

—

Coffee

18th. January, 1931.
PELITI'S

Beck's Beer

Indian butter fish, the pabda. Magur and shingi are brought live from the fish market, ensuring freshness, and are considered ideal for invalids and convalescents. Among the larger fish, rui (rohu) and bhetki weigh up to eight kilograms. Baskets of pink and silvery ilish (hilsa) match the shine on the glistening scimitar-like blade of the fishmonger's mammoth boti.

And the fish itself is eaten from top to tail. The head is fried or cooked with dal or rice. The Bengali believes that the fish head adds to his grey matter. The tail and bones are fried into a delectable charchari with herbs and red pumpkin.

Thrift is an integral part of Bengali cooking. In this land of plenty, the good housewife is loth to throw away any part of a fish or vegetable. Many of the vegetarian recipes are made up of roots and shoots, peels and scrapings. The tastiest dishes on the menu are sometimes khosha charchari (combinations of stalks, peels and fish bones).

The shopping done, the scene shifts to the ranna bari (cookhouse). The storage, cooking and eating areas in a Bengali home were a separate unit and the domain of the womenfolk. This barrack-like cookhouse was a row of rooms running parallel to a wide airy veranda often used as the dining space.

In an orthodox Bengali home, fish and vegetables were cooked over separate fires, rice over another and meat, if cooked at all, was done on a portable bucket fire outside the kitchen. Fowl was forbidden, but when the menfolk developed a taste for the bird the cooking was done out of sight in the bawarcheekhana, the new bawarchee's workshop.

The most important aspect of a joint family in Bengal was eating together, food from the same handi (cooking pot) prepared in the same henshel (hearth). The bunch of keys to the bhandar ghar (storeroom) was securely tied to the sari of the ginni or chatelaine—controller of the household. Depending on the size and station of the family, there were one or more storerooms.

The staple, rice, was stored for the year in enormous terracotta jars and allowed to age. There was always a small store of the long-grained, fragrant Basmati from Peshawar for polau. The Dehra Dun variety now used is said to have been introduced by the family of Amanullah Khan, the Afghan ruler who was exiled to India in the last century. Wheat was not grown in Bengal and was not a supplementary cereal till the Japanese entered World War II and the ration system for rice, wheat, sugar and textile materials was introduced for the first time in Calcutta.

Pure golden mustard oil, that pungent Bengali cooking medium, was stored in zinc lined tins. In another row, eighteen kilogram tins of the best ghee were specially transported from far-away Khurja in undivided Punjab. This was the householder's way of coping with shortages and minor famines. Spices were kept fresh in glazed brown and white jars. On wooden shelves stood the same kind of jars in larger sizes, containers for homemade pickles and preserves.

Before cold storage days, some of the shelves were lined with a layer of sand on which the new potatoes were laid in neat rows. During the mango season space was found for baskets of these summer delights from the mango orchards of North Bengal. Begum Pasand and Khirsapath were gently unpacked and placed on slatted shelves and turned from time to time for perfect ripening. As these turned from green to gold, their heady scent enticed the children who would steal into the storeroom and salt away a fruit or two. Clay pots of molasses, casein and homemade sweetmeats were suspended on giant hooks from the ceiling safe from marauders of all kinds.

Times have changed and the storeroom has shrunk to a cupboard tucked away in a corner of an apartment in a multi-storeyed complex anywhere in the concrete jungle. The contents remain the same on a diminishing scale with additions of varieties of patent sauces, pastas, soup cubes and packets of pre-cooked food.

Cooking utensils in contemporary urban kitchens have

changed beyond Grandma's imagination. Modern
implements have elbowed out the handcrafted kitchenware
of measuring bowls, earthen pots, bamboo stirrers and iron
karais (woks). But the tawa (griddle) and the handi hold
their own. The greatest invention since the wheel, in the
kitchen, is surely the pressure cooker. Today's child learns
to count by its whistle. The traditional karai and tawa with
new shiny copper bottoms make for comfortable cooking.

The hatha (ladle), khunti (metal spatula), jhanjri
(perforated spoon), chimtey (tongs) and sharashi (pincers to
remove vessels from the fire) made by the village
blacksmiths by heating and beating pure iron are being
replaced by aluminium and stainless steel equivalents.

The gleaming pyramid of conical-shaped brass and
wood rice measures from Bankura used to stand on the
storeroom floor. These have now been elevated to artefact
status and hold their own in many an ethno-chic drawing
room.

Metal pots and pans were probably popularized by the
peripatetic Muslims. The use of brass, copper and bell metal
was gradually replaced by the lighter aluminium until
health hawks began to pontificate on the hazardous
reaction of container and contents. The saucepan probably
came with the English memsahib and the handleless
modification, the rimmed deep flat-bottomed dekchi is a
hallmark of the Indian kitchen.

The convenience of packeted spice powders has almost
silenced the gourmet's cry for the finesse of freshly ground
spices. In fact, the latter are almost a luxury these days.
But die-hards insist on hand-grinding mustard with chilli
and a little sugar and salt to dispel the bitterness and bring
out the real punch. While food processors and blenders have
wiped away the tears from chopping and grinding onions,
the twin corner-stone of most Calcutta kitchens is the sil
nora.

The fertile land and enervating climate are said to have
made the Bengali an easygoing person but his economic
pragmatism makes him take to labour and fuel-saving

devices like a duck to water. The oven in its many models
has become a kitchen basic. The reader will find
recipes—once cooked on a cowdung, wood or coal fire or in
the embers—adapted to emerge almost perfect from a gas,
electric or the microwave oven.

It is really amazing that in a mega city at the end of the
twentieth century heads pop out of windows whenever the
cries of the bikriwala (rag-and-bone man), the quilt-maker,
the knife-grinder and the grinding stone cutter are heard
in the street below. The stone cutter re-notches geometric
patterns and the lucky fish motif worn smooth by use on the
heavy sil, the pentagonal stone slab. The nora is the smooth
black stone moving partner. This inseparable pair is often
handed down from mother-in-law to daughter-in-law. With
the nuclear family gaining ground, a young housewife
setting up her home will take along an experienced matron
to buy the best sil nora at the fair.

Calcutta's annual religious melas (fairs) are among the
many rural vestiges that the city will never outgrow. Many
of the villages in West Bengal are identified by a particular
craft, usually utilitarian and always beautiful.
Craftspersons come in to set up shop at the Charak Mela at
Puddopukkur in south Calcutta and on Beadon Street in
the north. The accent is on traditional kitchenware of clay,
stone, wood and bamboo. Old wooden chaki belon (round
pastry board and rolling pin) are replaced. Before metal,
ceramics and plastic became so easily available, wooden
platters and bowls held cut vegetables, spice powders and
salt. The sophisticated visitor buys them by the dozen as
plates for sizzlers and bowls for salads. The wooden hand
blender, the ghuntni, for puréeing dal is a safety measure
against power cuts.

Basketry is Calcutta's own handicraft. Baskets large
and small, lidded and unlidded, arrive for shopping, storage
and picnics. Baskets are ideal for keeping fries crisp and the
cholesterol conscious can happily indulge themselves being
assured that all excess oil has been drained off.

No visit to one of these melas is complete without a

taste of just-off-the-fire tele bhaja—onion rings, sliced brinjals and potatoes in a tasty lentil batter—fried in mustard oil on the roadside. Well-known citizens, among them the great scientist of the city, Professor Satyen Bose (of Bose-Einstein theory fame), have been known to travel from one end of the city to the other for these crunchy munchy mouthfuls.

The action in the kitchen begins with the cutting of fish and vegetables and the grinding of spices. Knives and peelers have made their debut but the boti, that unique cutting tool, has not yet been ousted. Boti, the Bengali woman's pride and joy and her proverbial weapon, is fitted on a wooden stand and held in place by the feet on the floor so that both hands are free. A table model is now in the market. The blade of the versatile boti varies and is sharp enough to cut off the head of the toughest carp or an errant husband!

In traditional joint families, the ginni sits cross-legged before her own personal boti. The cutting of vegetables is an important facet of her preparation. Each dish demands that its vegetables be cut in a particular shape. Gourd, brinjal, wax gourd and potatoes must be cut uniformly—cubed for chhenchki, quartered for jhole, and halved horizontally for dalna.

The pedestrian tuber was brought to Calcutta and christened vilayati alu (English potato) to differentiate the import from the indigenous ranga alu (sweet potato). Who brought the potato to India and when is a matter of conjecture. Dr K. T. Achaya wrote that the potato was a part of the banquet given by Asaf Khan for Sir Thomas Roe, the first English ambassador to the court of Jehangir in 1615. Around 1780, a 'basket of potatoes' was considered a fit enough gift to present to Warren Hastings, the Governer-General in Calcutta. The newcomer was treated with suspicion and it was a long time before the potato became a kitchen constant.

The tomato, called vilayati begoon (English brinjal), has undergone a sea change from the original South

American fruit. When the tomato reached Europe in 1550, it became an Italian favourite and was named the love apple. It has certainly made up for its late arrival in India by its presence in almost all vegetarian and non-vegetarian cooking.

The essence of Bengali cooking is the delicate balance between the main ingredients and its seasoning. The one must not overpower the other and the taste and appearance of the vegetable or fish should not be drowned in a heavy gravy. The cook is visibly upset if the appearance of every ingredient in the finished product is not just right. With careful preparation and cooking, a perfect meal is served.

Some dishes are twice-cooked, like a jhole (spicy stew). Vegetables are lightly sautéed and put aside. The fish is then fried. Ground spices are brought to the boil and vegetables are added and finally the fish. The reason is that all the ingredients need to be cooked to their proper consistency when removed from the fire. Santlano is the special term for this variation of sautéing. The trump card of Bengali cooking is the addition called phoron or sambhara which is a combination of whole spices fried and added either at the start or finish of cooking as a flavouring special to each dish.

Monsieur Daridan, the French Ambassador to India in the 1960s, remarked to his Bengali host in Calcutta that of all the foods in the world, only Chinese and Bengali food could compare with the sophistication of his native fare. Indeed the deceptively simple appearance of a Bengali meal is a combination of precision and balance and calls for every method of cooking. Rice and dals are boiled; bhaja is deep fried; chhenchki and charchari are braised or stir fried as the ingredients require; bhapey is steamed and there are a few dishes the ingredients of which are put into the dying embers of a wood or charcoal fire like jackfruit seeds, a tasty substitute for chestnuts, or fish in mustard sauce wrapped in banana leaves.

Variations on the menu are sukto, a mixture of vegetables, one of which must be bitter such as the bitter gourd or palta pata, the bitter leaf of the wax gourd. Sukto, served at room temperature, is strictly a luncheon starter in summer and on special occasions. The quickly made charchari is, as the name suggests, a fiery combination of vegetables and spices in which peels and scrapings are often included. A well-cooked charchari, dry, sharp and biting with just the right amount of fire, is the test of a competent cook. The laid back sister of the charchari is the dalna, again a combination of quartered vegetables cooked together with a heavier gravy, sweetened, of course, in West Bengal.

Ambole is a sweet-and-sour dish of fish, vegetables or fruit. A sharp tasting fruit makes a tasty ambole or chutney. Amra (hog plum), chalta (elephant apple), green mango with shole maachh (murrel) make lip-smacking amboles. An organized cook prepares the ambole first as it is served last and at room temperature and the fries come last straight out of the frying pan on to the thala.

A sweetened milk dessert is a palatable antacid. In Calcutta, mishti doi (sweetened yoghurt) bought from a Bengali sweet shop was the only outsider that the ginni allowed on her menu. Before the mishtir dokan (sweetmeat shop) had multiplied in every few feet of available space in every locality, yoghurt was set at home and eaten with a sprinkling of sugar. Natural yoghurt is not served and is only used as an ingredient in Bangla ranna but is accepted as the North Indian raita (seasoned yoghurt) and as dahi vada (fried lentil cakes in yoghurt).

Doi is not eaten at night by many because of its cooling properties and for fear of catching a chill. And so a large bowl of kheer (reduced milk) or rabri (fresh sweetened milk with squares of dried milk) when guests are invited to dinner, is the dessert attended by Calcutta's inimitable sandesh and rosogolla which we shall meet again in the last chapter. The use of chhana (cottage cheese) as a sweetmeat is peculiar to West Bengal and Bangladesh and we think that it may be an adaptation from Portuguese cooking.

In a secluded corner of the cookhouse, a widowed relative sits over her own stove. She has added delicate

nuances to the rich vegetarian cornucopia of Bangla ranna.
Her role in the kitchen warrants an explanation of her
situation. Up to the turn of the century, a ten- or
twelve-year-old girl was sometimes widowed and lived for
the rest of her life dressed in white with her hair cropped,
eating a radically vegetarian diet. Onions and garlic were
not allowed in her diet because of their alleged impassioning
properties. Today the widow's hidden treasury of recipes
have an added value as vegetarian volunteers grow in
strength the world over.

The humdrum routine of life was broken by the annual
visit of a widowed aunt. All the members of the family
gathered round her as she opened her tin trunk containing
goodies like bottles of kasoondi, a sauce made with ground
mustard slightly fermented to give that extra zing to a bowl
of moori (puffed rice) or as an accompaniment to fried
spinach. Kasoondi-making coincides with the green mango
season and the juice of the green mango was added for
flavour and as a preservative. She also brought out sweet,
chewy, layered aam satta delicately made by sun drying
individual layers of mango juice impressed in beautifully
handcrafted moulds. The rules of cleanliness and hygiene
are strictly observed to ensure their keeping properties.
During her stay, the family eagerly looked forward to tidbits
from her stove and fingers were licked clean of the subtle
tastes.

The Bengali looks forward to the fruits of the
season—mangoes in the hot weather, hilsa in the monsoons
and Darjeeling oranges in winter. Off-season fare is not for
this epicure and he turns up his nose at ashamayer ilish
(out of season hilsa) and will not touch fruit which has been
force-ripened with chemicals.

For a balanced and healthy diet there must be six
flavours on the plate according to Ayurvedic
thinking—bitter, pungent, astringent, sour, salty and
sweet—to stimulate the appetite, satisfy the palate and
digest what has been eaten. One or the other flavour
predominates and combined with textures to be chewed,

sucked, licked and gulped with suitable chomps and slurps—the better the meal the louder the sounds of appreciation—ending with a great fortissimo burp.

The basic standard meal, Khullana's bou bhaat is an indispensable guide for the menu-planner and is faithfully followed as it was recorded nearly five hundred years ago.

- Sukto : a predominantly bitter preparation of bitter gourd, brinjal, sweet potato and plantain
- Saag Bhaja : edible leaves, seasoned and fried
- Dal : pulses of a thick soup-like consistency
- Ghonto : vegetables, with or without fish, cooked together to a soft mush often with the addition of a little milk
- Jhole : meat or fish, with or without vegetables, cooked in a light gravy
- Ambole : sweet-and-sour dish of fruit, vegetables or fish
- Pitha : cakes of rice flour or sweet potato, steamed or fried in syrup
- Kheer : reduced and sweetened milk

Eating is a ritual. Just as the cook bathes before entering the kitchen so is the diner spruced up before he sits cross-legged in front of a platter. Bell metal, marble and on very special occasions, silver thala bati (platter and bowl) have been replaced by stainless steel and chinaware. Indian custom demands that an empty plate is not placed before the diner. Around the upper edge of the platter, salt, lime, a chilli or two and small portions of appetizers—bitters in summer, and brinjal fried in batter in winter may perhaps be served beforehand.

The food is served in bowls of different sizes arranged around the plate beginning with the dal on the extreme right, ending with the sweet on the left. Since the meal is eaten with the right hand, the glass is placed on the left. The manner of serving has been modernized for convenience but the sequence of courses has not changed.

Good cooks time their rice to within minutes of serving straight from the pot to the platter with the precision of a hi-tech rice cooker. A teaspoon of hot ghee follows to bring out the flavour of the first mouthfuls.

The appetizers are eaten first—fried spinach, julienne potato chips, tiny fried whitebait or dal boris—mixed with a little rice and a dash of lemon juice. To distract you for just a moment, we digress to tell you about bori and bori-making which is quite an event in many Calcutta homes. The ladies carry their bowls of handmixed seasoned lentil batter to the flat rooftops, spread lengths of muslin on to which they now carefully place the blobs of batter and leave to sun dry. The bori blobs are collected and stored in containers ready for frying or as an addition to ghontos, dalnas, jholes and amboles.

Now to return to the meal. The items are rotated—bhateys or poras of potato and brinjal and in season, the delightful roasted jackfruit seed. The diner does not help himself. The cook comes round with a dish at a time and fills the bowls around the top of the platter from right to left with dal, ghonto, a hot-pot of vegetables and spices, embellished with crushed boris or topped with fresh grated coconut, maachher jhole (fish stew), mangshor qorma (meat curry) and ambole or chutney in a stone bowl. Doi and sweets come last. Hands and mouth are washed and the diner adjourns to the boitakkhana (drawing room) for a paan from an ornamented paan daan.

Citizens of the City of Sweetmeats like sugar in their dal and tarkari, the generic name for all vegetable dishes. Like Chinese food and ajinomoto, the people on the Indian side of the Gangetic delta say that half a teaspoon of sugar brings out the taste and improves the colour of whatever is cooking. The East Bengali's preference for a greater variety and sharper tastes have found a place in the city's cooking pots as have these refugees from erstwhile East Pakistan, a home in the city.

Social occasions were of paramount importance to the

businessmen of the city built on trade and commerce and
outsmarting one another was a part of the culture. First rice
eating, marriage and death ceremonies were occasions for
competition as much as keeping of tradition. Often taboos
were overlooked and innovations were included in
traditional menus for the sake of one-upmanship. Perhaps
this and the fact that Calcutta's culture is one of a
cosmopolitan port is epitomized in a Paka Dekha feast in
the home of a Bengali banian (comprador). It is at the Paka
Dekha that the 'go ahead' signal for the marriage
arrangements is given. The best of fare served on this
occasion is often an adaptation of imported cuisines—bhetki
fish and prawn cutlets coated with crumbs and fried, polau
and mutton kalia, Moghlai paratha or layered Daccai
paratha or the typical Calcutta wheat bread, the
radhaballabi, always served with alur dom. The more exotic
dishes are galda chingrir chiney kebab, the ultimate in
style—crayfish stuffed with reduced milk, almonds,
pistachios and raisins and fried in ghee.

Our reader may well ask, 'Why chiney kebab?' Rare or
exotic items from outside Bengal were prefixed by the word
'China' or 'chiney' (Chinese). For example china salit is
lettuce and chiney badam, the modest peanut. The
compliment was returned by the British. They added
'Bengal' before the names of some of the tropical flora and
fauna like Bengal gram and the Bengal Black, a species of
goat. And, of course, the emblem of West Bengal, the
majestic Royal Bengal Tiger.

The marriage feast is usually an evening affair, held
outdoors in elaborately designed pandals, temporary
structures of bamboo covered with cloth which is intricately
folded, pleated and gathered. Liveried boys of one of the
dozens of good caterers in the city stand behind tables
decorated with raw vegetable sculptures, fruit and flowers,
loaded with a mixed à la carte from chholar dal to chilli
chicken. Guests still look forward to a sit-down meal served
in the traditional style. There are some homes where, no
matter how modern and unconventional they may usually

be, when it comes to a marriage in the family no departure from tradition is tolerated. Doi and sweets are ordered well in advance at the family's favourite shop or made to order by the family moira (sweetmeat maker).

Cosmopolitan Calcutta rejoices, mourns and celebrates the festivals of its communities with a *joie de vivre*. Eating a surfeit of the particular fare of the feast is the Bengali's forte. During the four-day Durga Puja fiesta the city does not go to bed. The annual return of the goddess from her abode in the Himalayas in autumn is a time of family reunions. Married daughters also return with their children to the home they grew up in. Exchange of gifts, visits to as many of the thousand puja pandals as possible, eating favourites old and new are all part of Calcutta's grandest celebration. On Bijoya, the goddess returns to Kailash after her four day sojourn and the sadness of her departure is dissipated by visiting relatives accompanied by a marathon sweet-eating affair. A glass of siddhi is offered on Bijoya with sweets in a few homes. Siddhi is an infusion of bhang (dried leaves of *cannabis sativa*) in thickened milk liberally mixed with almonds and sugar. *Cannabis sativa* has long been known as the cure for a multitude of ills. Just a glass of siddhi whets the appetite and brings a smile to the sternest face and giggles to the ginni.

Children look forward to Saraswati Puja and their first helping of the coconut-shaped narkeli kool after the fruit has been offered to the goddess. The weather is still pleasant at the end of January or beginning of February. Great handis of khichuri are stirred in the larger temporary kitchens constructed for the Puja in some schools and smaller ones in homes.

The next day is Sheetal Shashti, one of the very few days when the hearth is not lit and food cooked the day before is eaten cold. As we have said, leftovers were given away but panta bhaat is the exception. Rice left overnight in a bowl of water is the peasant's thrift measure and his source of Vitamin B. Sheetal Shashti has a special menu of panta bhaat and gota siddho, a delicious casserole of whole

moong dal roasted with whole vegetables, the
kitchen garden go into the pot—green pe
tender horse radish, baby brinjals, small p
new jackets, sweet potatoes and spinach, roo,
This is flavoured with peppercorns, garam masa.
leaves and slices of ginger. Before removing from the stove
a little mustard oil is poured over it which acts as a natural
preservative.

The monsoon is the most dramatically beautiful season
in West Bengal and the emotional Bengali expresses
himself through recitations, songs and eating. Football is
another monsoon madness and office attendance is thin on
the afternoon when the two ace rival teams, Mohun Bagan
and East Bengal, kick-off on the Maidan. Victory for East
Bengal means a run on hilsa as fans get together to
celebrate with shorsey ilish (hilsa in mustard). Prawns hit
the high-water mark when Mohun Bagan wins.

Daily shopping and cooking rituals may appear
unnecessary today. But the hot and humid climate dictated
this practice and was endorsed by religious sanctions to
ensure the serving of healthy food.

Arandhan on any one day in the Bengali (monsoon)
month of Bhadra (mid-August–mid-September) is another
of the few occasions when 'stale' food is eaten. Arandhan
literally means 'not cooking'. This custom finds an urban
interpretation in the kitchen of Calcutta's old families. Each
has added its own preferences to the meal, entirely prepared
the day before. Therefore the rules of hygiene become more
rigorous. The cook wears not a cap but a surgeon's mask
while the special meal of monsoon vegetables—arum
leaves, a fritto misto of seven kinds of edible leaves, hilsa
and shrimps—are cooked in new utensils. The Chandras of
Jhamapukur serve hilsa and a sweet fritter of mashed ripe
banana and coconut. The cooked food is left overnight
carefully covered with new kitchen towels. The rice is left
to soak in a shallow stone vessel containing water. The next
morning the hearth is cleaned and decorated with alpana,
symbolic designs on the floor made with rice paste. A cactus

.anch is placed in the well of the fire. The plant symbolically represents the snake goddess, Manasa (in Bengali the cactus is called manasa). The K. C. Das family of rosogolla fame use the white over-sized feather duster-like kash phool (grass flowers) for decoration in their kitchen. Friends and relatives are invited to partake of the cold feast.

Arandhan is a lingering of the animistic worship of Manasa. The rains bring the reptiles out of the wet earth and into the warm, dry kitchens in the countryside. The all-pervading belief is that if the snake goddess has been propitiated and all the rules of Arandhan have been observed in letter and in spirit, the food does not 'go off' the next day. And there are many stories which support this belief.

Women have a very clear view of their responsibilities towards the prosperity of their family and clan. Food is a moral proposition and certain ideals are expressed in the preparation and consumption of food. The intellectual organization behind the making of pitha reinforce the mother and wife as important contributors to the preservation of the family and the clan.

Pitha or puli in their many manifestations are the seminal sweets of Dravidian southern and eastern India. In an agrarian land, the essential ingredients of pitha are rice, coconut and date palm juice.

Boiled or steamed, fried and in syrup, pitha is eaten during the harvesting month of Poush (December-January) and ending in a three day festival called Pitha Parban. The Lahiri Choudhurys, originally from East Bengal, now Bangladesh, have been residents of the city for half a century. Renuka Devi Choudhurani, a doyenne of Bengali cuisine, has left a valuable legacy in notebooks of not only how to cook family favourites but the religious observances connected with festival fare. Their home is now a blend of the cuisines of the two Bengals. It is not surprising that her son takes enormous pride in all matters pertaining to victuals in any language and voices the opinion that food is 'an indicator and a part of culture'. Dhriti Kanta and his wife, Sheila, celebrate Pitha Parban with a pitha party in their study in south Calcutta—an interlacing of food for the mind and pitha for the palate. The guests guzzle pitha and puli while the host waxes eloquent on the two pitha traditions. It became clear to us that not only the pitha but other recipes in the Bangla Ranna chapter of this book were partitioned long before 1947 when East Pakistan and West Bengal became parts of two nations.

Traditionally, ashkay pitha, a cake of steamed rice-flour dipped in nolen gur (date palm juice of a particular consistency), is tasted first followed by ranga alur pitha, bhapa puli, manoranjan pitha, soojir (semolina) puli, chirer (pressed rice) puli and the old time winner, gokul pitha, the god Krishna's favourite. Their repertoire adds to Calcutta's own savoury soru chakli and moong saoli.

The emotional Bengali readily names dishes after Very Important Persons who appreciate them. Adventurous Calcutta cooks serve Husseini curry—meat cubes, pearl onions and ginger slices skewered on six-inch sticks. Who Hussein was, is not known. Maybe he was a great chef, a gourmet or both. He has been immortalized by his curry.

Like the city, Calcutta's cooking pots have open lids into which Portuguese Bandel cheese, Armenian dolma, Jewish mahashas, Southeast Asian malai kari and Chinese chow have arranged themselves to cook with a special Calcutta flavour.

The Islamic invasion was the beginning of a whole new chapter in the history of Bengali cuisine. The conquerors had already entered the Punjab and the Gangetic valley and established the Delhi Sultanate. With Bakhtiar Khalji came Turkish and Persian mercenaries to the fertile land of forests and rivers in 'Bangal' by the thirteenth century. And with them came the joys of camp cooking, al fresco eating and onions. The common onion, according to Dr Meera Chatterjee, a nutrition expert, was used 'on wounds in Babylon, as embalming material in Egypt, in poultices to cool and dry wounds in Greece, in moxibustion in China and

on burns in medieval Europe'. But it was taboo in the
Bengali kitchen until the coming of the nawabs in the
eighteenth century. The kebab and paratha in their
numerous elaborations entered the precincts of the Bengali
kitchen.

We start this chapter with suktoni or sukto as it is familiarly called. The ingredients were available to the early Bengali at home with the addition of spices from abroad, brought in by mariners.

» This is the classic suktoni. The ingredients can be varied according to taste and availability.

Suktoni or Sukto

Mixed Vegetables with Bitter Gourd

Serves 6

Ingredients:
- 100 gms medium sized potatoes
- 100 gms sweet potatoes
- 100 gms white radish
- 100 gms drumsticks
- 100 gms plantains (kacha kala)
- 100 gms broad beans (sheem)
- 100 gms small bitter gourd (ucchhe)
- 100 gms unpeeled brinjal
- 2 tbsp mustard oil
- 12 small matar dal bori
- 2 tsp ginger paste
- 1 tsp black mustard paste
- ½ tsp carom seed paste
- 2½ cups water
- salt to taste
- 2 bay leaves
- 1 tsp ghee
- 2 tbsp milk
- roasted panch phoron

Method:
Peel and cut lengthwise into 1½-inch pieces the potatoes,

sweet potatoes, white radish, drumsticks, plantains, broad beans, small bitter gourd and brinjal.

Heat the mustard oil to smoking in a wok. Reduce heat and fry the matar dal bori. Remove from pan and keep aside. In the same oil sauté the two kinds of potato, the drumsticks and bitter gourd for 3 minutes over medium heat. Add the rest of the vegetables and pour over them the ginger paste, black mustard paste and carom seed paste mixed in the water and strained through a fine muslin strainer. Add salt to taste, cover and cook until the vegetables are done. Add the boris, bay leaves and the ghee, cook for another 2 minutes. Add the milk, cover and remove from heat. Serve at room temperature, after sprinkling roasted powdered panch phoron on it.

Lal Saag Sukto

Red Spinach Cooked with Bitter Gourd

Serves 6

Ingredients:
- 200 gms red spinach (lal saag)
- 150 gms bitter gourd (karela)
- 100 gms medium sized potatoes
- 100 gms medium sized ridged gourd (jhingey)
- 150 gms brinjal
- 2 tbsp mustard oil
- 2 tbsp coriander powder
- 2 tbsp ginger paste
- 4 tbsp water
- 1 tbsp ghee
- 2 bay leaves
- ½ tsp whole black mustard seeds
- 1 tsp sugar
- salt to taste

Method:
Clean and cut off the tough stems from the red spinach.

Chop the leaves and tender stems. Remove the large seeds from the bitter gourd and slice finely lengthwise. Peel the potatoes and cut each lengthwise into 8 pieces. Peel the ridged gourd and cut into 1-inch rounds. Remove the stem from the brinjal and cut lengthwise to match the potatoes.

Heat the mustard oil in a wok until smoking. Reduce heat and add all the vegetables except the spinach. Sauté for 5 minutes. Add the coriander powder, 1 tablespoon ginger paste, sugar and salt to taste. Mix well, add the water. Cover and simmer over a low fire until the vegetables are almost done. Add the spinach and cook until the leaves are tender.

In a separate pan heat the ghee until smoking. Lower heat and add the bay leaves and the mustard seeds. When they stop sputtering, pour in the sukto, cover and simmer for 2–3 minutes. Finally, add 1 tablespoon ginger paste, cover and cook for 1 minute and remove from the fire. Serve at room temperature.

» Madhab Shaoo who has a vegetable stall at Calcutta's Beck Bagan market, always sells cauliflower with the leaves on. The leaves and stalks, says Shaoo, with other peels and scrapings combine into a stinging charchari (see text Chapter 2).

Khosha Charchari

Stir Fried Peels and Scrapings

Serves 6

Ingredients:
- 1 tsp cumin
- 1 tsp poppy seed
- 1 tsp turmeric
- 4 dry red chillies

- 1 tsp mustard seed
- 1 large onion
- 5 cloves garlic
- ½-inch piece ginger
- old potato peels
- red pumpkin peels
- bottle gourd (lauki) peels
- stalks and tender leaves of the cauliflower
- 100 gms small new potatoes
- a few leaves of spinach
- shells of green peas

   (The vegetables should measure about 4 cups)

For phoron
- 3 tbsp mustard oil
- 1 tsp panch phoron
- 2 dry red chillies (whole)
- 2 bay leaves
- 1 tsp sugar
- salt to taste

Method:

Grind together the cumin, poppy seed, turmeric, four dry red chillies, mustard seed, onion, garlic, and ginger. Cut into 1-inch pieces the thickly cut peels from old potatoes, red pumpkin, and bottle gourd. Cut to match the stalks and tender leaves of cauliflower. Quarter the small new potatoes in their jackets. Add the leaves of spinach and green pea shells.

   Heat the mustard oil to smoking in a wok. Reduce heat slightly and fry the panch phoron, two dry red chillies and bay leaves till the chillies turn colour. Add ground spices and stir fry for 1 minute. Add all the vegetables together and mix well, turning them thoroughly. Add the sugar and salt. Cover and cook over gentle heat until the vegetables are soft but separate and the oil comes to the surface. No water must be added to this dish.

   The same ingredients mixed together with a grating of coconut may be cooked in a tightly closed pot over a low flame or a moderate oven to make Bati Charchari.

» Tender purplish stalks of arum which appear in the monsoons combine with ground coconut and roasted moong beans to make this ghonto.

Kochu Saager Ghonto

A Spicy Mish-mash of Arum Leaves

Serves 4-6

Ingredients:
- 3–4 stalks arum
- 2 cups water
- 1 tsp turmeric
- a handful roasted moong beans
- 1 tsp coriander powder
- 1 tsp ground black pepper
- 2 green cardamoms (peeled and seeded)
- 1 tbsp ghee
- 1 tsp aniseed (whole)
- 2 bay leaves
- 2 whole dry red chillies
- 1 tbsp ground coconut
- 2 tbsp milk
- 2 tsp sugar
- salt to taste

Method:

Wash and string the stalks of arum. Cut it into 3-inch pieces and soak in lime water for half an hour. Drain, wash and boil in the water in a pan with the turmeric and roasted moong beans until the dal is soft and the stalks almost mushy. Drain and mash well. Add the coriander powder, ground black pepper, green cardamoms, sugar and salt. Heat the ghee in a wok and fry the aniseed, bay leaves and chillies. When the chillies turn colour add the arum mixture and mix well. Cover and cook until the oil comes on top. Add the ground coconut and the milk. Mix well.

When hilsa is cooked into jhal or paturi, the head is

cooked sometimes with arum stalks. The same procedure
as above is followed, only 2 tablespoons of ginger paste is
added with the spices, the hilsa head is broken, coated with
turmeric and fried in mustard oil and added to the stalks
before it is fried. If the fish head is to be included, the
cooking medium should be a mixture of oil and ghee.

» As we said earlier, the platter set before the Bengali
  diner is never empty. A slice of lime, a little heap of
  salt and some fries are served beforehand. To the
  array of julienne fried potatoes, tiny boris, rounds or
  slices of brinjal and crisp whitebait, we add this
  creation of greens by Minakshie.

Palang Saag, Dhoneypata and Methi Saag Bhaja

Fried Spinach and Coriander and Fenugreek Greens

Serves 4-6

Ingredients:
- **500 gms young spinach leaves**
- **250 gms fenugreek greens**
- **250 gms coriander greens**
- **1½ tbsp mustard oil**
- **1 medium onion (finely sliced)**
- **2–3 tomatoes (chopped)**
- **½ tsp turmeric**
- **½ tsp chilli powder**
- **2 tbsp unsalted peanuts**
- **salt to taste**

Method:
Remove the stems and the middle rib from the spinach
leaves. Pick the leaves of the fenugreek greens and the

coriander greens and discard the stems. Chop all leaves into small pieces.

Heat the mustard oil in a frying pan or wok to smoking. Add the onion and tomatoes. Stir fry for a couple of minutes. Add the turmeric and chilli powder. Reduce heat and continue to stir fry taking care that the onion remains soft, for about 7 minutes. Add the greens and salt to taste. Cook uncovered until all the moisture from the leaves has been cooked down and the leaves are still moist and tender. Add the unsalted peanuts and mix well. Stir fry for another 4-5 minutes and take off the fire.

» The recipe for this highly spiced pumpkin relish was handed down to her family by the late Renukana Dasgupta. In Chittagong, Bangladesh, where the recipe originates, sun-dried shrimps in shells were used. These are generally available in any store selling dried fish or Oriental groceries. Fresh shrimps may be substituted, and remember a little goes a long way.

Kumro Bonthi

Shrimp and Pumpkin Relish

Serves 6

Ingredients:
- **500–600 gms fresh shelled shrimps or 100 gms dried shrimps**
- **3 kg sweet red pumpkin (coarsely chopped)**
- **12–14 cloves garlic (chopped)**
- **750 gms onions (chopped)**
- **2 tbsp turmeric paste**
- **1½ tsp red chilli paste**
- **300 gms mustard oil**

- **8 green chillies**
- **salt to taste**

Method:
Soak the dried shrimps for 2 hours in cold water. Heat oil in a large wok. Fry the chopped garlic and onions till brown. Add turmeric and chilli paste and stir until the smell of the turmeric disappears. Add shrimps and cook stirring, until they are slightly brown and there is no smell of fish. Add coarsely chopped pumpkin, reduce heat and cover to release water from the vegetable. Uncover, increase heat and stir constantly until the water has dried. Add salt and 4 slit green chillies. Stir until the colour is a rich brown and the consistency like a rich dough. If it appears too dry, add a tablespoon of pre-heated mustard oil.

To serve, place in a bowl and garnish with 4 green chillies standing upright in the bonthi. Tastes best eaten with plenty of plain boiled rice.

» The next recipe is a general favourite any time of the day.

Pata Bhaja

Batter Fried Spinach Leaves

Serves 6

Ingredients:
- **large single leaves of spinach**
- **3 tbsp flour**
- **1 cup water**
- **1 cup mustard oil**
- **salt to taste**

Method:
Make a fairly thin batter of the flour, water, salt, and a few

drops of mustard oil. Heat the mustard oil in a wok to smoking. Reduce heat. Dip large single leaves of fresh spinach in the batter and fry them crisp and golden. Serve immediately. (Pumpkin flowers may be treated the same way.)

Remember spinach contains a lot of natural salt, so dishes with spinach require less salt than normal. Also, all leafy vegetables cook down to sometimes half their quantity. It is wise to use more than less if the spinach is to be the only ingredient in a dish.

» Chapor is a freshly made bori, an essential ingredient of chapor ghonto, one of the luminaries of Bengali cuisine.

Chapor or Chapri

Freshly-made Split Pea Cakes

Makes 6 - 8 chapors

Ingredients:
- **200 gms matar dal (split peas)**
- **1–2 green chillies (split, seeded and finely chopped)**
- **oil**
- **¼ tsp salt**

Method:
Wash and soak the split peas overnight. Drain and grind it with the green chillies. The dal should be ground coarsely. Add the salt and whip the batter well.

Heat a griddle well and grease it with a little oil. Make 2-inch or 3-inch round cakes ¼-inch thick and place them one at a time on the hot griddle. Cook over medium heat until the underside is brown; turn over and cook until the cakes are crisp, pouring a little more oil if necessary to prevent burning and sticking. Remove from griddle and keep aside until needed.

Chapor Ghonto

Mixed Vegetables with Split Pea Cakes

Serves 6 - generously

Ingredients:
- **100 gms medium potatoes**
- **100 gms wax gourd (potol)**
- **100 gms ridged gourd (jhingey)**
- **100 gms brinjal**
- **25 gms chholar dal (Bengal gram)**
- **chapor (broken into small bits) made from 200 gms split peas (see recipe above)**
- **2 tbsp mustard oil or ghee**
- **2 bay leaves**
- **2 dried red chillies**
- **1 tsp panch phoron**
- **1 tbsp ginger paste**
- **1 tsp sugar**
- **salt to taste**

Method:
Soak the chholar dal (Bengal gram) overnight. Peel and dice the potatoes. Dice the wax gourd, ridged gourd and brinjal. Drain the water from chholar dal.

Heat the mustard oil or ghee in a wok till smoking. Reduce heat and add the bay leaves, chillies and panch phoron. Stir fry until the chillies change colour and the panch phoron sputters. Add the vegetables, the chholar dal and the chapor. Stir fry and let the vegetables cook in their own juices on low heat. Add the sugar and salt. When the vegetables are quite soft, add the ginger paste. Mix well and take it off the fire.

Variations:
- Replace chholar dal with 2 tablespoons of grated coconut which may be added with the ginger. Grated coconut may also be added as a garnish before serving.

» The next recipe may be called a vegetarian muri ghonto—thor or banana stem replaces the fish head.

Thor Muri Ghonto

Banana Stem Cooked with Rice

Serves 6 - 8

Ingredients:
- 2 12-inch pieces banana stem (thor)
- 1 cup Basmati rice
- 2 medium sized potatoes
- 1 tbsp raisins
- 2 tbsp oil
- 1½ tbsp poppy seeds
- 1 tbsp cumin powder
- ½ tbsp dhania powder
- 1 tsp chilli powder
- 100 gms ghee or oil
- 4 bay leaves
- 4–5 green cardamoms
- 6–8 cloves
- 2-inch stick cinnamon
- water as required
- turmeric
- salt to taste

Method:
Cut the two 12-inch pieces of banana stem[*] into julienne strips, mix in a little turmeric and salt and leave it to soak

[*] Always grease your fingers before cutting banana stem and banana flower.

for one hour. Wash and soak the Basmati rice separately for about 10–15 minutes. Dry the rice out as much as possible by strewing it in a large plate or platter. Peel and dice the potatoes into ½-inch pieces. Wash the raisins and soak them in ½ cup water. Fry the potatoes until they just turn brown, drain and keep aside. Do the same with the raisins. Grind the poppy seeds and mix in the cumin powder, coriander powder, chilli powder and a couple of tablespoons of water. In a wok heat ghee or oil, add the bay leaves, green cardamoms, cloves and cinnamon. Stir fry for a couple of minutes then add the mixture of poppy seeds, cumin, coriander and chilli. Fry this until the spices change colour and you get the aroma of cooked spices. Add the rice and stir fry for 5–7 minutes. Now add the banana stem after squeezing out all the water and kneading it to a pulp. Mix this in well with the rice and then add approximately 1½ to 2 cups of water and salt to taste. Cover and simmer over medium heat until the rice is nearly done.

Add the fried potatoes and raisins, stir, reduce heat, cover and cook until the rice is done. When you are adding the potatoes and raisins check the quantity of ghee/oil in the rice and banana stem mixture. If you think it is too dry, add 2 tablespoons of ghee. Remove from fire.

» This simple dish should be made at the onset of winter when new potatoes and tomatoes and the green onion sprouts appear in the market.

Piaj Koli, Alu Piaj O Tomator Tarkari

Onion Sprouts with Potatoes, Onion and Tomatoes

Serves 4

Ingredients:
- **500 gms onion sprouts**
- **200 gms potatoes**
- **200 gms onions**
- **200 gms tomatoes**
- **2 tbsp oil**
- **1 tsp panch phoron**
- **1 tsp turmeric powder**
- **1 tsp sugar**
- **salt to taste**

Method:

Cut the onion sprouts into 1½-inch pieces. Peel and cut the potatoes, onions and tomatoes into thin rounds. Heat the oil to smoking in a wok, reduce heat and add the panch phoron. As soon as the oil stops sputtering, add the potatoes and onions. Stir fry for 2 minutes and add the tomatoes. Stir fry over medium heat for 5 minutes and add the turmeric powder, sugar and salt. Reduce heat and cook covered for 7–10 minutes until the potatoes are nearly cooked, the onions soft and the tomatoes pulpy. Add the onion sprouts, mixing well. Increase heat and cook for another 5 minutes until the onion sprouts are soft and the oil comes to the surface. No water must be added to this dish.

» The preparation of the broad flat beans (sheem) with a coriander paste is another quick and easy winter dish. Care must be taken that the sheem does not curl, and is served in one flat layer in a dish. This dish is best cooked in a large frying pan.

Sheem Aur Dhoney Saag

Broad Beans with Green Coriander

Serves 6

Ingredients:
- **400 gms broad beans (sheem)**
- **400 gms green coriander**
- **4–6 green chillies**
- **2 tbsp oil**
- **½ tsp nigella seeds**
- **1 tbsp ginger paste**
- **3 tsp sugar**
- **salt to taste**

Method:
Grind the green coriander to a paste with the green chillies, 1 teaspoon of sugar and salt. Top and tail the broad beans and leave them whole, washed and dry.

Heat the oil to smoking in a wok, add the nigella seeds. Reduce heat and add the ginger paste and stir fry for 3–4 minutes. Add the broad beans and mix well, distributing them evenly in the pan. Stir the coriander paste and pour over the broad beans. Add 2 teaspoons of sugar and salt to taste. Simmer over medium heat until the water is absorbed and the beans are tender. Turn them once, cook for another minute and remove from fire. Leave them in the pan in which they were cooked until they can be lifted into a flat serving dish.

» The next two recipes are also winter fare, classy enough for parties.

Kamala Phulkopi

Cauliflower with Oranges

Serves 6

Ingredients:
- 3 oranges
- 1 kg cauliflower
- 4 potatoes
- 4 tbsp oil
- 2 bay leaves
- garam masala of 4 cloves, 2 green cardamoms, 2-inch stick of cinnamon
- 1 tsp turmeric
- 1 tbsp ground ginger
- 2 ground onions
- 1 tsp chilli powder
- 2 tsp cumin powder (optional)
- ½ cup water
- 3–4 green chillies
- 1 tsp sugar
- salt to taste

Method:
Peel the oranges and remove seeds and skin, keeping only the pulp. Cut the cauliflower into 1-inch flowerets. Peel and cut the potatoes into 1-inch pieces. Wash and coat lightly with turmeric. Heat the oil to smoking in a pan, reduce heat and add the vegetables and sauté them till they are a light brown. Remove from the pan and keep aside. In the same oil, fry the bay leaves, and the garam masala till there is a fragrance from the spices. Add the turmeric, ground ginger, ground onions, and chilli powder. You may add the cumin powder if you like the flavour. Saute until the spices change colour. Sprinkle a few drops of water to prevent burning. A

teaspoon of sugar added to the spices brings out the colour. Add the vegetables, sprinkle salt to taste and put in the pulp of two oranges, reserving the rest for garnishing. Mix well and cover and cook over gentle heat, taking care that the vegetables are not too dry. A little water may be sprinkled from time to time, or ½ cup of water added to the dish while cooking. Add the chopped green chillies 5 minutes before you remove the pan from the fire. There should be very little gravy in the pan. To serve, decorate with the remaining orange pulp.

Beet Hingi

Beetroot with Asafoetida

Serves 4 - 6

Ingredients:
- 2 large beetroots
- 2 large potatoes
- 1 gm crushed asafoetida
- water
- 1 tbsp coriander powder
- ½ tsp turmeric
- 1 tsp chilli powder
- 2½ tbsp yoghurt
- 2 tbsp oil
- 1 tsp mixture of whole fenugreek, whole aniseed, whole carom seeds (teen phoron)
- 1 tsp carom seed powder
- 2 green chillies (finely chopped)
- 1 tbsp lime juice
- salt to taste

Method:
Peel and dice the beetroots and potatoes into small cubes. Dilute the crushed asafoetida in 2 tablespoons of water. In 3 cups of water mix the coriander powder, turmeric and chilli powder. Sieve into a pan and bring to a boil. Add the

vegetables and simmer for 15–20 minutes or until they are done. Remove from heat and add the yoghurt and salt. Return to fire and simmer gently for another 5 minutes. Heat the oil to smoking. Reduce heat and add the mixture of whole fenugreek, whole aniseed and whole carom seeds. Fry for 1 minute and pour over the vegetables. Cover, simmer for a minute and take off the fire.

Just before serving, add the asafoetida, stir, cover and cook for a further two minutes. Add the powdered carom seeds and the green chillies. A large tablespoon of lime juice gives a fresh tang if the beetroot is too sweet. Mix well and serve.

» The next dish, an egg and brinjal bhatey has been contributed by Ms Swarupa Das, the granddaughter of C. R. Das. It is served at the Bengal Club buffet table.

Khagina

Brinjal and Hard-boiled Egg Appetizer

Serves 6 - generously

Ingredients:
- **500 gms brinjal**
- **2 eggs (hard boiled)**
- **1 large onion (chopped fine)**
- **1 tsp cumin powder**
- **1 tsp coriander powder**
- **¼ tsp chilli powder**
- **½ tsp turmeric**
- **1 tsp ginger paste**
- **½ cup oil**
- **2 bay leaves**
- **1 tsp garam masala paste**
- **1 green chilli (finely chopped)**

- 1 tsp green coriander (chopped)
- 2 tsp sugar
- salt to taste

Method:
Boil or scorch the brinjal until soft. Cool and skin. Separate
the yolks from the whites of the hard-boiled eggs. Chop the
whites. Mash the yolks and add to the brinjal with the
chopped onion, the cumin powder, coriander powder, chilli
powder, turmeric and ginger paste. Heat the oil to smoking
in a wok, reduce heat, add the bay leaves and fry for 2
minutes. Add the brinjal mixture, salt to taste and the
sugar. Stir over a medium fire until the brinjal leaves the
sides of the pan. It should be moist and mushy. Mix in the
chopped egg whites, the garam masala paste and chopped
green chilli. Add the chopped green coriander and remove
from fire.

» The fish's head so dear to the Bengali has recently
   gained a place on the menus of fashionable
   restaurants in South East Asia. We present here a
   recipe from Durga Pada Barik.

Chirey Muri Ghonto

Fish Head with Beaten Rice

Serves 4

Ingredients:
- 300 gms head of rui (or any other large carp)
- 100 gms beaten rice (chirey)
- mustard oil for deep frying
- 100 gms potatoes
- turmeric
- ½ cup chopped coconut
- 100 gms mustard oil

- **1 tbsp ghee**
- **1 tsp cumin seeds**
- **2 cloves**
- **2 green cardamoms**
- **1-inch stick cinnamon**
- **100 gms onion (chopped)**
- **1 tsp ginger paste**
- **1 tsp chilli powder**
- **¼ tsp turmeric**
- **1 cup water**
- **1 tsp sugar**
- **salt to taste**

Method:

Clean the fish head and coat with turmeric and salt. Fry it in mustard oil in a wok and keep aside. Peel and cube the potatoes, coat them with salt and turmeric. Fry the chopped coconut in mustard oil. In 100 grams of mustard oil fry the beaten rice and drain.

Heat the ghee in a wok and fry the cumin seeds and cloves, green cardamoms, and cinnamon. Add the chopped onion, ginger paste, chilli powder, turmeric. Fry until the spices turn colour. Break the fish head and add to the spices. Add the potatoes, coconut, beaten rice, sugar and salt to taste and 1 cup of water. Simmer covered until the water is absorbed and the gravy coats the fish and other ingredients.

» Alur dom is the classic accompaniment to luchi in a
Bengali meal. Paradoxically, even though the
non-Bengali regards alur dom as essentially a
Bengali dish, the Bengali regards it as an import and
prefixes it with 'Kashmiri' or 'Moghlai'. We have
chosen two recipes for alur dom; the first is to be
served with a party meal and the second for a luchi
meal at home.

Kashmiri Alur Dom

Curried Potatoes from Kashmir

Serves 6

Ingredients:
* 1 kg old potatoes
* 250 gms ghee
* 2 green cardamoms
* 3–4 cloves
* 2 1-inch sticks cinnamon
* 2 bay leaves
* 4–6 Kashmiri chillies (soaked in water and ground to a
  paste)
* 1 tsp turmeric
* 1½ tsp ginger paste
* 250 gms yoghurt
* a pinch asafoetida
* 1 tbsp milk
* 50 gms grated dehydrated milk (khoa)
* 1 tbsp ghee or butter
* 1–2 tbsp sugar
* salt to taste

Method:
Peel the potatoes and prick them all over with a fork. Soak
them in water for an hour. Prick them over once or twice
during soaking so that they are quite soft. Drain and pat
dry with a clean towel.

Heat the ghee to smoking in a wok and reduce heat. Fry the potatoes on low heat until half cooked. Drain well, place on absorbent paper (newspaper is excellent) and keep aside. Pour out all but 2 tablespoons of ghee. Heat and add the green cardamoms, cloves, cinnamon and bay leaves. Stir when the spices smell fragrant, add the Kashmiri chilli paste and ginger paste. Fry gently for another couple of minutes. Lightly beat the yoghurt till smooth and add to pan (for best results take the pan off the fire to prevent the yoghurt from curdling). Simmer the mixture on low heat for 5 minutes then add the potatoes, sugar and salt. Mix, cover and simmer till potatoes are cooked. Add a pinch of asafoetida soaked in a tablespoon of milk and grated dehydrated milk and coat the potatoes evenly with the gravy. Remove from fire. Stir in a tablespoon of hot ghee or butter before serving.

Alur Dom

Curried Potatoes

Serves 4

Ingredients:
- **500 gms small potatoes**
- **1 tbsp ghee**
- **2 tbsp oil**
- **3 green cardamoms**
- **4 cloves**
- **1-inch stick cinnamon**
- **2 bay leaves**
- **1½ tbsp onion paste**
- **½ tbsp ginger paste**
- **1 tsp turmeric**
- **1 tsp chilli powder**
- **3–4 green chillies (slit)**
- **1 tbsp lime juice**
- **4 tbsp milk**
- **1 tsp sugar**
- **salt to taste**

Method:
Boil the small potatoes in a pan and skin them. Heat the ghee and oil together in a wok to smoking. Reduce heat and fry the green cardamoms, cloves, cinnamon and bay leaves until they give out a fragrance. Add the onion paste, ginger paste, turmeric, and chilli powder. Fry on medium heat for 5 minutes. Add the potatoes, sugar and salt to taste and stir for another 5 minutes. Add the green chillies, lime juice and milk. Simmer for 2 minutes, take off the fire and keep covered.

» Malai Curry, or 'Malay Curry' as it is called in some very old cookbooks, is probably an adaptation of a Malaysian import and has been in the repertoire of the Calcutta housewife for a long time. The turn-of-the-century cookbook by 'A twenty-five year resident' gives a delightful recipe which includes lemon grass. There is little doubt that the name of this curry has changed from Malay to Malai in the last hundred years.

Like so many dishes, it seemed to have gone 'out of fashion' for a while but came back in the post-war era to become the favourite among lovers of good food.

The version given here, one of many, is from an old Calcutta family, as prepared for the wedding of a daughter, fifty years ago.

Chingri Maachher Malai Curry

Prawn Malai Curry

Serves 6

Ingredients:
- **1 large coconut**

- 2 cups hot water
- 500 gms medium sized tiger prawns (bagda chingri)
- turmeric
- 2 tbsp ghee
- 2 green cardamoms
- 4 cloves
- 1-inch stick cinnamon
- 2 bay leaves
- 4 green chillies (slit)
- ½ tsp ground mace (jaitri)
- salt

Method:

Grate the coconut and extract the cream by squeezing the flesh through a piece of muslin. Add hot water to the residue coconut and squeeze out the milk. Keep the milk and cream separately.

Coat the tiger prawns lightly with turmeric and salt and sauté for 2 minutes in hot ghee in a pan. Remove from pan and keep aside. In the same ghee, fry the green cardamoms, cloves, cinnamon and bay leaves. When there is a fragrance from the spices, add the coconut milk and let it simmer for 5–7 minutes. Add the prawns and chillies and salt to taste. Let it simmer for 10 minutes. Add the ground mace and simmer very gently for another 2 minutes before adding the cream from the coconut.

Variations:

- Increase quantity of mace to 2 teaspoons and leave out the garam masala of green cardamoms, cloves and cinnamom.
- Add ½ teaspoon of ground garlic and 2 teaspoons of ground ginger to the ghee after frying the prawns.
- Add ½ teaspoon of Kashmiri chilli powder.

» This delicious oven cooked dish can be done in the microwave oven or on top of the stove on a very low flame. We give instructions for oven cooking.

Doi Chingri

Tiger Prawns Cooked in Yoghurt

Serves 4

Ingredients:
- **250 gms small tiger prawns (shelled and cleaned)**
- **2 medium sized potatoes (cut into ⅛-inch thick rounds)**
- **2 medium sized onions (thinly sliced)**
- **8 cloves garlic (chopped)**
- **1 tsp chilli powder**
- **1 tbsp ginger paste**
- **50–75 gms plain yoghurt**
- **2 green cardamoms**
- **4 cloves**
- **2-inch stick cinnamon**
- **2 bay leaves**
- **4 tbsp ghee or vanaspati**
- **2 tsp sugar**
- **salt to taste**

Method:
Pre-heat the oven to 350°F, 180°C. Mix together all the ingredients. Arrange in an oven proof dish, pour any extra yoghurt mixture over the prawns to cover them. Cover the dish and cook in oven for 30 minutes.

For the Microwave Oven:
Mix all the ingredients except the prawns and ghee. In a glass pan, heat the ghee for 2 minutes on high heat in the microwave oven. Take the pan out and place in it all the ingredients except the prawns. Cook on low heat for 10 minutes. Remove pan, add the prawns and mix well. Cook

on low heat for 5–7 minutes. Cover with a piece of cling film with holes in it while cooking.

This recipe does well for chicken, mutton or fish, but the timings are, obviously, different.

» The epitome of all things Bengali is maachher jhole. For better or worse, in sickness and in health, the Bengali must have his maachher jhole. It can be made with any fish. We give here a rui recipe.

Rui Maachher Jhole

Spicey Carp in a Vegetable Stew

Serves 6

Ingredients:
- **500 gms rui**
- **salt**
- **turmeric**
- **150 gms medium sized potatoes**
- **150 gms young wax gourd**
- **100 gms drumsticks**
- **6 medium kalaier dal boris with asafoetida (hing)**
- **1 cup mustard oil**
- **1 tsp turmeric**
- **1 tsp chilli powder**
- **1½ tsp cumin powder**
- **1½ tsp coriander powder**
- **3 cups water**
- **1 tsp panch phoron**
- **2 dry red chillies**
- **2 bay leaves**
- **1 tsp sugar**
- **salt to taste**

Method:
Cut the rui into 3/4-inch thick steaks and lightly coat with

salt and turmeric. Peel and quarter the potatoes lengthwise, peel the wax gourd in strips and halve them lengthwise. Clean and cut the drumsticks into 2-inch pieces. Fry the kalaier dal boris with asafoetida in a cup of smoking mustard oil in a wok and keep aside to drain. In the same oil fry the fish steaks and keep them aside. Pour out all but 2 tablespoons of oil and sauté the prepared vegetables in it for 3–4 minutes. Mix the turmeric, chilli powder, cumin powder and coriander powder in 3 cups of water and add to the vegetables. Add the sugar and salt to taste, cover and cook until the vegetables are almost done. Add the fish and boris and cook for another 5 minutes. Heat 2 teaspoons of mustard oil to smoking in a small frying pan or ladle and fry in it the panch phoron, dry red chillies and bay leaves, until the chillies turn colour. Pour over the jhole and cover and simmer for 3 minutes. It is best to add the phoron just before serving, as it helps to retain the flavour.

Variations:

- The ways of cooking jhole are legion. The phoron may be added before sautéing the vegetables or at the end. In winter the fish may be bhetki and the vegetables new potatoes, cauliflower, peas in pods and broad beans. For the invalid the addition of plantain and green papaya is advisable, the boris should be left out. Ginger paste is a welcome addition to the mixed spices. The spices may be fried with the vegetables and so on.

» Jhal and jhole are the inseparable twins on a Bengali
   menu, the one alternating with the other in everyday
   life. They may be vegetarian or not as pleases the
   cook.

Borar Jhal

Black Lentil Balls in a Mustard Sauce

Serves 4–6

Ingredients:
- **100 gms split dried black lentils**
- **4 green chillies**
- **½ tsp ginger paste**
- **a pinch asafoetida**
- **1 cup mustard oil**
- **1 tsp nigella seeds (kala jeera)**
- **2 tbsp paste of black and yellow mustard seeds, 2 green
  chillies, 1 gm salt, 1 tsp sugar mixed with 3 cups water**
- **½ tsp sugar**
- **½ tsp salt**

Method:
Soak the black lentils for half an hour, drain and grind them
with 2 green chillies, salt, sugar, ginger paste and
asafoetida. Whip for 7–10 minutes by hand and for 2
minutes in a blender. Heat 1 cup mustard oil to smoking in
a karai, reduce heat and drop level tablespoonfuls of the
batter into it carefully so that they form into balls (boras)
as they fry to a golden brown and come to the top of the oil.
Remove them with a slotted spoon and leave to drain while
you make the sauce.

Pour out all but 2 tablespoons of oil from the wok. Heat
the oil to smoking and fry the nigella seeds until they give
out their fragrance. Add the paste mixed in water. After it
comes to the boil, let it simmer for 10 minutes. Add the
boras, mix well with the sauce and remove from the fire.

The boras will absorb some of the sauce, but there should be enough left to eat with rice.

Variations:

• The same sauce is made for fish. The amount of water is halved as fish cooks quickly and does not absorb water. The fish is lightly coated with turmeric and salt and fried for a minute or two on either side and then placed in the sauce until it is done. The best fish to use is any variety of small fresh water fish, especially the koi or climbing perch.

» For most festive occasions, this light sweet concoction of rice and spice is the base with which the rich curries are eaten. It can be identified with paramanna, of which we have talked in the last chapter, with modifications.

Bangla Polau

Bengali Pilaff

Serves 12–15

Ingredients:
• **3 kg Basmati rice**
• **12 cups water**
• **a pinch saffron colouring**
• **200 gms ghee**
• **150 gms cashew nuts**
• **50 gms raisins**
• **5 gms whole garam masala of cinnamon, cloves and green cardamoms**
• **½ grated nutmeg**
• **1 tsp mace powder**
• **1 tbsp garam masala powder**

- 1 tbsp screwpine (kewra) water
- 1 tbsp rose water
- rose petals/jasmine flowers/mogra flowers for garnishing
- 100 gms sugar
- salt to taste

Method:

Wash the rice and soak it for an hour. Drain the rice. Bring the water to the boil in a pan, add rice and a pinch of saffron colouring. Let it come to the boil again, skimming off the scum as it rises. Cover and let it simmer over medium heat until half cooked. Drain the water from the rice and preserve it.

Heat the ghee over medium heat in a pan and sauté the cashew nuts, raisins and whole garam masala until there is a fragrance from the spices. Add the rice, sugar, salt to taste, the grated nutmeg, mace powder, garam masala powder, screwpine (kewra) water and rose water. Mix well, cover with a tight fitting lid, reduce heat to minimum and cook for another 5–7 minutes by which time the rice should be quite done, and the grains separate. In case the rice is still not quite ready, add a little of the liquid in which it was cooked, cover and leave it on a slow fire for 3–4 minutes. Keep it covered until ready to serve, heat for 5–7 minutes before serving. Garnish it with a sprinkling of rose petals in winter, and jasmine flowers or mogra flowers in summer.

» The originator of the next recipe was Mrs Lila Ray who introduced it on the menu of Suruchi, a Bengali restaurant run by the members and trainees of a women's welfare organization. It was adapted by Chandradeep Das Gupta for Food Shop and is now much in demand at Calcutta parties. We include it in this book as a tribute to them. This recipe is not for beginners.

Palang Chhanar Kofta

Curried Spinach and Cottage Cheese Balls

Serves 12–15

Ingredients:

For the spinach
- 3 kg spinach
- 200 gms potatoes
- 1 tbsp arrowroot
- 200 gms flour
- 1 tsp sugar
- 1 tsp salt

For the cottage cheese
- 500 gms cottage cheese
- 1 tsp oil or ghee
- 2 bay leaves
- ½ tsp nigella seeds
- 1½ tsp ginger paste
- a pinch of saffron
- 25 gms raisins
- ½ tsp sugar
- ½ tsp salt

For the koftas
- 1½ cups oil

For the gravy
- **8 tbsp oil**
- **100 gms onions**
- **15 gms garlic**
- **25 gms ginger paste**
- **coconut milk from 2 large coconuts (mixed with 6 cups hot water)**
- **8–10 green chillies (optional)**
- **1 tsp sugar**
- **½ tsp salt**

Method:

Spinach
Remove the stems and any hard bits from the spinach. Peel, boil and mash the potatoes. Steam the spinach in a pan until quite soft and squeeze out all the water. Mix the spinach and potatoes with the arrowroot, salt, sugar and flour. Mix them well with your hands.

Cottage cheese
In a wok heat the oil or ghee, add the bay leaves and nigella seeds. After 2 minutes add the cottage cheese, salt, sugar, ginger paste and a pinch of saffron. Mix well and fry for a maximum of 3–4 minutes, taking care that the cheese does not stick to the bottom of the pan.

Remove from fire and keep aside with the raisins.

Koftas
Divide the spinach into 30 portions and do the same with the cottage cheese. Oil your hands, take a portion of the spinach and flatten it into a disc on the palm of your hand. On this place a ball of cottage cheese with a raisin in the centre. Cover the cheese completely with the spinach mixture and roll into a ball (kofta). You will have 30 koftas. Heat 1½ cups of oil in a wok to smoking. Reduce heat and fry 3–4 koftas at a time until the spinach turns a dark green. Remove from oil with a slotted spoon and keep aside.

Gravy

Extract the coconut milk by soaking the grated coconut meat in 2 cups of hot water for half an hour. Squeeze out milk through a piece of muslin.

Prepare the gravy 15 minutes before serving and assemble the dish just before it goes to the table for best results. Remove all but 8 tablespoons of oil from the wok, and heat till it smokes. Add the onions, garlic and ginger paste, with the coconut milk mixed in hot water, salt and sugar. The green chillies may be added.

Add the koftas, simmer for 5 minutes and serve immediately. If the gravy has to be made ahead of time, bring it to the boil before adding koftas.

» The yellow split Bengal gram is chholar dal in Bengal. It is the favourite party dal and is cooked thick, flavoured with spices and garnished with coconut and raisins. It takes longer than most other dals to cook.

Chholar Dal

Yellow Split Peas

Serves 4 - 6

Ingredients:
- **250 gms chholar dal (Bengal gram)**
- **6 cups water**
- **5–6 green chillies (split)**
- **1 tsp turmeric**
- **3 tsps sugar**
- **salt to taste**
- **2 tbsp oil or 1 tbsp ghee**
- **2 bay leaves**
- **white meat of half a small fresh coconut diced small**
- **50 gms raisins (cleaned)**
- **2-inch piece cinnamon**

- 3–4 small cardamoms
- 4–6 cloves
- 2 dried red chillies
- 1 tsp cumin seeds

Method:

Heat a griddle well, reduce heat and roast separately a garam masala of cinnamon, cardamoms and cloves; also roast the dried red chillies and cumin seeds. Grind the garam masala and the other spices separately to a fine powder. Bring the water to the boil in a pan and add the chholar dal (split Bengal gram). Take the scum off the dal and reduce heat. Cook until it is half done. Add the split green chillies, turmeric, sugar and salt to taste. Cover and cook until done over a medium fire. The dal should be stirred occasionally, as it tends to stick to the bottom of the pan.

In a small frying pan or ladle, heat the oil or ghee to smoking. Reduce heat and add the bay leaves and the diced white coconut meat. Fry until the coconut is a light brown. Pour this over the dal. Add the raisins. Cover and simmer for 5 minutes. The dal should be thick and sweet. To finish, sprinkle the powdered garam masala, the red chilli powder and cumin seed powder over the dal and cover. Do not stir until ready to serve.

» Roasting the split moong bean is unique to Bengali cuisine and we give you a variation with aam ada, galingale, which has caught the palate of the world in Thai food.

Aam Ada Diya Bhaja Moong Dal

Roasted Split Moong Beans with Galingale

Serves 4–6

Ingredients:
- 250 gms small grained split moong dal (moong beans)

- 5½ cups water
- 1 tsp turmeric
- 1 tsp red chilli powder
- 4 green chillies
- 1 tsp ghee or 2 tsp oil
- 1 tsp cumin seeds
- 2 red chillies
- 1 bay leaf
- 2 tbsp galingale paste (aam ada)
- 1 tsp sugar
- 2 tbsp milk
- salt to taste

Method:

Heat a griddle well and roast the moong dal to a golden brown. Cool and wash. Bring the water to the boil in a pan. Add the dal, turmeric powder and red chilli powder. Remove scum as it rises to the top, cover and simmer until the dal is half-cooked. Add salt to taste and the green chillies and complete cooking.

In a small frying pan or large ladle, heat the ghee or oil to smoking. Reduce heat and fry the cumin seeds, red chillies and bay leaf, until the chillies turn colour. Add to the dal and simmer covered for 2–3 minutes. Add the galingale paste, sugar and milk. Allow the dal to remain on the slowest fire for it to absorb the flavours for another two minutes. Heat through without boiling before serving. Good with rice or luchis.

Variations:

- Leave out the galingale and use 1 teaspoon ginger paste with turmeric and chilli powder. Temper with garam masala, dried whole red chilli and 1 bay leaf. Add a handful of shelled green peas or 3 dried jackfruit seeds and 2 medium potatoes (peeled and diced) to the dal while cooking. Leave out all other spices except turmeric. Add a teaspoonful of ghee before taking off the fire.
- Moong dal is sold ready roasted in Calcutta as bhaja mooger dal.

» In Bengal, red split peas are known as masoorir dal. It is most commonly used for everyday meals. It is one of the cheaper dals, with a high protein content, and easy to cook. The basic method of cooking the dal is the same, varied by changing the phoron.

Masoor Dal

Red Split Peas

Serves 4 - 6

Ingredients:
- **250 gms masoor dal (red split peas)**
- **5 cups water**
- **1 tsp turmeric**
- **1 tbsp oil or 1 tsp ghee**
- **4 dried red chillies**
- **½ tsp ground carom seeds**
- **½ cup green coriander leaves (chopped)**
- **4 green chillies (split)**
- **salt to taste**

Method:
Bring the water to the boil in a pan. Add the masoor dal (red split peas) and turmeric. Remove scum from the dal and reduce heat. Add salt to taste and simmer uncovered until the dal is cooked. Stir with a ghuntni (dal stirrer) to break the grains.

In a small frying pan heat the oil or ghee to smoking. Reduce heat and fry in it the dried red chillies and ground carom seeds. Fry for 1–2 minutes until the chillies turn colour. Pour over the dal and cover and simmer for 2 minutes. Before serving add the chopped green coriander leaves and split green chillies.

Variations:
- Thin the dal with ½ a cup of water after it is

stirred. Temper it with 1 teaspoon of nigella seeds
and 4 split green chillies fried in mustard oil. Add
a few drops of lemon juice and a grating of lemon
rind before serving.

- Boil 1 chopped onion with the dal. Temper it with
  ½ an onion finely chopped, 2 cloves of garlic finely
  chopped and 2 dried red chillies fried in ghee until
  the onions are crisp and brown.

» The entry of button mushrooms in a big way into the
Calcutta markets led us to include this dal with a
foreign flavour.

Mushroom Masoor

Red Split Peas with Mushrooms and Spices

Serves 4–6

Ingredients:
- 5½ cups water
- 250 gms masoor dal (red split peas)
- 1 tsp turmeric powder
- 100 gms small button mushrooms
- 2 tsp coriander powder
- 2 tsp cumin powder
- ¼–½ tsp chilli powder
- 1 tbsp ginger paste
- 3–4 split green chillies
- 1 tbsp ghee
- 1 tsp panch phoron
- 3 tsp sugar
- salt to taste

Method:
Bring the water to the boil in a pan and add the red split
peas and the turmeric powder. When half cooked, add the

small button mushrooms cut in half or quartered depending on their size, coriander powder, cumin powder, chilli powder, ginger paste, split green chillies, sugar and salt. Stir well and simmer covered until the dal is cooked.

In a small frying pan or ladle, heat ghee to smoking. Reduce heat, add panch phoron and fry until it sputters. Add to dal and let it come to the boil. Remove from fire.

» We know that the preparation of banana flower (mocha) is a tedious affair, but the end result is so good that we had to include this vegetarian paturi before we introduce the classic fish recipe.

Mochar Paturi

Banana Flowers Wrapped in Banana Leaves

Serves 6

Ingredients:
- 250 gms prepared banana flower
- 200 gms wax gourd (potol) (diced small)
- 125 gms onions (coarsely chopped)
- ½ tsp chilli powder
- ½ tsp turmeric
- 8 green chillies
- 125 gms yellow & black mustard (equal quantities)
- 1 tsp sugar
- ½ cup mustard oil
- 2 tbsp water
- ½ tsp salt

- 5 banana leaves
- thread

Method:
To prepare the banana flower, peel off the red covering sheaths of the spadex and pick out the yellow flowers.

Remove the stamens from the centre and the tough calyx at the bottom. Chop the tender flower petals and soak them in water with a teaspoon of turmeric for an hour. Drain and squeeze out the water.

Take the prepared banana flower and mix it with the diced wax gourd, coarsely chopped onion, chilli powder, turmeric, 6 green chillies slit down the middle, and a paste made with the yellow and black mustard, 2 green chillies, sugar and salt and 2 tablespoons of water and mustard oil.

From 5 banana leaves cut 10 pieces to fit your griddle (tawa). A non-stick pan serves well to make paturi. Place 5 layers of leaf and put the banana flower mixture in the middle, cover with another 5 layers and fold them under the banana flower mixture. Bring the bottom leaves over the top leaves to make a packet and tie it with thread to keep it together. Place the greased griddle (tawa) on high heat and grill the packet until the leaves burn off one by one to the last leaf. Flip the packet carefully and repeat the process. Leave in the packet till it is ready to serve. Reheat and serve in the packet—to be cut at the table.

» We chose for our readers two rather exotic recipes for fish which have been much appreciated by our guests.

Ilish Maachh Aur Anaras

Hilsa with Pineapple

Serves 4

Ingredients:
- **600 gms hilsa**
- **turmeric and salt for marination**
- **2 tbsp mustard oil for light frying**
- **4 slices pineapple**
- **4 tbsp mustard oil**
- **2 bay leaves**

- 4 cloves
- 4 green cardamoms
- 2 1-inch sticks cinnamon
- 1 tsp turmeric
- 1 tsp chilli powder
- ½ tsp Kashmiri chilli powder
- 1 tbsp ginger paste
- 1 tbsp aniseed paste
- ¼ cup water
- 1 onion (cut in rings)
- salt to taste

Method:

Cut the hilsa into 8 pieces, crosswise and coat lightly with turmeric and salt and set it aside for half an hour. Heat 2 tablespoons of mustard oil in a wok and lightly fry the fish and keep aside. Do not use this oil again for this dish. Cut the pineapple slices and coarsely blend them in a blender. Set aside with the juice in a bowl.

Heat the rest of the oil in a pan, add the bay leaves, cloves, green cardamoms and cinnamon. Fry for 3 minutes and add the turmeric, chilli powder, Kashmiri chilli powder, ginger paste and aniseed paste. Fry over moderate heat until the spices change colour. Add the pineapple and salt to taste. Add the water and simmer for 5 minutes. Add the fish and carefully spoon the spices over it. Cover and cook for 15–20 minutes, turning the fish once, taking care it does not break. Brown the onion cut in rings and sprinkle over the fish before serving. This is optional.

Posto Pomfret

Pomfret with Poppy Seeds

Serves 4

Ingredients:
- 500 gms pomfret
- 3 tbsp mustard oil

- **2 dried red chillies**
- **1 tbsp curry leaves**
- **1½ tsp coriander seeds**
- **1½ tsp cumin seeds**
- **2 whole dried chillies**
- **1 tbsp poppy seeds**
- **½ cup water**
- **1 tsp mustard oil**
- **a few green chillies (slit)**
- **1 tsp sugar**
- **salt to taste**

Method:

Heat the mustard oil to smoking in a pan, reduce heat and add the dried red chillies, curry leaves, fry for 2 minutes. Add the coriander seeds, cumin seeds, whole dried chillies, poppy seeds, all freshly ground together to a fine paste. Stir fry over high heat, sprinkling it with water as you fry. When the spices turn colour, add the water and bring to the boil. Add the sugar and salt. Add the pomfret cut in slices, turn down the heat and simmer for 10 minutes or until the fish is done. Before taking it off the fire add the mustard oil and a few slit green chillies for taste.

Ilish Maachher Paturi

Hilsa in Banana Leaves

Serves 4 - 6

Ingredients:
- **500 gms hilsa**
- **25 gms yellow mustard seeds**
- **25 gms black mustard seeds**
- **2 green chillies**
- **½ tsp salt**
- **1 tsp sugar**
- **1 tsp turmeric**
- **½ cup mustard oil**

- **banana leaves**
- **thread**

Method:
Cut the hilsa into 6 steaks. Make a paste of the yellow and black mustard seeds with the green chillies, salt and sugar. Mix with the turmeric and mustard oil. Lightly salt the fish. Cover with mustard paste evenly.

Cut the banana leaves into 12 rectangles and place them in 6 crosses. Place a piece of the seasoned fish in the centre of each cross and tie up into envelopes. Place in an oven-proof dish and cook in a preheated moderate (350°F, 180°C) oven for 15–20 minutes. Maachher paturi can be made with fillets which must be cut a little smaller than pieces meant for frying. Calcutta fishmongers will do it on request.

» Parshey is a delicious small freshwater fish, best eaten in winter when it is full of roe. The one central bone structure makes it easy to tackle and it is equally good fried, in a jhal or jhole. We have chosen an unusual roast, excellent for a party.

Parshey Maachher Roast

Spicy Roast of Parshey

Serves 4

Ingredients:
- **500 gms parshey**
- **turmeric and salt for marination**
- **5 tbsp ghee**
- **1 medium onion**
- **1-inch piece ginger**

- ½ tsp red chilli powder
- ½ tsp Kashmiri chilli powder
- 1 tbsp vinegar
- 3–4 green chillies
- ½ cup water
- 1 tsp sugar
- salt to taste

Method:

The parshey should ideally be of equal size, full of roe if possible. Score them down the sides and coat them with turmeric and salt and set aside for half an hour. Heat 4 tablespoons of ghee in a large heavy bottomed frying pan and fry the fish lightly. Lift, drain and keep aside. Grind the onion and ginger to a paste. Add another tablespoon of ghee to the pan and heat to smoking, reduce heat, add the red chilli powder, Kashmiri chilli powder. Stir fry till the spices turn colour, for about 5 minutes. Be careful not to cook too quickly, or the chillies will burn and lose colour. Add the vinegar, sugar and salt. Add 3–4 green chillies and stir fry for 2 minutes. Add ½ cup water and let it simmer and add the fish gently into the gravy, spooning it over to cover the fish. Cover and cook for another 5 minutes, turning the fish once. Remove from fire. This is a delicate dish and must be handled with care, or it looks messy.

Variations:

- The same recipe can be used for cooking carp (rui maachh). With the addition of a handful of raisins and thinly sliced almonds during the last basting of the fish, rui maachher roast becomes a dish to serve at a Paka Dekha ceremony where a marriage contract is sealed (see text).
- As an alternative to parshey, trout or any freshwater or estuarine fish can be used. Parshey fish is available in other Indian cities.

» Green mangoes are said to be a preventive for
sunstroke, so it is consumed in many forms in the hot
dry months of April and May, before the rain breaks.
Aam jhole is a light and simple ending to a summer
meal.

Kancha Aamer Jhole

Spicy Stewed Green Mangoes

Serves 6

Ingredients:
- 3 green mangoes
- 3 cups water
- 2 tsp oil
- 1 tsp black mustard seeds
- 1 whole dried red chilli
- 3 tbsp sugar
- 1 tsp salt

Method:
Stone and cut the green mangoes into quarters lengthways.
Peel them if the peel is very tough. Bring the water to the
boil in a stainless steel pan with the sugar and salt. Add
mangoes and cook on a medium fire till soft. Heat the oil in
a ladle and fry the black mustard seeds and whole dried red
chilli till they sputter. Pour over the mangoes. Cover. Serve
cold.

Variations:
- Kool (the Indian plum) can be treated this way,
  but the sweetening should be with molasses.
     These jholes should have a syrup thin enough to
  sip out of a cup. Check the jhole for sweetness. If
  the mangoes are very tart, add extra sugar to
  taste.

» Kancha Aamer Chutney is thicker, sweeter and more dressy than the last recipe—good with luchi.

Kancha Aamer Chutney

Green Mango Chutney

Serves 6

Ingredients:
- **3 green mangoes**
- **turmeric**
- **1 tbsp mustard oil**
- **1 tsp black mustard seeds**
- **2 dried red chillies**
- **1 tsp ginger (finely sliced)**
- **1½ cups water**
- **1 tbsp raisins**
- **4 tbsp sugar**
- **salt to taste**

Method:
Stone and cut the green mangoes into 6 pieces each and coat them lightly with turmeric and salt. Heat the mustard oil in a stainless steel pan and fry the mustard seeds and dried red chillies. Add the mangoes and sliced ginger. Fry gently for 3 minutes and add the water. When the mangoes are half done, add the sugar and raisins. Cook gently till done. Serve at room temperature.

» This recipe for tomato chutney stays well in the refrigerator for at least a week—from Mrs Sudha Ray's recipe book. In Calcutta this chutney is cooked in March when tomato prices are low, and the chutney can be made in bulk and preserved with half a teaspoon of sodium benzoate added at the last.

Tomato Chutney

Makes 1 kg

Ingredients:
- **2 kg tomatoes (quartered)**
- **2 cups sugar**
- **1 cup vinegar**
- **2 tsp chilli powder**
- **4 tsp garlic (ground)**
- **2 tbsp raisins**
- **2 tsp ginger (sliced)**
- **4 dried red chillies (cut in pieces)**
- **4 green chillies (chopped)**
- **salt to taste**

Method:
Cook together all the ingredients in a stainless steel pan. Simmer on a gentle fire until the tomatoes are pulpy and thick.

Topa Kooler Achar

Preserved Indian Plum

Makes 750 gms

Ingredients:
- **1 kg topa kool**

- **250 gms mustard oil**
- **a pinch of turmeric**
- **50 gms chilli powder**
- **250 gms cane sugar molasses**
- **250 gms sugar**
- **50 gms freshly roasted and ground panch phoron (more cumin and less fenugreek)**

Method:

Wash and dry the topa kool. Dry them for a day in the sun. Heat the mustard oil in a stainless steel pan, add a pinch of turmeric and the chilli powder. Add the kool, stir on medium heat boiling slowly. Add the cane sugar molasses and sugar. Cook for 15 minutes. Before taking off the fire, add the freshly roasted and ground panch phoron. The consistency should be slightly sticky.

    Cool and bottle.

» Three kinds of pitha are eaten over the three days of Pitha Parban in mid-January (see text). The primeval steamed pitha has been described in Chapter I. The following are versions of fried pithas and pithas in syrup.

Nonta Puli

Sweet Potato Cakes with a Green Pea Filling

Makes 12 Cakes

Ingredients:

For dough

- ½ kg sweet potatoes
- 2–2½ tbsp rice flour
- 2 tbsp flour
- 1 tsp oil

For filling
- 1 cup shelled peas
- 1½ tbsp oil
- 2 tsp powdered aniseed
- 1 tsp freshly ground black pepper
- 1 tsp sugar
- salt to taste

To assemble
- 3/4 cup oil

Method:

Dough
Boil and skin the sweet potatoes and mash with the rice flour, flour and oil. Knead to a pliable dough, cover and keep aside.

Filling
Grind the shelled peas to a smooth paste. Heat the oil in a wok and add the peas with the powdered aniseed, freshly ground black pepper, sugar and salt. Fry gently for about 5 minutes. If the peas are fresh they will cook in that time. If they are too dry, add a quarter cup of water and continue cooking until the water dries up and the peas come off the sides of the pan in a mass.

To assemble
Divide the sweet potato mixture and the green pea mixture into 12 balls each. Take a ball of sweet potato in your hand and shape it into a small cup. Fill it with the pea filling and seal, shaping it into a small torpedo.

Heat the oil in a wok to smoking, reduce heat and fry the pithas a few at a time to a golden brown. Drain and serve hot or at room temperature.

Ranga Alur Rasher Pitha

Sweet Potato Cakes in Molasses

Makes 12 pithas

Ingredients:

For dough
- ½ kg sweet potatoes
- 2 tbsp oil
- 3 tbsp flour
- 1 tbsp rice powder

For filling
- 1 grated coconut
- 1 cup milk
- 1 cup molasses

For syrup
- 250 gms liquid date palm molasses
- 2 cups water

To assemble
- 2 cups oil

Method:

Dough
Boil and skin the sweet potatoes. Mash them well. Rub the oil into the flour and rice powder. Mix thoroughly with the potatoes.

Filling
In a wok put the grated coconut, milk, molasses. Stir over medium heat until the mixture leaves the sides of the karai. Remove the karai and keep it covered on a greased plate.

Syrup
Boil together the liquid date palm molasses and the water

for 2 minutes in a pan. Cool.

To assemble
Divide the sweet potato dough into 12 portions. Take each
portion into the palm of your hand and shape it into a cup.
Fill it with a portion of the filling and shape it into a 2-inch
torpedo. Heat 2 cups of oil in a wok to smoking, reduce heat
and fry a few pithas at a time on a low fire until they are a
deep golden brown. Put them into the syrup. Serve at room
temperature.

» This recipe is from the notebook of Renuka Devi
  Choudhurani, who was a great cook. It is not easy to
  perfect and is a good example of pitha-making being
  a leisure craft. It requires time, patience and skill.
  The end result is worth it.

Monoranjan Pitha

Little Cakes of Coconut and Semolina in Thickened Milk

Makes 30 pithas

Ingredients:
- half a coconut (ground)
- 100 gms semolina
- 30 gms dehydrated milk (khoa)
- 60 gms sugar
- 1 litre milk
- 1 tbsp ghee
- green cardamom seeds (ground)

Method:
Grind half a coconut and mix it well with the semolina,
dehydrated milk (khoa) and sugar. Boil and reduce the milk
in a pan to a little more than half the original quantity and
allow it to cool. Cook the ground coconut mixture in a wok

over moderate heat until it leaves the sides of the wok. Shape into tiny half-moon shaped cakes and place them on a greased plate. Heat the ghee in a frying pan and spread it all over to grease the entire surface of the pan. Fry the pithas a few at a time on very gentle heat, turning them over carefully so that they brown evenly. This is the tricky bit. The oil should not be too deep in the pan and the heat really low. Place them carefully in the thickened milk as you lift them from the pan.

Sprinkle the dish with ground green cardamom seeds.

» Malpoa in many versions is common all over India. This is a Bengali variation.

Malpoa

Yoghurt Pancakes

Makes 9 malpoas

Ingredients:
- **250 gms unsweetened yoghurt**
- **2 tbsp flour**
- **1 tsp whole aniseed**
- **½ cup ghee**

Method:
Blend the yoghurt with the flour in a bowl. Add the whole aniseed. Mix well. Heat the ghee in a wok and add a tablespoon of yoghurt at a time and fry until brown and crisp at the edges. Remove from the ghee and drain on paper. Place in a bowl of sugar syrup (see below).

For Syrup
Mix 1 cup sugar in 2 cups cold water and stir until the sugar dissolves. Place a pan on medium heat and bring the

mixture to the boil. Boil until the syrup is thick. Cool. Add
the malpoas one at a time as they are fried.

» The last recipe in this chapter is not as sweet as it
  should be but Husseini Curry takes us on to how and
  why the Muslims came to Calcutta and enriched our
  kitchen.

Husseini Curry

Skewered Meat Curry

Serves 4

Ingredients:
- **500 gms mutton**
- **250 gms small pearl onions**
- **3–4 ½-inch piece ginger**

For gravy
- **4 tbsp ghee**
- **2 bay leaves**
- **4 green cardamoms**
- **4 cloves**
- **1-inch piece cinnamon**
- **1 medium onion (chopped)**
- **1 tsp chilli powder**
- **1 tsp turmeric**
- **1 tsp ginger paste**
- **1 medium onion (ground)**
- **4 tbsp whipped yoghurt**
- **2 cups mutton broth**
- **1 tsp sugar**
- **salt to taste**

Method:
Boil and drain the mutton. Reserve the stock. Cut the
mutton into 3/4-inch cubes. Peel the pearl onions. Slice

ginger very thinly into rounds. For this dish you need small skewers. Ideally, they should be cut from bamboo to fit your cooking vessel, but small metal skewers will do too. Skewer alternately, a slice of ginger, a cube of mutton and an onion, beginning and ending with ginger.

Gravy

Heat the ghee in a pan. Add the bay leaves, green cardamoms, cloves and cinnamon. Fry for 2 minutes, add the chopped onion and brown. Add the chilli powder, turmeric, ginger paste and the ground onion. Fry for 5–7 minutes, sprinkling with water to prevent burning. Take the pan off the fire, add the whipped yoghurt. Return it to the fire, add the sugar, salt to taste and mix well. Add 2 cups of mutton broth and cook for 5–7 minutes. Place the skewers carefully in the pan and spoon some gravy over them. Cover and simmer gently until the onions are cooked. There should be a thickish gravy in the pan. To serve, place the skewers side by side on a flat dish and spoon gravy over them.

Variations:

- This curry may be made with chicken, in which case the meat should be skewered uncooked.
- There is an Anglo-Indian version using beef and veal.

Chapter 3

Dastar Khwan

New foods and flavours travelled on the dastar khwan along the well-known land routes to the subcontinent with the Muslim invaders and conquerors from Central Asia. The end of the twelfth century was the beginning of a cross-current which, over the next five hundred years saw the adoption of new adab qaidas (manners and mores) and different dastoors (conventional customs). The invader brought his rich kingkhabs (brocades) and makhmul (velvet), tailored coats and pantaloons and the taste of meats, drinks, spices, and essences.

A totally new type of meat-heavy diet appeared which may best be described as camp food with a long shelf life. Some of the new culinary terms—kebab, kalia and qorma—have become a part of Bangla ranna.

Kebabs, Kalia and Qorma

Above all the taste of onion and garlic for flavour, so long out of favour, were introduced. In partnership with the local green ginger they have become hardy stalwarts in the modern Indian kitchen, though there are still some homes where the twosome is taboo.

The food philosophy pronounced in the Holy Koran is similar to that of other holy books, that the Maker is the Giver of Food and the followers of Islam pray before and after meals and are taught never to waste food.

The food dictates strictly followed are halal and haram—that which is permitted and that which is forbidden. Scaleless fish and crustaceans fall into the ambiguous grey area called makruh.

Ingredients were brought from different parts of the Mughal Empire and the North Western frontiers. Long-grained rice came from Peshawar and fruits like the apple and apricot from Kashmir. Grapes and melons were grown near Agra and oranges in Bengal.

Ain-i-Akbari mentions the remarkable range of fruits in the Delhi markets—pineapples, guavas and custard apples—which had only recently been introduced from the New World via Europe.

In the mid-nineteenth century, baskets of fruit travelled on the newly opened railways to the fruit markets in Calcutta.

In their twilight hours, the piquancy had evaporated from the power of the Mughals in Delhi. The kitchen fires smouldered and the fragrance of polau was stronger in the subahs (provincial courts) of Dacca and later Murshidabad, the new capital of Bengal.

The last sultans, pampered by the gentler climate, lost some of the virility of the soldier and ruler and indulged the softer characteristics of their sensitivity and a passion for things beautiful. They cultivated the wild rose and the tropical mango to perfection. Eau de rose played in the fountains and was sprinkled on polau. Calcutta mango-eaters today dream of the advent of summer and the small sweet hybrid Begumphuli, and the delectably fragrant Himsagar from the orchards of Malda in North Bengal.

Delving into culinary archives we discover *Nimat Nama*, an exquisitely illustrated pre-Mughal book of recipes, and the *Ain-i-Akbari* by Abul Fazl, a most accomplished man of letters in Akbar's court. Besides the varied subjects contained in this book's many volumes, there is a description of the three classes of cooked dishes. The first is called Safiyuna which is meatless. The ingredients are rice, khuska, khichra or khichri, the seasoned gluten from wheat, dal, leafy vegetables, halwa and sherbat. The second class included polau and biryani (meat cooked with rice) or harisa, halim, and qutub (meat cooked with wheat), while the third comprised yakhni, kebab, kalia, and dopiyaza (do piaza, meat cooked in ghee with twice the quantity of onions). The story goes that Mullah Do Piyaza was one of the nine jewels of Akbar's court. He was a gourmet and a gourmand and no mean cook to boot. The dish dopiaza is an example of his culinary ingenuity.

The Mullah's home was open house and by dinnertime the guests were well over the list. To keep the party going, the Mullah would clap his hands from time to time indicating to the kitchen that more onions should be added to the meat curry. And thus did Mullah Do Piyaza accidentally discover that the proportion of double the quantity of onions to meat was quite the best. And so was created the dopiaza (Do - 2, piaza - onions). The missionary Samuel Purchas wrote in the seventeenth century of 'one they call deu pario (dopiazza), made of venison cut in slices, to which they put onions and herbs, some roots, with a little spice and butter: the most savoury meat I have tasted and do almost think it that very dish which Jacob made ready for his father, when he got the blessing.'

Like many Orientals, the Muslims follow a strict ritual before starting to cook. The bawarcheekhana (kitchen) is ruled by the Muslim bawarchee (cook) whom we shall meet again in the next chapter. He must be pak saf (clean and pure) having done gosul wazoo, a bath complete with ablutions as done before namaz (prayer).

Muslim food in Bengal has been a domesticated al fresco cuisine. The ingredients and methods of cooking depended largely on local conditions and availability. Spices were dealt out with a heavy hand for wet grinding, dry pounding or chopping. They roasted, grilled, baked, fried or stewed their meats, first doused in highly seasoned marinades, both to tenderize and flavour often tough and high viands. Shikar, a favourite sport of badshahs and sultans, provided a rich variety of flesh which had to be cured to be made edible. From the elk to the sparrow, the hunter from Central Asia shot anything his eye spied and roasted it on a spit.

Muslim cooking methods in Calcutta still suggest an impromptu stove. There are no elaborate preambles to the preparation of the ingredients. A dry fry or braising on the tasst (griddle) is preferred. Gravy is optional, which is understandable in a diet where bread is the staple food. Vegetables were not a part of the cooked menu and is a later introduction. Fruit, fresh and dried, is still preferred.

The preparation and cooking of the kebab is done in many ways on an open fire. Cubes of meat are skewered into boti kebab. In passinda kebab the meat is ground and rolled round an iron skewer. Cakes of mince are turned on a tasst into tikkia kebabs. The ghoti kebab is stirred in a pot to a paste. Handi kebab takes its name from the vessel in which it is cooked. Another favourite for large get-togethers in rezala. Calcutta families have their own recipes and each one stakes a claim for the best and of course the original. And if the domestic front temporarily collapses, Sabir's restaurant in central Calcutta produces the goods with unquestionable authenticity. Sabir was undaunted by meatless Thursdays and Fridays promulgated in the state and fish rezala appeared on his menu.

Roti is the generic name for Indian breads and the Muslim bread basket is a baker's bounty. There are breads big and small, soft and hard, fried, baked, rolled, patted, filled and baked on a griddle. Many kinds of bread were introduced into the land of the rice-eating Bengali—the griddle and baked breads, chapatti (light, thin, unleavened bread), naan (thick leavened bread), tandoori roti (baked on the sides of a clay oven), rumali roti (large thin chapatti, folded like a gentlemen's handkerchief) and the fried breads: paratha, soft, semi-soft and the layered Daccai paratha, an Indian cousin of the French milles feuilles. Rotis are rolled to shape every mood and occasion, from Spartan battle fare to the luxury of an imperial banquet. They complement kebab and qorma. They are eaten plain or soaked in soorwa (soup) or wrapped round halwa or dipped in raita (seasoned curd with grated cucumber). Bread is indeed the staff of life for the Muslim. The bakar khani roti was named after Bakar Khan, Governor of Bengal, who had this cream-cracker like bread baked out of necessity so that it would last throughout his long winter tours. The Khan Chowdhury family of Malda still leaven the khmberi roti with juice of the date palm as it was in the deserts of Arabia. Is it any wonder that, in Calcutta, Muslim bakers have a closed shop of the pau roti (loaf bread) business.

Muslim cooking came to Calcutta's Chitpur. The air around was redolent with aromatic mixtures of Amburi and Badshah Pasand tobacco briquettes and kebabs turning on charcoal fires in front of walk-in eating houses on Chitpur Road, once the only link between the town and Delhi. Vestiges of nawabi culture linger on in Chitpur.

It was after the fall of Murshidabad when the Nawab of Bengal, Zafar Ali, came to Calcutta that nawabi food made its headway in the city. With the Nawab came the frills and flounces of his court and his bawarchees with dekchi, tasst and seekh and a whole new cuisine. The cooks took a little time to find their ladles in a land that was so green and lush and where fish was so plentiful in the waterways that crisscrossed the delta and its fertile hinterland. Perhaps the Bengali Muslim took to fish and vegetables because both are so abundant. He created green

jackfruit qorma and kanch kala kofta out of plantains. He
innovated additions including mahey polau, a fish polau, of
which using hilsa was the master stroke.

The travelogues of visitors to India from the fourteenth
century onwards speak of the courtly Muslim 'mat manners'
and eating customs which they witnessed for the first time
in northern India. Ibn Batuta, the greatest Muslim
traveller, journeyed in AD 1333 from his native Tangier
through Khorasan and Kabul, over the Hindu Kush
mountains to the Indus valley. He visited Delhi on an
invitation from Mohammad bin Tughlak and his
observations are interesting.

'Before the dinner begins, the chamberlain stands at
the head of the simat (carpet spread for the dinner) and
performs the khidmat (bow) in the direction of the Sultan,
and all present do the same. The khidmat in India consists
of bowing down to the knee as in prayer. After this the
people sit down to eat; and then are brought gold, silver and
glass cups filled with fine sugar and water perfumed with
rose water which they call sherbat. The chamberlain's
resounding call "Bismillah" (a grace) echoed through the
hall . . . . The dishes followed in a set pattern at a grand
dinner and often consisted of forty sumptuous courses.'
('Muslim Cross Current' by K. T. Achaya in *Science Age*,
June 1985, pp. 39–44.)

Qashaq (spoon) and karad (knife) were used for serving
food and carving meat and glass carafes for chilled water
and sherbat. Food was eaten with fingers off large metal
plates set on a dastar khwan (tablecloth).

Batuta proceeds to give an idea of the order of service.

'To begin with khubi (loaves) are served which are very
thin and resemble cakes of bread; then they (chamberlains)
cut the roasted meat into large pieces in such a manner that
one sheep yields from four to six pieces. One piece is served
before each man. Also they make round cakes of bread
soaked in ghee; and in the midst of these place the sweet
called subunia (a mixture of almond, honey and sesame oil).
On every piece of bread is placed a sweet cake called khisti

(which means bricklike), a preparation of flour, sugar and ghee. Then they serve meat cooked in ghee, onion, and green ginger in China dishes. Then is brought a thing called samusak, minced meat cooked with almonds, walnuts, pistachios, onions and spices placed inside a thin bread and fried in ghee. In front of every person is placed from four to five of such samusak. Then is brought a dish of rice cooked in ghee on the top of which is roasted fowl (dojaj, that is pulau with murgh mussalam), next a kind of sweet which is called hashimi (and then) alqahiriya (a kind of pudding borrowed from Qahira). At the end of the meal fuqqu, a wine made from barley, is served and "Bismillah" is called out in thanksgiving. Spices wrapped in betel leaves and tied with a red silk thread are offered . . . . Everyone bows to the amir and takes his leave.' ('Early Travellers Tales' by K. T Achaya in *Science Age*, May 1985.)

Chewing of paan (leaf of the *Piper betle*) was a Hindu adoption embellished into a sophistication in the Sultanate. Abdur Razzak of Herat, an ambassador from Samarkand at the court of the Zamorin of Calicut in the mid-fifteenth century, pronounced praises on the habit of chewing betel-nuts which he said, ' . . . deserves its reputation. It lightens up the countenance and excites intoxication like that caused by wine. It relieves hunger, stimulates the organs of digestion, disinfects the breath, and strengthens the teeth. It is impossible to describe, and delicacy forbids me to expiate on its invigorating and aphrodisiac qualities.' Dentists and doctors in the twentieth century may not uphold Razzak's ode to the paan.

The common man's meal reads like a feast in the Indian context today. Breakfast of naan (a flat loaf) with kebab or kofta (minced meat balls) with rice and soorwa, a soup from trotters, or the richer neharia on a cold winter's morning. To sweeten the taste, firni, halwa or kheer prepared with milk, pappy rice, sugar and dried fruits akin to the Bengali payesh was served.

The Nawabs of Bengal carried the traditional ice making secrets from Delhi. Large square pits, two feet deep,

were dug in the cooler winter months. The bottom was lined
with rice husks on which were placed a number of shallow
porous terracotta pans filled with boiled water. These were
left undisturbed and in the morning the layer of ice that had
formed was carefully collected and preserved in fifteen foot
deep wells specially lined with straw and rough blankets.
The mouth of the well was sealed and a thatch roof was built
over it. Ice was mixed with saltpetre and used to cool
sherbat and freeze kulfi in summer.

Kulfi in metal cones is India's first ice cream. It must
be remembered that the Muslims came from a much colder
climate and no sooner had they established themselves than
they became homesick. They could now afford to think of
the luxury of ice in a tropical country and even sent for ice
from the mountains!

Calcutta has been the refuge of many a court in exile.
Certain charismatic characters in modern Indian history
with whom Her Majesty's Government crossed swords and
wished to remove forever from the sphere of their influence
were exiled to the malarial swamps in Calcutta's suburbia.
And this is how, after the slaying of Tipu Sultan at the battle
of Seringapatam, the Tiger of Mysore's two begums and
twelve sons, their entourage, together with his elder
brother's family came to Calcutta from South India in the
early nineteenth century. They were interned in
Tollygunge, then an insalubrious marshland, and given
handsome stipends. With the begums, concubines and
khawasses (ladies-in-waiting) another undercurrent, that
of Deccan cooking, edged its way into Calcutta and is now
perhaps not always identifiable except in the sweet Mysore
paak.

Just behind the Shahi Masjid in Tollygunge stands a
dilapidated red brick mansion known as Nawab Kothi, the
home of Sahabzada Mohammed Maqbool Alam, the sixth
generation descendant of Tipu's only brother, Prince Karim
Shah. Maqbool's charming begum, Sherbanoo, fondly
remembers her grandmother-in-law, Begum Sahiba
Anjumanara, a legend in the locality. The story goes that

whenever she travelled in her curtained Chevrolet, the menfolk did not appear on the road leading from her house. Before her story ends, an aroma wafts into the bedroom-cum-living room of the Alams from the little kitchen separated only by a curtain. What's cooking? One of the hundred meat recipes of the great lady, handed down by word of mouth and now Sherbanoo's proud possession.

Fifty years later came another royal exile, Wajid Ali Shah, and a more elaborate adaab quaida and a new taste was added to the Calcutta Muslim flavour of food—the Avadhi flavour from Lucknow. Handsome Humayun Mirza spoke with great pride about his great-great-grandfather, Wajid Ali Shah, the last king of Oudh (Avadh). A patron of the arts, a writer himself, he was an expert on the light romantic classical thumri. Deposed by the British in 1857 and exiled to Metiabruz on the outskirts of Calcutta, he built a mini Lucknow. Naseem Ara Mirza, better known as Jani Begum, Humayun's mother, told us of features peculiar to the Shahi (royal) kitchen. The Nawab's food was recommended and tested by a hakim (a doctor of the Unani system of medicine). Masoor dal was boiled in a clay handi with an Asrafi mohur (gold coin) as was peosi (egg-based pudding) and stirred in a copper lagan (utensil). Gold is believed to have therapeutic value but was it not also a nawabi extravagance? Wajid Ali's late night dinner was an array of dishes—polau, vegetable bhujia (stir fries), shami kebabs and shahi machhli ka qorma, to mention a few. The latter is a carp cooked in mustard oil, a Bengali adoption. Shahi semai cooked over a slow fire and maybe peosi with fifty eggs was the pudding. A glass of burhani (yoghurt, garlic and chilli) was prescribed by the hakim as a digestive. Wajid Ali only drank chilled water and a ready remedy for a cold was at hand in besan roti (gram-flour bread) eaten with a chutney of garlic and green chilli.

India's trade with the Middle East is as old as the hills. From the seventh century onwards Arabs came overland and in dhows making their presence felt in Sind and along the Coromandel coast. They reached Calcutta many centuries later when other traders, the Bohras and the Khojas and the Iranis, merchants from Persia (Iran), already established on the west coast of India, came to Calcutta with the building boom at the end of the last century. They traded in hardware, tea, rice and timber and traded all the way to Burma. N A Siddiqi, an expert Bokhara carpet-mender in Calcutta, is often mistaken for a Kashmiri. He came as a young man with his father from Arabia in 1920. A connoisseur not only of carpets but also of food, his eyes light up as he recites a recipe dear to his heart for stuffed whole fish.

Zarina Patherya, who belongs to the fourth generation of the oldest Bohra family in the city, takes pride in their specialized cooking and has the recipes on her fingertips. As she expounds on the intricacies of the hulba and harisa, Mudar, her son, talks of the best meat in Calcutta sold in Colootala and Zakaria Street in the neighbouring Chitpur area. Patherya goes on to talk about patthar gosht, meat cooked on a heated slate placed at an angle of forty-five degrees. The mutton, cut into paper-thin slices, is first marinated in ginger, garlic, green chillies and raw papaya and then seared on a hot slate imported from Karbala. Commercially-made stone slabs can now be heated in large ovens. Each of these communities added their own taste to Calcutta's bawarcheekhana and so the cooking pots of Calcutta began to multiply.

The Maharajas of Burdwan were among the largest landowners in India. At a dinner at Bijoy Manzil, their palace in Calcutta, some of the specialities are very different from the general run of Bangla ranna. Dr Pranay Chand Mahtab tells us how his ancestor, Abu Rai, a settler from the Punjab in the seventeenth century, helped to feed the stranded Mughal army marooned in the torrential monsoons. Abu Rai's bazaar became the Mughal army's commissariat and in recognition of a kind deed, Emperor Aurangzeb gave Abu Rai a title. And so it was quite natural that some of the Mughal recipes like the kasta kebab and the loung paratha (with cloves) marched into the Burdwan kitchens. With the abolition of the zamindaris of Bengal, the landlords, great and small, had perforce to reduce their establishments. The last Maharaja of Burdwan said to his valet, 'Poncha, I have a craving for maachh begooner kalia.' The ever faithful Poncha, now the general factotum, produced four king-sized pieces of rui fish cooked with brinjals in a rich curry—a tasty example of the integration of cuisines.

The avant-garde intellectuals of Bengal in the 1940s remember Jahanara Begum's salon in Calcutta. They met to share poetry, to sip her sherbat and partake of her superb refreshments. A stunning beauty, the Begum was a versatile artiste. Her forte was a whole goat roasted on the spit served with murgh mussalam and biryani.

Rubee Noor, a member of the Legislative Assembly of West Bengal, is famous for her murgh polau which she serves to celebrate Independence Day in her Calcutta home.

Bengali Muslims like bhuna gosht, a variation on the do piaza and tikkia kebabs and parathas at festival time. Their daily fare consists of maachher jhole, spiked with onions and garlic, alu or begoon bharta (potatoes or brinjals charred over a fire and mashed with a few drops of pungent mustard oil, chopped onions and chilli) and a masoor dal with onions and panch phoron.

Today, at the great festivals of the two Ids, mountains of sewai (vermicelli) and dates rise beneath the slender minarets of the Nakhoda Masjid. Impromptu restaurants with benches and folding chairs open on the narrow, ever busy Chitpur Road and in other parts of the city during the month of Ramzan ending in the sighting of the Id-ul-Fitr moon.

During Ramzan, the month long fast is broken daily at Iftar, with a sip of water at sunset and the fruit of the desert, the date, followed by cucumber, piazzi (onions deep fried in lentil batter) and samosa (deep fried, three cornered, vegetable or meat filled pastry) which has descended from the samusak of Ibn Batuta's journal. Before modern medicine made us cholesterol conscious, the date was prescribed by the hakim as a natural blood thinner. Sherbat is served. A traditional Iftar food is halim, a substantial, nourishing soup of meat, lentils and cereals. Iftar parties have become the fashion in large cities. The table is laden with rich qorma, sizzling kebab and chaap (curried rib chops).

Sara Gangjee, according to custom, sends cooked food to friends and to the poor during the month of Ramzan. And at the end of the thirty days, Id is celebrated with a mammoth community prayer on Calcutta's Red Road. Later in the day, Kabulis dance with handkerchiefs on the Maidan.

Winter brought train loads of small traders to Calcutta from Kabul. These turbaned Kabuliwalas, towering a good one foot above the local people, carried enormous sacks on their backs. They went from door to door peddling dried fruits and nuts, asafoetida, saffron and surma (kohl). Mothers used the large but gentle Kabuliwala as a bogeyman who would, they told naughty children, carry them away in their bundle.

It may be interesting to know a little about some of the religious and social occasions at which some of the dishes, for which the recipes are given, are served. The most striking is a biryani cooked with qurbani (sacrificial meat) at Bakr-Id, celebrating Ibrahim's readiness to sacrifice his son Ismael and Allah's reward for his faith.

The month of Muharram is observed in mourning for the tragic Battle of Karbala. There was very little to eat and a khichra was put together with whatever there was in the house. In commemoration, majlis or prayer meetings are followed not by a scratch meal but a delicious khichra of cereals and lentils, often with a bit of meat, the ingredients shopped for specially in the market.

Sab-e-Barat is a time of remembrance of the dead, like All Souls Day. Candles are lit in homes, mosques and imambaras. Paratha and halwa made of lentils, semolina, wheat, carrots and eggs are shared on this day. A speciality is anda halwa, the plebeian peosi of the Shahi kitchens of Metiabruz.

The rakabdar, the master cook engaged to produce a wedding feast, supervises the preparatory steps with a keen eye and a seasoned palate. Then he examines the gilded saffron scented heaps of biryani carefully and tastes the succulent piece of chicken in a thick golden red gravy of murgh mussallam before the guests are served. The traditional dessert is zarda polau, a confection of sweetened rice dressed with nuts and raisins sprinkled with rose water.

What strikes us about Mughlai food is its presentation. Mounds of polau appear in imperial glory, dressed in tabac (edible gold and silver leaf) sprinkled with rose water or a few drops of the headier attar, slivers of almonds and pistachios and a showering of rose petals.

On a Sunday morning, Calcuttans in search of a change from their humdrum daily breakfast fare, willingly queue up for Tibetan momo, Chinese dim sum and South Indian idli and dosa and the very Bengali 'hot hot' singara and jilipi. And where did the singara and jilipi come from, but the kitchens of the travelling Tartars. Sweetmeat shops make the golden jilipi between seven and nine in the morning. It is fascinating to watch the dexterity with which the sweetened Bengal gram batter is squeezed through a muslin bag, making crisp fried golden concentric rings in a wok of boiling ghee then gently lifted out and dipped into a hot sugar syrup. Waiting his turn at a mistanna bhandar (sweet store) in south Calcutta, a litigating Bengali, thinking of the morrow's court case, commented that to the twisted mind of his adversary this convoluted confection was a straight line.

Two hundred years ago the bawarchee brigade was firmly ensconced in the Chitpur area of the Black Town, as the 'native quarter' of Calcutta was known. The butcher, the baker and the candlestick-maker followed, leaving their families in the adjoining districts of Midnapore, Chhapra and Muzzaffarpur, and lodged in the servants' quarters in the compounds of the bungalows in the White Town—the English quarter. It is here that their repertoire was added to by their fair employer, the memsahib.

In the next chapter, we meet a mixed group of Europeans who came to Bengal in the seventeenth century and painted a fabulous picture of the East with 'its strange food and drinks'. Francois Bernier, a doctor who attended to Emperor Aurangzeb and spent seven years in India (AD 1659–66), writes charmingly about the beauty and allurement of Bengal three hundred years ago. Bernier foresaw Calcutta's sweet tooth, inherited maybe from the Portuguese in their settlement at Hooghly famous for murabba (preserved fruits in syrup). We succumb to the temptation to quote once again, this time from Bernier's diary.

'In a word, Bengal abounds with every necessity of life . . . (all of which) has given rise to a proverb among the Portuguese, English and Dutch, that the kingdom of Bengal has a hundred gates open for entrance, but not one for departure.' ('The West's Devouring Look' by K. T. Achaya in *Science Age*, July 1985.)

Enter the Firinghee.

We start this chapter with two breakfast dishes which are Calcutta's favourites—a recipe from Mrs Zarina Patherya.

Paya

Soup of Goat's Trotters

Serves 6

Ingredients:
- **4 goat's trotters**
- **2 onions (sliced)**
- **6 cloves garlic**
- **1-inch piece ginger (sliced)**
- **2 tsp coriander powder**
- **6 cups water**
- **2 tbsp oil**
- **2 cardamoms**
- **4 cloves**
- **1-inch piece cinnamon**
- **2 bay leaves**
- **1 onion (sliced and browned in oil)**
- **chopped coriander leaves**
- **slices of lime**
- **salt to taste**

Method:
Singe and clean the goat's trotters well. Pressure cook them for 30 minutes with the 2 sliced onions, cloves of garlic, sliced ginger, coriander powder and salt in the water. When the soup is ready, heat the oil and fry the cardamoms, cloves, cinnamon and bay leaves. Pour over soup and mix in the sliced browned onion. Mix well and boil for another 2 minutes. Serve with chopped coriander leaves and slices of lime.

Roghni Roti

Whole Wheat Griddle Bread

Makes 10 rotis

Ingredients:
- **500 gms whole wheat flour**
- **50 gms ghee**
- **1¼ cup milk**
- **water**
- **½ tsp salt**

Method:
Mix the whole wheat flour with the salt, ghee, milk and water in a bowl to make a stiff dough. Knead well and leave aside for an hour. Knead again and divide into 10 portions. Roll out into fairly thick circles. Score with a knife and cook on a griddle. This roti can be baked in a moderate oven (350°F, 180°C) for 15 minutes.

» Muslim food in Calcutta is synonymous with kebab and paratha and the kebab shop has travelled from Coolootola in the North to the wheel barrows all over the city.

Handi Kebab

Kebab in a Pot

Serves 12

Ingredients:
- **2 kg boneless lamb (cut in 1½ inch cubes)**
- **2 kg onions**
- **3 tbsp ginger (ground)**

- 1 tbsp garlic (ground)
- 350 gms yoghurt
- 4–6 tbsp oil or ghee
- 6 bay leaves
- 8–10 dry red chillies, preferably Kashmiri chillies
- 2 tsp sugar
- salt to taste

Method:

Cut the boneless lamb. Halve and slice the onions. Mix the lamb with two-thirds of the onions, ground ginger, ground garlic, sugar, salt and yoghurt. Allow to marinate for several hours, preferably overnight, in a glass or ceramic dish.

Heat 4–6 tablespoons of oil or ghee in a deep pan to smoking and reduce heat. Add the bay leaves, fry for 2 minutes. Add the lamb in marinade. Stir fry over high heat for 10–15 minutes. Lower heat to a gentle simmer and cook for at least another half an hour. This part of the cooking can be done in a moderate oven (300°F, 150°C) for about 45 minutes.

Before serving, place the lamb on a very high flame and stir fry for 10 minutes with the remaining one-third portion of onions and the chillies. As the lamb cooks over high heat the oil should come to the surface. Taste for salt and serve with roghni roti or naan.

» The next recipe is from Jani Begum of Avadh.

Shami Kebab

Minced Meat Kebab

Makes 25 - 30 kebabs

Ingredients:
- 1 kg meat (finely minced)

- **3 onions (sliced)**
- **1-inch piece ginger**
- **8 peppercorns**
- **1-inch stick cinnamon**
- **2 large black cardamoms**
- **2 eggs**

Filling
- **onions, garlic, green chillies, green coriander (chopped)**
- **flakes of fresh orange**
- **1 cup oil**

Chutney
- **50 gms green coriander**
- **50 gms mint**
- **6 cloves garlic**
- **4 green chillies**
- **2 tsp sugar**
- **salt to taste**
- **juice of half a lime**

Method:
Boil the finely minced meat with one sliced onion, ginger and peppercorns ground with cinnamon and black cardamoms in a pan. Cook till the meat is almost a paste and quite dry. Throw out the ginger. Brown 2 sliced onions, grind them and add to the meat. Mix in the eggs. Make the meat into balls, and flatten each on the palm of your hand and form into a cup. Fill it with a teaspoon of the filling of chopped onions, garlic, green chillies and green coriander and a few flakes of fresh orange. Reshape into balls and flatten into 2-inch discs. Heat the oil in a wok and fry the kebabs a few at a time.

Grind together the green coriander, mint, garlic, green chillies, sugar, salt and the lime juice to make the chutney.

» The king of kebabs is surely the raan kebab, spiced,
   marinated and roasted to a turn.

Raan Kebab

Spiced Roasted Leg of Lamb

Serves 8

Ingredients:
- 1½–2 kg leg of lamb

Marinade
- 1 tbsp poppy seeds
- 4 1-inch pieces cinnamon
- 6 black cardamoms
- 6 green cardamoms
- 4 cloves
- 2 tbsp aniseed or fennel
- 1 tbsp cumin
- 2 medium onions
- 6 cloves garlic
- 1-inch piece ginger

- 1 cup oil or ghee
- 6–8 bay leaves
- 2 tbsp yoghurt
- 2 tsp Kashmiri chilli powder
- salt to taste

Method:
Prick the leg of lamb with a fork or skewer until the meat
is loosened from the bone.

Make a marinade by grinding together the poppy seed,
cinnamon, black cardamoms, green cardamoms, cloves,
aniseed or fennel and cumin to a powder and mixing with a
paste of the onions, garlic and ginger.

Rub the marinade well into the lamb, pricking it again
so that the spices permeate. Let it rest for 24 hours in a glass
or ceramic dish, turning in once.

Heat the oil or ghee in a pan large enough for the leg. Add bay leaves, fry for 2 minutes and take it off the fire. When the oil has cooled a little, add the yoghurt, Kashmiri chilli powder and salt. Return it to the fire and stir for 2 minutes. Put in the lamb and brown on both sides over a medium flame. Reduce heat to a gentle simmer, cover and cook until the meat is tender, basting it frequently with the juices that run out of it.

This dish it best done in a moderate oven (350°F, 180°C) for one and a half hours. Since it is difficult to get good mutton in Calcutta, we would suggest that a piece of green papaya be ground with the onions. This helps to tenderize the meat and improve the taste. The cooked leg should be tender enough to eat with a spoon.

» Rezala is a Calcutta Muslim speciality. Every family has its own special recipe. The meat normally used is that of the fattened castrated goat, the khashi, which in most parts of India would be called mutton. The cut is from the upper rib and neck, and has some bone and some fat. Young lamb may be used instead of khashi. A recipe from Begum Unaiza Khan Chowdhury.

Rezala

Meat and Yoghurt Curry

Serves 8

Ingredients:
• **1 kg mutton**

Marinade
• **2 medium onions**
• **2-inch piece ginger**

- **8 cloves garlic**
- **1 tbsp coriander powder**
- **400 gms yoghurt**

- **200 gms ghee**
- **10 small onions**
- **6 dried sour plums (alu bokhara)**
- **1 tbsp pistachios, almonds, cashew nuts (chopped)**
- **10–15 green chillies**

Method:
Cut the mutton into fairly big pieces. Grind the onions, ginger and garlic to a smooth paste. Mix in the coriander and yoghurt to make the marinade. Marinate the meat for an hour in a glass or ceramic dish. Heat ghee in a pan till it is smoking, reduce heat slightly and fry the meat in its marinade over a fairly high flame for 5 minutes. Reduce heat and simmer until the meat is half done. Add the small onions and dried sour plums, chopped pistachios, almonds and cashew nuts, and the green chillies halved and seeded. Cover and simmer till the meat is tender.

Minakshie collected another recipe for shahi rezala which follows the same method but includes ¼ teaspoon turmeric, a few bay leaves, 2 green and black cardamoms each and 10 peppercorns in the spices. A cup of milk is added halfway through the cooking and ¼ cup light cream and a pinch of saffron added at the end.

» A recipe from Mrs Sara Gangjee.

Muslim Roast

Spiced Cubes of Mutton

Serves 6

Ingredients:
- **1 kg mutton cut in 2-inch pieces**

Marinade
- **250 gms yoghurt**
- **2 tbsp ginger paste**
- **1 tbsp garlic paste**
- **1 tsp chilli powder**

- **4 tbsp oil**
- **4 large onions (finely chopped)**
- **1 cup water**
- **2 cloves**
- **2 green cardamoms**
- **2-inch piece cinnamon**
- **2 bay leaves**
- **1 tsp powdered garam masala**
- **a pinch of saffron soaked in 1 tbsp rose water**
- **salt to taste**

Method:

Marinate the mutton pieces in the mixture of yoghurt, ginger paste, garlic paste and chilli powder for 12 hours.

Heat the oil in a pan and fry the finely chopped onions until brown. Add the meat and the marinade. Fry over high heat, stirring until the liquid is absorbed and the meat is well browned. Add the water and cloves, green cardamoms, cinnamon, bay leaves and salt to taste and cook over a slow fire until the water is absorbed and the meat tender. Before serving, sprinkle powdered garam masala, and the saffron soaked in rose water.

» The Do Piaza has been an attraction on the dinner
table from the days of the *Nimat Nama* (see text). The
centuries have surely seen it undergo many a change,
but it remains a favourite dinner recipe. We chose a
simple but delicious adaptation by Mrs Sita Pasricha
courtesy Mrs Tara Sinha.

Do Piaza

Serves 4

Ingredients:
- **500 gms mutton or beef**
- **1 kg onions (quartered)**
- **6 cloves garlic (finely chopped)**
- **1-inch piece fresh ginger (cleaned and finely sliced)**
- **750 gms yoghurt**
- **4 tsp coriander seeds**
- **1 tsp turmeric**
- **2 tsp cumin seeds**
- **1 tsp cloves**
- **4-inch stick cinnamon**
- **10 dry red chillies**
- **2 bay leaves**
- **1 tsp peppercorns**
- **6 large cardamoms**
- **6 tbsp ghee or butter**
- **salt to taste**

Method:
Cut the meat into small pieces. Beat the yoghurt till smooth.
Mix all the ingredients except the ghee or butter, and place
them in a deep pan with a tight fitting lid. Cover and bring
gently to the boil, and simmer until all the liquid has been
absorbed. If the meat is not cooked, add a little water and
cook till dry. Add the ghee or butter and fry the curry gently

for 5 minutes, taking care not to break the pieces of meat.
Serve with chapattis.

» The Muslim cook's forte is bread making. From his
  large repertoire, we have chosen a few which are good,
  eaten freshly made. A recipe from Begum Unaiza
  Khan Chowdhury.

Bakar Khani Roti

Bakar Khan's Bread

Makes 4 rotis

Ingredients:
- 1 kg flour
- 100 gms ghee
- 6 tbsp water
- a mixture of molasses and water in which a pinch of
  saffron has been soaked
- poppy or nigella seeds
- 2 tbsp sugar
- 1½ tbsp salt

Method:
Mix the flour with the ghee, sugar and salt until the mixture
resembles breadcrumbs. Add the water to make a stiff
dough. The dough must not be dry, but too much water will
make the bread tough. Knead the dough until it leaves the
fingers, cover and keep it aside for an hour.

Divide the dough into 4 equal sized balls and roll each
into a large, fairly thin circle. Spread ghee on this and fold
in four to make a square. Roll out again, fairly thick this
time. Sprinkle each square with a mixture of molasses and
water in which a pinch of saffron has been soaked, sprinkle
a few poppy seeds or nigella seeds. Bake on a greased
griddle, turning once, for 20 minutes or in a pre-heated oven

(350°F, 180°C) for 12 minutes.

This bread travels well and was taken by Bakar Khan, Governor of Bengal, on his tours of the districts (see text).

Khmberi Roti

Leavened Bread

Makes 12 large rotis

Ingredients:
- 1 kg whole wheat flour
- 1 tsp fresh yeast
- 4 cups warm water
- 3 tsp sugar
- 2 tsp salt
- 1 tsp baking soda
- ½ cup yoghurt

Method:
Dissolve the fresh yeast in the warm water and 1 teaspoon of sugar until it is frothy. Mix the whole wheat flour with salt, 2 teaspoons of sugar and the baking soda. Mix in the yeast and the yoghurt. Add enough hot water by hand to make a soft dough. Knead the dough until it leaves your fingers, about 5 minutes. Cover and leave to rest for at least 2 hours. Roll out into fairly thick rounds, and cook on a griddle, holding it over an open flame to make it puff up. Kept in an airtight tin, this roti keeps fresh for three or four days.

» A recipe from Jani Begum of Avadh.

Shirmal

Flaky Bread

Makes 8 shirmals

Ingredients:
- **500 gms flour**
- **100 gms ghee**
- **milk**
- **saffron**
- **½ tsp salt**

Method:
Mix the flour with the ghee and salt; add enough milk to make a stiff but not dry dough and knead for 8 minutes. Divide the dough into 8 portions and roll them out fairly thick shaping them into heart shapes. Place on a heated griddle and cook for 5–7 minutes on a medium flame on one side. Turn over, glaze with milk and saffron and cook for another 5–7 minutes. This bread may be baked in a pre-heated (350°F, 180°C) oven for 15 minutes.

» A recipe from Mrs Suraiya Gupta.

Paratha

Makes 12 parathas

Ingredients:
- **500 gms flour**
- **2 tbsp ghee**

- **2 tsp sugar**
- **water**
- **½ tsp salt**

Method:

Rub the ghee into the flour and add the sugar and salt. Knead with enough water to make a soft and pliable dough for 8–10 minutes and leave to rest two hours. Roll out into a large thin circle, stretching it with your hands as much as possible. Spread ghee on this and cut it into 12 strips of equal width. Roll each strip into a cylinder and place it flat side up. Roll out into 8-inch circles. Cook on a well-greased griddle over medium fire until brown and crisp on both sides, about 3 minutes on each side.

Laong Paratha

Paratha with Cloves

Makes 4 laong parathas

Ingredients:

Dough
- **250 gms flour**
- **milk**
- **½ tsp salt**

Filling
- **200 gms mutton (minced)**
- **ghee**
- **2 onions (minced)**
- **1-inch piece ginger (minced)**
- **5 cloves garlic (minced)**
- **1 tsp fresh ground pepper**
- **1 tsp garam masala**
- **1 tbsp Worchestershire sauce**
- **dill (chopped)**
- **coriander leaves (chopped)**
- **4–5 green chillies (chopped very fine)**

- **salt to taste**
- **48 cloves**

Method:

Dough
Sift the flour with the salt. Add enough milk to make a soft dough. Knead for 8 minutes. Shape into a ball, cover and set aside.

Filling
Heat 2 tablespoons of ghee to smoking in a wok. Lower heat, brown the onions lightly. Add the garlic and ginger. Fry for 3 minutes. Add the minced mutton and fry until the meat turns brown. Add pepper, garam masala and Worchestershire sauce, dill, coriander leaves and green chillies. Add salt to taste. Stir to mix, cover and put on a low flame for 15 minutes. Take it off the fire and cool.

To assemble
Divide the dough into 16 portions and roll each out into 4 x 4 inch squares. Spread a square lightly with ghee. Take 2 teaspoons of the filling and spread it evenly on a square of dough. Place another square of dough on the filling. Repeat until you have 4 layers. Pin down the edges with 12 cloves. Make 4 parathas in this manner. Heat ½ cup ghee in a deep frying pan and fry the parathas one at a time until they are brown and crisp, turning them once. Serve hot.

» A Muslim meal in Calcutta immediately conjures up thoughts of biryani, murgh mussalam and rezala from Royal Hotel or Sabir or Shiraz. We went to great lengths collecting family recipes. This biryani recipe is from Abdool Shakoor whose job it was to drive and whose interest it was to cook.

Biryani - I

Rice Cooked with Meat and Spices

Serves 8 - 10

Ingredients:

Stage one
- 2 kg meat cut into large pieces
- 50 gms garlic
- 100 gms ginger
- 25 gms dried red chillies
- 50 gms cumin
- 6 green cardamoms
- 4 black cardamoms
- ½ nutmeg
- 500 gms yoghurt

Stage two
- 100 gms ghee
- 50 gms onions (thinly sliced)

Stage three
- 200 gms ghee
- 4 bay leaves
- 4 cups hot water
- salt to taste

Stage four
- 1 kg Basmati rice
- 50 gms ghee
- 150 gms yoghurt

- **1 cup water**
- **salt to taste**

Method:

Stage one
Grind together the garlic, ginger, dried red chillies, cumin, green cardamoms, black cardamoms and nutmeg. Mix the ground spices and the yoghurt with the mutton and leave to marinate for 2 hours in a deep glass or ceramic dish.

Stage two
Heat the ghee in a frying pan and fry the thinly sliced onions crisp and brown. Drain and set aside.

Stage three
Heat the ghee in a deep pan to smoking, reduce heat and add the bay leaves. When they turn colour, add the meat and the marinade, and salt to taste. Stir fry on low heat until all the natural juices have been absorbed and the meat is dry and the oil comes to the top. Add the hot water, stir and allow to simmer covered till the meat is three-fourths done. At this stage, there should be a thick gravy in the pan.

Stage four
In a large pan, bring plenty of water to the boil and cook the rice with the salt until the rice is half done. Drain. In a large pan, arrange the cooked meat with the gravy, spreading it out evenly so that there are no gaps between pieces. Spread half the fried onions over the meat. Spread the rice over the meat and onion layers. Mix together 1 cup water, ghee and yoghurt. Spread this mixture evenly over the rice and cover with a layer of fried onions. Cover the pan. Seal the rim with dough made with flour and water. Heat a large griddle over a high flame.When it is hot, reduce heat to low and place the pan of meat and rice on it. Cook for 35–40 minutes, shaking the pan from time to time to prevent sticking. This part of the cooking can also be done in an oven set at 350° F, 180° C.

Optional

- Whole potatoes peeled, boiled in turmeric water and lightly fried may be added over the layer of meat before adding the rice.
- Biryani is a meal-in-a-dish served with chopped cucumbers, onions, tomatoes and a plain yoghurt raita.

» Biryani, murgh mussallam and zarda polau are three classic dishes served at Muslim weddings in Calcutta. We give a second and more festive recipe from Sara Gangjee, followed by one for murgh mussallam.

Biryani - II

Rice Cooked with Meat and Spices

Serves 8 - 10

Ingredients:

Stage one
- **1 kg mutton**
- **750 gms medium sized potatoes**
- **15 cloves garlic**
- **3-inch piece ginger**
- **5 green chillies**
- **50 gms coriander leaves**
- **2-inch square green papaya**
- **2 tsp cumin seeds**
- **8 cloves**
- **1 tsp saffron**
- **2 cups yoghurt**
- **turmeric**
- **salt**

Stage two
- **1 kg Basmati rice**
- **6 cloves**
- **4 cardamoms**
- **¼ tsp black caraway (shah jeera)**
- **1-inch piece cinnamon**

Stage three
- **2 cups ghee**
- **750 gms onions (sliced)**
- **1 tsp red chilli powder**
- **1 tbsp powdered spices [3 green cardamoms, 3 black cardamoms, 1-inch piece cinnamon, 2 blades mace, 1½ tsp black caraway seeds (shah jeera)]**
- **1 tsp chilli powder**
- **6 alu bokharas**

Stage four
- **1 tbsp rose water**
- **½ cup ghee**
- **3/4 cup milk**

Method:

Stage one
Grind the garlic, ginger, green chillies, coriander leaves, green papaya and cumin seeds. Soak 1 teaspoon saffron in 2 tablespoons of hot water.

Cut the mutton into large pieces. The butcher will do this for you if he is told to cut the meat for biryani. Wash and rub the meat with salt. Keep aside for 15–30 minutes. Squeeze and rub dry with a cloth and coat with a few drops of yellow colouring (we prefer a pinch of turmeric). Mix the ground spices with the yoghurt and rub well over the meat.

Peel the potatoes. Make a cut in the centre of each and coat them with a pinch of turmeric.

Stage two
Wash the rice. Bring a pan three-fourths full of water to the boil and add the rice with the cloves, cardamoms, black caraway and cinnamon. Quarter-cook the rice, strain and

reserve the water.

Stage three
While the rice is boiling, heat the ghee and brown the sliced onions. Drain and keep aside. In half the ghee add 2 teaspoons of fried crushed onion and red chilli powder dissolved in water. Cook for a minute and add potatoes and fry lightly. Drain and set aside. Take a large flat-bottomed pan and arrange in it the pieces of meat in a single layer closely packed, leaving no space between pieces. Pour over it half a cup of the drained ghee, sprinkle the powdered spices and chilli powder. Place the potatoes over the meat in a layer and arrange the alu bokharas between the potatoes.

Stage four
Sprinkle the rose water and 1 teaspoon of saffron water and scatter the remaining fried onions over the potatoes. Spread the rice evenly over this layer and sprinkle the ghee, milk, and one and one-fourth cups of the reserved rice water. Pour the remaining saffron water in the centre of the rice and cover tightly, sealing the lid with dough of flour and water.

Place the pan over a high fire for 15–20 minutes while you heat the oven to very hot (450° F, 300° C). Put the pan into the oven for one and a half hours, lowering the heat to medium (350° F, 180° C) after 20 minutes of cooking. After the biryani is cooked, place the pan again on a medium flame for 10–15 minutes.

» A recipe from Begum Unaiza Khan Chowdhury.

Murgh Mussallam

Spicy and Aromatic Roast Chicken

Serves 4

Ingredients:
- 1¼ kg chicken
- 1 gm saffron soaked in 2 tbsp hot water for half an hour
- 1 egg
- 50 gms cashew nuts (cleaned and chopped)
- 50 gms almonds (cleaned and chopped)
- 50 gms raisins (cleaned and chopped)
- 15 gms pistachios (cleaned and chopped)
- 150 gms ghee
- 1 tbsp garlic paste
- 1 tbsp ginger paste
- 2 tbsp onion paste
- 1½ cups water
- chopped nuts and raisins
- few drops screwpine (kewra) essence
- salt to taste

Method:
Clean and skin the chicken. Pierce it all over with a fork.
Hard boil and shell the egg and put it in the stomach cavity
of the chicken with the chopped cashew nuts, almonds,
raisins, pistachios.

Coat the chicken with the soaked saffron. Truss it and
sew up the stomach vent.

Heat the ghee in a large pan. Put in the garlic, ginger
and onion paste and fry for 5 minutes on medium heat. Put
in the chicken and fry until the spices turn colour and the
oil comes to the top. Add 1 cup water, cover and cook till the
water dries. Add ½ cup water and some chopped nuts and
raisins. Before serving add a few drops of essence of
screwpine (kewra) and heat through.

The amount of water given is for a broiler chicken; double the quantity will be required for a country chicken.

Murgh mussallam can also be roasted in a medium oven, (350° F, 180° C), for half an hour, basting every 10 minutes.

» To counteract the fat in the rich polaus and curries, burhani, a yoghurt drink, is taken as an accompaniment. A recipe from Jani Begum of Avadh.

Burhani

A Flavoured Yoghurt Drink

Serves 8

Ingredients:
• **4 cups yoghurt**
• **4 cups water**
• **1 tsp salt**
• **2 tsp black pepper**
• **2 tsp cumin powder (roasted on a griddle)**
• **8 cloves garlic (chopped)**
• **green chillies to taste (chopped)**

Method:
Mix the yoghurt with the water in a glass or ceramic bowl. Add the salt, black pepper, cumin powder and chopped garlic. Mix well and serve cold. Burhani is made well in a blender. Add the chillies after blending.

» No one who has lived in Bengal for any length of time has been able to resist the fish in the rivers and tanks. Meat polaus have been adapted to fish. This recipe for hilsa polau comes from Dr Sonya Noor whose

family lives in Malda, North Bengal, where the
Ganga is full of this fish. It is brought into Calcutta
in season. Fish polau can be made with any firm white
fish like rui or bhetki.

Ilish Maachher Polau

Hilsa Polau

Serves 6

Ingredients:
- 1 kg hilsa
- 750 gms Basmati rice
- 1-inch piece ginger
- 2 medium onions
- 6 cloves garlic
- 350 gms yoghurt
- 200 gms ghee
- 2 green cardamoms
- 4 cloves
- 2-inch piece cinnamon
- 4 bay leaves
- hot water
- 3 cups warm milk
- 2–3 tsp sugar
- salt to taste

Method:
Cut the hilsa into half inch thick steaks (10–12 pieces).
Wash and semi dry the Basmati rice. Grind to a paste the
ginger, onions and garlic.

Mix the onion-ginger-garlic paste with half the yoghurt
(175 grams) and a little salt and marinate the fish for 1 hour.
Heat the ghee in a pan till very hot. Reduce heat and fry the
green cardamoms, cloves, cinnamon and bay leaves till they
are fragrant. Add the fish and marinade and fry for another
3 minutes. Lower heat, add half a cup of hot water and cook
for another 7 minutes on moderately high heat. The water

should have evaporated and the fish cooked. Remove the fish and set aside. Leave the gravy in the pan. Add rice to the pan and cook on high heat until it changes colour. Add 3 cups of hot water and warm milk, sugar, salt and stir well. Let it come to the boil, reduce heat, cover and cook for 10–12 minutes. The rice should be almost done but still moist. Remove the rice and butter the pan well. Layer it with rice and fish alternately beginning and ending with rice. Whip the rest of the yoghurt (175 grams) and pour it over the rice. Cover with a tight fitting lid. Preheat a griddle on a high flame, lower the flame and cook the polau on the griddle. The polau can also be baked in a preheated (300° F, 150° C) oven for 15 minutes.

Sonya says the best part of eating polau or biryani is to scrape the bottom of the pan for the bits which refuse to come out easily!

» Tehary is another dish of rice cooked with meat. This recipe is supposed to have originated in the kitchens of the Nawabs of Dacca. As mustard oil replaces pure ghee and beef replaces the traditional mutton, tehary was probably made for the lesser mortals of the Nawab's household.

Tehary

Rice and Meat Cooked with Spices in Mustard Oil

Serves 10 - 12

Ingredients:
- **2 kg beef (preferably undercut)**
- **1 kg long grained rice**
- **250 gms onions**
- **3 eggs (hard boiled)**
- **100 gms ginger**

- **50 gms garlic**
- **100 gms yoghurt**
- **250 gms onions (finely sliced)**
- **mustard oil**
- **hot water**
- **green chillies to taste**
- **½ nutmeg (grated)**
- **½ tsp mace**
- **salt to taste**

Method:

Cut the beef into one and a half inch cubes. Make a paste of the onions, ginger and garlic. Mix it into the beef with yoghurt and salt to taste and marinate for half an hour.

Fry the finely sliced onions crisp and brown, set aside. Heat 250 grams mustard oil in a pan till smoking. Add the beef and stir fry on medium heat till the natural juices are absorbed. Stir in 4 cups of hot water and allow the curry to come to the boil. Reduce heat and simmer till the meat is done and there is a thick gravy. Heat 250 gms mustard oil. Add the rice and stir fry until it changes colour. Add 8 cups of warm water and bring to the boil. Stir and reduce the flame, leave the rice to simmer approximately for 15–20 minutes or until it is nearly cooked. Mix in the cooked beef, green chillies to taste, grated nutmeg and mace.

Cook on a low flame until the rice absorbs all the liquid and the grains are quite separate.

Serve on a flat dish, garnished with browned onions and thickly sliced hard boiled eggs.

» To accompany tehary, we chose this simple egg curry
  made by Sofia Bibi whose husband runs an egg stall
  at the New Market.

Anda Tarkari

Egg Curry with Raw Eggs

Serves 3 - 4

Ingredients:
* **6 eggs**
* **2 tbsp mustard oil**
* **2 onions (chopped)**
* **2 tsp ginger paste**
* **2 tsp garlic paste**
* **1 tsp ground cumin**
* **2 tbsp water**
* **chopped coriander**
* **chopped tomato**
* **chopped green chillies**
* **salt to taste**

Method:
Heat the mustard oil to smoking in a deep frying pan.
Reduce heat and brown the chopped onions. Add the ginger
paste, the garlic paste and the ground cumin and fry for 3
minutes. Add the water and salt to taste and simmer for 1
minute. Lower heat and carefully break in the eggs. Spoon
the gravy over, cover and cook until the eggs are set. To
serve, cut into squares and garnish with the chopped
coriander, tomato and green chillies.

» The Muslim ways of cooking meat with cereals make nourishing meals-in-a-dish. Halim is eaten after a fast during the month of Ramzan.

Halim

Meat and Cereal Stew

Serves 12

Ingredients:
- ¼ cup toovar or arhar dal (red gram)
- ¼ cup chana dal (split dried Bengal gram)
- ¼ cup moong dal (moong beans)
- ¼ cup masoor dal (split dried red lentil)
- ½ cup rice
- 1 cup dalia (broken wheat)
- 1 kg shoulder of mutton
- 4 large onions (sliced)
- 4 large onions (ground)
- 10 cloves garlic (ground)
- 2-inch piece ginger (ground)
- 1 cup ghee or oil
- 2 tbsp turmeric
- 4 tbsp chilli powder
- 8 cups water
- 4 tbsp garam masala [10 green cardamoms, 10 cloves, 4-inch piece cinnamon, 10 black cardamoms, 1 tsp mace (roasted on a griddle and powdered)]
- wedges of lime
- chopped green coriander
- salt to taste

Method:
Wash the dals and the rice. Cut the mutton into small pieces.

Heat the ghee or oil in a 5 litre pressure cooker, add the sliced onions and cook till brown. Add ground onion, ginger, garlic and turmeric, and chilli powder. Fry until the spices change colour. Add the meat and stir fry over medium heat for 15 minutes. Add rice, dals and dalia. Mix thoroughly and stir fry for 10–15 minutes. Add salt to taste. Add the water and pressure cook for 1 hour over a medium-low flame. As the dalia tends to stick to the bottom of the cooker it is best to uncover the cooker at least twice and stir the halim. Continue cooking until nearly all the water is absorbed and the oil comes to the surface. Add the garam masala. Serve with wedges of lime and chopped green coriander.

Halim can also be cooked without pressure—it would require 10 cups of water, 2 hours of cooking time and frequent stirring in a pan.

» A recipe from Mrs Zarina Patherya.

Harisa

Meat and Wheat with Spices

Serves 6

Ingredients:
- 250 gms boneless mutton
- 250 gms dalia (broken wheat)
- 3 onions (chopped)
- 4–6 green chillies (chopped)
- 1 tbsp garlic paste
- 1 tbsp ginger paste
- 2 tbsp roasted sesame seed paste
- 1 tbsp ginger powder
- 1 tbsp aniseed powder
- 4 large black cardamoms (peeled and crushed)
- 4 green cardamoms (crushed)
- 6 cloves (crushed)
- 4-inch piece cinnamon (crushed)
- 6 cups water
- 1 cup milk or cream
- 2 tbsp ghee

- 1 onion (sliced)
- powdered garam masala (2-inch piece cinnamon, 6 peppercorns, 2 green cardamoms, 2 black cardamoms)
- 1 tbsp ginger (cut fine)
- 2 tbsp mint leaves (chopped)
- sliced ginger
- wedges of lime
- salt to taste

Method:

Cut the boneless mutton into pieces and mix with the dalia, chopped onions, chopped green chillies, garlic paste, ginger paste, roasted sesame seed paste, ginger powder and aniseed powder. Add the peeled and crushed black cardamoms, crushed green cardamoms, crushed cloves, crushed cinnamon and salt. Cook in a pressure cooker with the water over a medium-low flame for 1 hour. Uncover once during cooking and stir well, as the dalia tends to stick.

Release pressure, remove lid and mix the soup well with a stirrer or in a blender to make a thick creamy soup. Add 1 cup milk or cream and mix well.

Heat the ghee and fry the sliced onion until lightly browned. Add the garam masala powder; add the finely cut ginger, and chopped mint leaves. Stir fry, add to the soup and cover. Before serving, heat the soup well, stir thoroughly and pour into bowls. Serve chopped mint, sliced ginger and wedges of lime separately.

» For those who like brain, this is a simple, quick dish. A recipe from Mrs Sara Gangjee.

Brain with Methi

Brain with Fenugreek Greens

Serves 4 - 6

Ingredients:
- 4 sheep's brains

- **100 gms fenugreek greens**
- **salted water**
- **1 tsp turmeric**
- **2 tbsp oil**
- **1 tsp coriander powder**
- **1 tsp cumin powder**
- **1 tsp chilli powder**
- **salt to taste**

Method:
Wash and clean the sheep's brains and boil them in salted water with the turmeric. Break them into chunks. Boil and drain the fenugreek leaves. Heat the oil in a wok and when it is smoking, take the wok off the fire and fry the coriander powder, cumin powder and chilli powder. Put the wok back on a low flame, add the fenugreek leaves, the brain and salt to taste. Stir until the brain gets the colour of the gravy.

» N. A. Siddiqi who cleans our carpets is an octogenarian Arab who came to Calcutta with his father from Sind. He gave us this recipe for cooking fish, which is very similar to the kok palla the Sindhis cook.

Whole Stuffed Fish

Serves 6

Ingredients:
- **1½ kg bhetki or any other white fish with a central bone structure**
- **lime**
- **salt**

Filling
- **3 large onions (sliced)**

- **2 tbsp ghee**
- **1 tbsp ginger (ground)**
- **2 tsp garlic (ground)**
- **1 tsp chilli powder**
- **50 gms mint (chopped)**
- **50 gms green coriander (chopped)**

Garnish
- **4 cloves garlic (chopped)**
- **4 green onions with tops**
- **mint (chopped)**
- **green coriander (chopped)**
- **chives (chopped)**

Method:
Scale the fish and split it down the middle to remove the bones, but do not separate the two halves. The fishmonger will do this for you.

Score the fish on both sides and rub with salt and lime and let it stand for a couple of hours.

Brown the onions in the ghee in a large frying pan, add the ground ginger, ground garlic, chilli powder, chopped mint, chopped green coriander and salt to taste. Stuff the fish with this mixture and put the two halves together. Tie it with twine and place it in a large greased baking dish in a moderate oven (350° F, 180° C) for 20–30 minutes. This can also be cooked over a vessel of hot water. When it is done, it should flake easily. Untie the fish and gently scrape off the skin. Heat some oil and fry the chopped garlic, green onions with the tops, a handful of chopped mint, green coriander and chives, until the herbs are just soft. Pour over fish and serve.

» The Muslim table did not include many vegetables but brinjal seems to have been acceptable. Later the local vegetables were adapted into highly spiced qormas and bhajis. A brinjal recipe from Mrs Zarina Patherya.

Baigan Bharta

Charred Brinjal Appetizer

Serves 12

Ingredients:
- **4 large brinjals**
- **4 tbsp yoghurt**
- **1 onion (chopped)**
- **3 green chillies (chopped)**
- **green coriander**
- **½ tsp cumin seeds (roasted and ground)**

Method:
Char the brinjals and skin them. Place them in a glass bowl. Mash them with the yoghurt, chopped onion, chopped green chillies and green coriander. Sprinkle roasted and ground cumin seeds.

» Enchor, the green jackfruit is called gachh pantha—tree mutton—for its meaty taste. We chose this preparation of enchor because it fits in with the Muslim cuisine in this chapter.

Enchorer Korma

Green Jackfruit Curry

Serves 6

Ingredients:
- **500 gms green jackfruit**
- **½ tsp turmeric**
- **2 tbsp oil**
- **2 tbsp ghee**

- 1 tsp cumin seeds
- 2–3 bay leaves
- 1 tbsp ginger paste
- 1½ tbsp onion paste
- 1 tsp red chilli powder
- 50 gms yoghurt
- 2 tsp sugar
- 3 green cardamoms
- 4–5 sticks cinnamon
- 3–4 cloves
- 1 tbsp raisins
- ½ cup hot water
- salt to taste

Method:

Grease your fingers and cut the jackfruit into large pieces. The vegetable seller in the market will do this for you. Boil the pieces with ¼ teaspoon of turmeric in a pan, drain and keep aside. Heat the oil and ghee in a large wok or pan to smoking. Reduce heat and add the cumin seeds and bay leaves. Fry until the spices are fragrant. Add ¼ teaspoon of turmeric, ginger paste, onion paste, red chilli powder, yoghurt, sugar and salt. Stir fry until the spices change colour. Add the green cardamoms, cinnamon, cloves—half crushed. Continue frying until the spices are a rich brown and the oil comes to the surface. Add the jackfruit and stir fry until they are well mixed, about 3 minutes. Add the raisins and continue frying for another 5 minutes. Add the hot water and simmer until it has been absorbed and the oil comes to the surface.

» This comes from the kitchens of the Maharajas of Burdwan, as told by Poncha—see text.

Maachh Beguner Kalia

Carp and Brinjal curry

Serves 6

Ingredients:
- **500 gms rui or any other large fish**
- **500 gms brinjals**
- **5 tbsp mustard oil**
- **2 bay leaves**
- **2 green cardamoms**
- **4 cloves**
- **2-inch piece cinnamon**
- **1 tbsp onion paste**
- **1 tbsp ginger paste**
- **1 tsp red chilli powder**
- **2 tsp sugar**
- **2 tbsp yoghurt**
- **salt to taste**

Method:
Boil, skin and bone the fish. Boil the brinjals, stem and skin them. Heat the mustard oil to smoking in a large wok. Reduce heat and fry the bay leaves, green cardamoms, cloves and cinnamon. When they are fragrant, add the onion paste, ginger paste, red chilli powder, sugar, salt to taste and yoghurt.

Stir fry gently until the oil comes to the top. Break the fish into large flakes and cut the brinjal into 2-inch pieces. Add these to the spices. Stir fry over medium heat until lightly browned but still moist.

» The recipe for this royal slice of bread came to us from the royal house of Avadh. Minakshie has cut it down to suit a contemporary kitchen, but that has not taken away its flavour.

Shahi Peosi

Royal Bread Toffee

Serves 12

Ingredients:
- ½ slice bread soaked in 1 cup milk
- 1 tsp saffron soaked in 2 tbsp milk
- 110 gms dehydrated milk (khoa)
- 15–20 almonds
- 125 gms ghee
- 12 eggs
- 60 gms sugar
- rose water
- chopped nuts

Method:
Grate the dehydrated milk (khoa). Soak, peel and grind the almonds. Heat the ghee and add the bread and milk and cook until thick in a pan. Remove from fire and let it cool. Separate the yolks from the whites of the eggs; beat the yolks till thick and yellow and the whites to a soft peak. Stir the yolks into the milk mixture with all the other prepared ingredients and sugar. Fold in the whites gently and place in a large greased oven proof dish—the nawabs used thick lined copper vessels—and bake in a preheated (300° F, 150° C) oven for 20 minutes. Test by inserting a knife into the toffee. If it comes out clean, the dish is ready. Sprinkle rose water and chopped nuts. This dish may be cooked on high heat in a microwave oven.

» Halwa is eaten with paratha at Shab-e-Barat (see text). Anda halwa keeps well. It is a perfect gift for a friend with a sweet tooth.

Anda Halwa

Egg Toffee

Serves 12

Ingredients:
* **12 eggs**
* **2 litres milk**
* **2 cups sugar**
* **½ tsp saffron soaked in 2 tbsp milk**
* **1 cup pure ghee**
* **1 tbsp almonds (blanched and slivered)**
* **1 tsp screwpine (kewra) essence**

Method:
Separate the yolks from the whites. Beat the whites till they are stiff in a bowl or in a food processor. Boil down the milk to one-third of the original quantity in a pan.

Heat the milk and egg yolks together with the sugar. Cook them over a very low flame, stirring all the time. Fold in the stiff egg whites and saffron. Stir in the ghee. Continue cooking gently, taking care that the mixture does not curdle. When close to setting, add the almonds and screw pine (kewra) essence. Beat well to remove all lumps. Pour into a greased dish and allow it to set. Cool and cut into diamond-shaped pieces.

» The grand finale to this chapter of sultans and slaves is a recipe for sewai, the traditional sweet offered at Id-ul-Fitr after the month of Ramzan. Our recipe comes from the house of the last Nawab of Avadh, Wajid Ali Shah, as told by his descendant Jani Begum. The quantities are for royal entertainment.

Sewai

Sweet Vermicelli

Serves 25

Ingredients:
- 2 litres milk
- 1 kg sewai
- 250 gms dehydrated milk (khoa)
- 2 kg sugar made into a syrup in 1 cup water
- 500 gms ghee
- 200 gms almonds (ground)
- ½ tsp saffron soaked in 2 tbsp milk
- 250 gms raisins

Method:
Cook down the milk to three-fourths of its original quantity. Grate the dehydrated milk (khoa).

Heat the ghee in a very large thick bottomed pan. Add the sewai and brown it gently if preferred, or leave it white, turning it in the ghee three or four times. Take the pan off the fire and add the milk, stirring quickly so that the sewai absorbs the milk. Add the sugar syrup and simmer very gently. Add the dehydrated milk (khoa), the ground almonds and the saffron. Take off fire and add the raisins. Stir well taking care not to mash the sewai. Place in a serving dish. The sewai must be separate yet tender and not too greasy.

Chapter 4

Firinghee Flavours

Bandel Cheese, Dolmas and Worcestershire Sauce

The Firinghees came from the Iberian peninsula, northern Europe, France, Greece, the British Isles and Asia Minor. They came over land and sea. They came to trade, to colonize and to convert to Christianity. In the beginning many died young as a result of disease and over-indulgence. Some chose to remain while others were guided by the destinies of their countries.

On the opposite bank of the river Hooghly from Calcutta, a brick and mortar legacy of Governors' residences, churches and court houses tell the broken tale of a mini Europe. The first Europeans to navigate the dangerous creeks and channels of the Sundarbans were the Portuguese. Driven out of their native land for one reason or another, they turned to piracy and were feared by the local inhabitants for their cruel ways. Others, like Pedro Tavares, came in the name of their God and in 1579 the Mughal Emperor Akbar granted a firman (permission) to Tavares to build a church and a town. He chose the salt port of Ogli because it was a good harbour and named it Bandel, from bandar, the Persian word for wharf. By the end of the century the Portuguese had settled down as merchants and lived in great luxury. They dressed in nawabi style, ate their duck buffadoo and prawn temperado and 'made merry with dancing slave girls, seamstresses, cooks and confectioners'. They plundered the Chittagong hill tracts and took away the tribal Mogs as galley slaves and servants, who quickly learnt the culinary art of their masters. The ships' biscuits, hard as stone, were the beginning of a long line of baking with flour, water and salt, later sweetened as shortbread and flaky millefeuilles, filled and flavoured for every occasion. The small discs of salted smoked Bandel cheese were probably made by the Mog cooks under Portuguese supervision. The cheese is now made in Calcutta and sold as Bandel cheese in two shops in the famous not-so-new New Market.

When the English were ready for housekeeping, the progeny of Portuguese intermarriage rowed across the river to seize the opportunities of employment. Portuguese merchants from the west coast of India also came hotfoot to Calcutta to make their fortunes. A God-fearing people, they built and endowed Catholic churches in the grey quarter of the town adjoining the English Tank Square settlement, the pukka white quarter. Many of them came from Goa and Goan cooking added zest to the culinary fare of Calcutta. Goa, Daman and Diu remained a Portuguese colony till 1961.

Sorpotel, a highly spiced mixture of meats, is a must at Christmas or a marriage feast in the Goan community. A Goan chicken curry eaten with sadam, a light puffy rice cake, is unforgettable and who can say no to a vindaloo or a spiced sausage.

A very different shipload, the Dutch, arrived in Chinsurah, a few kilometres upstream in 1625. This stolid breed of merchants brought with them wine and cheese. They happily integrated with the local people and their gifts to the Sandeshwar Temple are used for puja on festival days.

Baranagar, a few kilometres north of Calcutta and on the same side of the river, was once the haunt of the Dutch mynheers. H. E. A. Cotton writes in *Calcutta Old and New* that Streynsham Master, who visited the village in 1676, found a 'Hogg factory . . . where they kill 3,000 hogs a year and salt them' to preserve the meat for revictualing their outgoing ships. Baranagar, some say, derived its name from baraha (boar) and nagar (town).

Fluctuating with the political climate in the West, the socializing on both banks of the Hooghly waxed and waned. 'In peaceable times,' wrote one Mr Price, 'the European inhabitants of the English, French and Dutch settlements mingle together like a patriarchal family of old. Their plays, their Freemason's Clubs, their public halls on the birthdays of their several sovereigns are open to the three settlements. Everywhere you are regaled with a tankard of English beer, a bottle of French wine and a slice of Dutch cheese.'

In 1824, the British exchanged Sumatra for Chinsurah and it was goodbye to the Dutchman's bicentennial sojourn.

Next to arrive was the French East India Company. They set up Fort d'Orleans at Chandernagore, a few kilometres away from Dutch Chinsurah, in 1688. They brought with them the loaf of bread, feathery flaky millefeuilles pastry, sauces and dressings. The many layered khaja and Daccai paratha were already here in the homes of the Nawabs of Bengal. The native cook learnt to make it à la francais and called his work of art 'milly filly'.

The most significant contribution of the French to Calcutta's table is pau roti (loaf of bread)—the universal tiffin and breakfast food of today's Indian. Pau is said to be the corruption of *pain*, the French word for bread. Pau, however, is the Hindi word for feet which leads others to believe that, as with the grapes in the vineyards of France, the huge quantities of dough were kneaded by stamping feet. But in fact pau is the Portuguese word for a loaf of bread.

The gastronome sought out the Hotel de France on Chandernagore's Strand, lined with stately mahogany trees. The menu for dinner read something like this: 'Soupe aux Moules, Oeufs à la Toulonnaise, Filet de Beckti, Pomme de Terre et Petits Pois, Tarte de Pommes, Cafe au Lait.' The revels of yesteryear have been tempered by the law, for the Hotel de France is now a subjudiciary court. But we shall see how these very same courses reappeared on Calcutta tables.

Back to Burrabazaar. The hub of business activity in Calcutta was a veritable Tower of Babel in the eighteenth century as Armenian, Jewish, Greek and Arab traders wagged fingers, shook capped heads and clinched deals. Among the foreign communities who first made Calcutta their home were the Armenians from New Julfa in Persia (Iran). Before all else they built a wooden chapel in Old China Bazaar Street, which was replaced in 1722 by the Holy Church of Nazareth on Armenian Street. Calcutta also has an Armenian Ghat—both ghat and street are tributes to their philanthropy and business acumen.

The British accepted the Armenians, perhaps remembering that it was one of them who negotiated the important trading rights with Emperor Farrukshuyar in 1715. The Armenians have always maintained their identity and even as a very small group today, they celebrate Christmas on January 6 with a solemn service at their church. A lunch follows at the Burra Club, as the Armenian Club on Park Street is called, with a mixed menu of Armenian and Indian dishes. Serving bowls of cabbage dolma sit comfortably beside fish kalia and cauliflower bhaji. The priest blesses the food on the buffet table, says grace and the first spoonful of samit pilaff is served. Old Armenia lives on in the dolma. Once upon a time, grape vines grew on bamboo trellises in Armenian gardens for a taste of the real thing—minced meat and rice wrapped in the vine leaf. Today cabbage leaves make a good substitute. Friends, invited to share the Christmas lunch, also exchange recipes. The Armenians are a hospitable and generous people. They owned and managed boarding houses and, later, hotels in the city. Arathoon Stephen, like many other Armenian boys and young men, was sent to Calcutta in the last quarter of the nineteenth century almost penniless. Stephen worked hard as a jeweller's assistant in a shop situated on the property which he eventually purchased, plot by plot, and built the Grand Hotel, a landmark in the city and in the history of hoteliering in India. Despite their dwindling numbers, two Armenian ladies still run hotels in the good old boarding house tradition.

Shalom Cohen was the first resident Jew in Calcutta, although by no means the first to visit this great commercial entrepôt. He arrived from Aleppo via Bombay and Surat in 1799 and felt at home near the Armenian and Portuguese settlements around Moorgihatta. The area around the Roman Catholic Cathedral on Portuguese Church Street is still called Moorgihatta—literally 'market for chickens', a favourite meat of the new settlers.

The later immigrants were from Baghdad and they steadily increased in numbers. The Calcutta Jewry prospered. A third synagogue in the city, the magnificent Maghen David was built by Elia David Joseph Ezra in 1884. When India became independent, many Jews migrated to Israel and other countries. The hundred strong community today regard themselves as part of the Sephardic group. Their kosher kitchens contribute some tasty additions to gourmand Calcutta.

Beside the great bazaar where they traded, another colourful colonnaded market—Tiretta Bazaar—spread out its exotic wares.

Edward Tiretta, a friend of Casanova, was exiled from his native Venice and came to seek his fortunes in Calcutta's Ali Baba caves. He was the City Civil Architect, a prosperous post no doubt for in 1783 he acquired the market. The Portuguese, Armenian, Jewish and Greek residents of the villas around this grey quarter of the city snopped for canaries in cages or leopard cubs as their fancy chose. Here all the ingredients for their mahashas, vindaloo and pilaff were available, and of the best quality, for the Ihudis as the Jews were called settled for nothing but the best.

At Nahoum's on a Saturday in Calcutta's New Market, Norman Nahoum has the time of day for everyone and a fresh cheese cake for his friends. Nahoum & Sons is the only shop where Jewish cheese, plaited or in blocks and unleavened bread has gentile patronage. The cheese makes a delicious addition to a salad or can be eaten on a piece of toast. His shop is always full of people—old customers, visitors from up-country and tourists from abroad living in the small hotels around the market.

Jewish kitchens functioned under the eagle eye of an elderly lady. The admonition from the Old Testament: 'Thou shalt not cook the kid in its mother's milk', was strictly adhered to and utensils were kept completely separate for dairy and meat foods. Aloo makallah, a potato preparation, is perhaps their best-known and most appreciated dish in Calcutta. The potato is coated with turmeric—an addition by the Indian cook—salt and pepper and deep fried to a crisp. The Armenian dolma is the Jewish mahashas—tomatoes, brinjals and capsicums stuffed with rice, minced meat and herbs of which mint is essential. The links in the culinary chain across the trading posts from London to Shanghai connect the meat filled pastry samusak of the Muslim feasts to the Jewish sambusak, a cheese filled pastry. Indians have adopted this and converted it into the samosa in the north and the three cornered Bengali singara.

Muslim cooks from Midnapore worked in affluent Jewish homes and learnt the customs and cuisine earning their clan the title of 'Jewish Cooks'. In turn, their sons inherited the cooking skills which were sometimes better than the memsahib's! They are now, like the Mogs, a vanishing breed.

The Jewish calendar has its movable High Holy days. Yom Kippur, the Sabbath of Sabbaths and a Day of Atonement, is observed with prayers. April is a month of festivals in Calcutta—Easter for the Christians, Poila Baisak, the first day of the year for Bengalis, Baisakhi for the Punjabis, Bohag Bihu for the Assamese and Passover for the Jews, commemorating their deliverance from bondage. The women have a busy time spring-cleaning the house and the Jewish women are particular that every surface in the kitchen is scrubbed clean of all traces of leaven. A senior member who lived in Calcutta described the baking of mussa by Jewish women in the Beth El Synagogue before the feast. Mussa, a wafer-thin, flat, unleavened bread, is eaten dipped in halek made from date juice—boiled, thickened and garnished with almonds and walnuts—a nostalgic link with the land from where they came. Mussa appeared in the Colootola wayside shops around the Beth El Synagogue and other communities discovered that this crisp bread went well with soorwa or stew.

Armenian and Jewish residents of Calcutta had a similar social life. The Galstauns, the Stephens, the Ezras and the Cohens owned racehorses, kept lavish tables at which ladies in frills and flounces, jewels and saris, enjoyed their hospitality. What is more, they gave of their bounty most generously to the poor in the country of their domicile. In every old hospital there is at least one ward donated by a Sassoon, an Ezra or a Galstaun. Calcutta's Zoological Garden has an Ezra House and a Gubbay House. And so it was with the earlier Portuguese merchants, the Barettos and the D'Souzas, who built churches, endowed orphanages, homes for the aged and served on committees of educational institutions. The flavours of their foods are reminiscent of a time when Calcutta was truly cosmopolitan, a home for world trade and commerce.

Meanwhile the East Indiamen unloaded cargoes and ships' cooks. They taught the bawarchee and the Mog cooks to boil, to bake and to fry as the sahibs would like it. The quality and choice of ingredients was not always in their favour. Often the ingenuity of the Indian apprentice saved the day. One excellent example is the Worcestershire Sauce, its Indianness disguised only by its name for it is a pungent mixture of spices and vinegar used to mask the taste and smell of meats that had risen higher than they should have.

The life of the British community in the early days was symbolized in messing at the East India Company's general table. The main consideration was economy. This was found contrary to the findings because the expenses of the table were three times that incurred by individual board wages to Company servants. The 'wicked native servants' were blamed but unmentioned to Leadenhall Street was the fact that the dinner (lunch) and supper had fifteen courses which included 'kishmishes, Bengal Goats, Sugar Candy, Almonds, Brahminy Bull, Turkeys, Geese, Sheep, Rabbits and Lime' and of course, wine flowed like the Hooghly. The prescribed mess menu was an abstemious 'salt fish, rice for supper and nine courses for dinner'!

There was a saying that when the Portuguese settled down in a new place, their first priority was a church; for the Dutch, it was a fort and for the English, a tavern. And punch houses and taverns sprouted like beans in eighteenth-century Calcutta. Major Harry Hobbs gives a very readable account of old taverns in India in *John Barleycorn Bahadur*.

Apollo's Tavern, full of flies, was set up in Lall Bazaar in 1758, just beyond the Old Fort. Buntings strung across the street leading to eating houses, grog shops and brothels earned the street the nickname 'Flag Street'. Today it is the headquarters of the Calcutta Police.

Twenty years later, when refrigeration was still unheard of and ice a far cry on the Tropic of Cancer, Mr J. Tresham advertised that besides supplying 'Dinners, Suppers or Cold Collations on the shortest notice' he also prepared 'Biscuits of all kinds; tarts and tartlets fresh every day' and for 'up-country' and long sea voyages 'Potted Beef, Veal, Mutton, Ducks, Geese and Pigeons, Collard Beef,

Mutton, Pork and small Pigs, Fish, Coreach, Mince Meat, Plumb Cakes, Jams and Marmalades of all kinds' guaranteed for six months.

Fresh oysters are not seen in Calcutta anymore but two hundred years ago, the booming oyster business brought these delicacies to the table at almost every meal. Mr Robert Rishton offered in 1781, 'oysters every week'. The Harmonic Tavern had a well to keep the oysters fresh. Shipments of 'pearl oysters' came to Calcutta from Ceylon and were put up for auction in lots of 12,000. The successful bidders kept them in the sun to open and eagerly searched for pearls.

The centre of social life in Calcutta, the Harmonic in Lall Bazaar, boasted the 'handsomemost house in the Settlement'. Humorous Hobbs adds: '. . . and one of the advantages of a pub over a club is that you never know who may come into it. In a club you often know only too well.' Those were the days of 'eating, drinking to excess, gambling and shouting' and the tamasha at the tavern lasted till three in the morning.

Monsieur Le Gallais had a tavern near the famous Harmonic frequented by Richard Barwell, a member of the Governor-General's Council. Le Gallais was much in demand. The second Masonic Lodge of Bengal—Lodge Industry and Perseverance—was installed at Brother Le Gallais's on the second Friday of every month. He catered for a New Year's dinner hosted by 'His Lordship' at the Old Court House. The numerous guests dined on turtle, turkeys and 'other good things' and drank twenty-four 'loyal toasts' to an accompaniment by the Grenadiers who fired a blank cartridge out of the window after each toast. The first St Andrew's Dinner was held at Le Gallais and it is not improbable that haggis was on the menu as it was till recently specially flown in from bonny Scotland to the residence of the British Deputy High Commissioner.

James Augustus Hickey's *Bengal Gazette* has pride of place as Calcutta's first newspaper but was more like the tabloids in Britain that soak up every piece of gossip. It was not royalty this time but the 'Topsi Mutchees' (mango fish) that got caught in its black and white net. We read that at meetings in the late eighteenth century the eating of mango fish was a priority on the agenda! One retired colonel swore it was worth a journey to Calcutta just to eat 'Topsi-Mutchees lightly crumbed and fried'.

In 1830 business in Calcutta suffered a depression and many firms declared insolvency. With recovery around 1845, small traders opened shop. Wine Merchants head the list followed by 'Bakers and Confectioners, Tailors, Habit Makers, Boot, Shoe & Harness Makers, Milliners & Dressmakers and a dozen General Shopkeepers'.

About this time the Moravian missionaries brought not only their trades but Spartan foods like German bread. These traders found temporary homes in the many boarding houses, one of them, O'Brien's Chop House, in Radha Bazaar—the watch and clock market today—but nothing more is said about either O'Brien or his chops.

Caviare was an accompaniment to drinks at Calcutta's bars and food poisoning was not uncommon after eating meals in 'doubtful places'—even 'the best'. A rhyme made up by a victim in the koi hai style is worth a mention.

You're quite all right inside the bar
But Khubburdar, the caviarre (*sic*).

John Spence is, according to Hobbs, the originator of hotels in Bengal. The earliest mention of Spence's Hotel is in 1830. After a long sea voyage around the Cape, on a diet of salt beef and hard biscuits, with 'one tablecloth to last the voyage', the weary traveller guided to Spence's beholds a snow white tablecloth and its 'beautiful array of ham, eggs (fresh for a change), a superb kind of fish from the salt water lakes called a becktee or cockup fried, boiled rice, muffins, tea, coffee, etc. Plaintains, radishes, small prints of butter in a handsome cut-glass vessel of cold water and a bouquet of flowers.'

Its situation was well-placed, just a stone's throw from Government House now Raj Bhavan. It had an almost unbroken tradition of excellent managers, barmen and stewards from the P & O Shipping Lines who kept the flag flying till the 1970s. The hotel doors were finally closed and later reopened to admit a bank.

A break came unexpectedly for Calcuttans on board the *S S Tuscany* making 1833 a memorably cool and comfortable year. It was ice. The reader may relax with a taken-for-granted iced drink and enjoy the believe-it-or-not anecdotes that circulated when this luxury arrived in Calcutta.

J. Stocqueler, a colourful journalist and editor of *The Englishman*, the leading daily newspaper in Calcutta, was rudely awakened by his old faithful who could not wait to give him the news that burruf (ice) had arrived from America. 'There it lay,' wrote Stocqueler later, 'in a square mass of the purest crystal, packed in felt and fragrant pine dust. A quantity of rosy American Baldwin apples reposed upon the surface of this glacier . . .' Back in his office, the facile editorial pen wrote on: 'How many Calcutta tables glittered that morning with lumps of ice. The butter dishes were filled; the goblets of water were converted into miniature arctic seas with icebergs floating on the surface. All business was suspended till noon, that people might rush about to pay each other congratulatory visits and devise means for perpetuating the supply. Everybody invited everybody to dinner to taste claret and beer cooled by the American importation.'

Another story related that a lady reclining on her veranda noticed something large and white shining on her grass tennis court. She put on her topi (hat) and went out to investigate. To her dismay, she discovered a lump of precious ice. The khitmatgar (house steward) was sent for and scolded for throwing away so valuable a commodity. Surprised at his memsahib's outburst, he replied in bewilderment, 'But huzoor, that is the stale ice of yesterday.'

The American captain of the *Tuscany* was presented with a gold cup by the Governor-General, Lord Bentinck, and the romance of American ice was listed as an achievement of his government. A subscription was raised for the erection of an Ice House. And anyone who could afford an icebox invested in one of those zinc-lined wooden contraptions.

Calcutta's banqueting tables took on an arctic hue with peaks of ice and ornately sculpted swans bearing caviare. Cold soufflés, aspics, mousses and galantines were washed down with plenty of chilled loll shrob (red wines).

The Great Eastern Hotel opened in 1841 on Old Court House Street leading to St Andrew's Kirk and was the second oldest hotel in the British Empire. David Wilson, affectionately called Dainty Davie, was the owner of this hotel with a 'Multiple Shop' on the ground floor—the forerunner of the departmental store. In 1883 'it was said, a man could walk in at one end, buy a complete outfit, a wedding present, or seeds for the garden, have an excellent meal, a burra peg (double) and if the barmaid was agreeable, walk out at the other end engaged to be married.'

The climate of Calcutta was conducive to ease and, coupled with Calcutta's definition of food as 'what is eaten between meals', prompted the Great Eastern Hotel to offer a service to customers in their horse-drawn gharries. They would pull up for a tiffin at a rupee a plate of 'steak or chop, bread and vegetables,' and of course, a burra peg. When Shirley Tremearne was managing the Hotel, he would preside at a Sunday tiffin for his friends. The tiffin served was 'half a dozen choice spirits, hors d'oeuvres, turtle soup, pâté de foie gras, asparagus and ices washed down with extra dry champagne'. A similar meal reads today, consomme royale, chicken liver or prawn pâté, asparagus from Bhutan and green mango ice washed down with excellent Indian Marquise De Pompadour sparkling champagne.

Monsieur Boscolo started his catering career in Calcutta as a chef in the Great Eastern Hotel. He took over the Continental Hotel on Chowringhee in 1894. Two years later Mark Twain was a guest here for three days. Calcutta

was all set to wine and dine the American whose reputation
as a storyteller had preceded him. Unfortunately, he was
confined to his room with bronchitis for the greater part of
his stay and was unable to enjoy the excellent French
cuisine, for which the Hotel was well-known till 1920. Since
1993, Quality Inn stands in place of the old Continental.
Among the multi-cuisine served, we are glad to note that
Bangla ranna has climbed the five-star heights here, at last.

The evolution of eating places in colonial Calcutta
followed the English pattern, from taverns and coffee
houses to hotels and clubs, some more exclusive than others.

The club culture of Calcutta was essentially British and
singularly masculine. Expatriates, separated from family
and friends, recreated some of the familiar features of life
back home in their clubs. The Bengal Club (1827) is the
oldest in the subcontinent and was very much the burra
sahibs' club till over a decade after Indian independence. In
the old days, ladies were admitted on sufferance on rare
occasions so much so that a member, who was obviously a
lady's man, suggested a bibikhana in 1939. A generation
later, ladies enjoy all the club facilities. In the Reynold's
Room they confer over a cup of coffee with the Steward,
P. K. Dutta, on the recipe for the club's special Apple Pie or
the choice of beckti Normande or steak and kidney pie or a
cooked leg of ham in pineapple and cherry sauce. Two weeks
before Christmas, Dutta's little office is invaded by
members eager to be the early birds for his mince pies and
roast turkey. Christmas lunch is an institution, with all the
Club's specials on the buffet table in the main dining room.

The chhota sahibs not to be left out, cavorted at the
Saturday Club and the not so pukka sahibs decided to start
the 300 Club admitting Indians. In Boris Lissanevich, a
cabaret artiste and ex-cadet of the Russian Imperial Navy,
an ideal Secretary was found. The Club opened its doors on
the ground floor of an art deco extravaganza known as
'Philip's Folly'. As the night wore on, couples spilled out on
to the wooden dance floor in the garden. The musician and
the chef were Russian. Not surprisingly shashlik and

chicken à la Kiev were the specialities of the house.

The Calcutta Club was started in 1907 to fulfil the growing need of a meeting place for like-minded people overcoming barriers of race and religion. Banquets were a regular feature of the Club in its early days when Calcutta was the capital of British India.

The Platinum Jubilee Book of the Club waxes eloquent on the excellence of its food heightened by a philosophy 'that makes the Bekty served here different from the fish on any other table'. The culinary treasures are described as 'both liberal and conservative . . . a famous collection of Indian and Western dishes . . . stewed Turtle Soup presented in a tureen of appropriate design and Minced Partridge Pie garnished with assorted liquored cherries.' Calcuttans dining on a surfeit of turtles and partridges may have been responsible for endangering the species and the current ban!

A very senior member ecstatically remembers one old time favourite, Steak Romain: 'A fairly thin slice of grilled beef, on top of that grilled ham, on top of that mushrooms and on top of that a good appetite.'

The two-hundred-year-old Neel Kuthi of indigo-planter, Richard Johnson, has been the Tollygunge Club house for a century. Set amid ninety-five acres, it retains the ambience of a country club. On one of those rare occasions when the club was all white, a prominent Indian member of the Calcutta Bar was invited to a Golightly ball and remembered the barbecue fork dinner with spits turning whole sheep and suckling pigs with apples stuck in their mouths on the table. Hot drop scones liberally spread with jam or pâté are still served after a game of golf or a cross country ride at the Tolly.

In order of vintage, the Royal Calcutta Golf Club (RCGC) is the oldest and at one time staked a claim with the Calcutta Rowing Club for the best steaks East of Suez. Christmas Tiffin in 1931 was Rs 3 and sixty years later members paid sixty times as much for a similar menu indicating a rise in the cost of living. Products of the Club kitchens are taken home sometimes, no doubt as a peace offering for a prolonged nineteenth hole round, which brings to mind that from the Cocktail Bar at the RCGC (the scene of the nineteenth hole) where members were 'soothed by the clucking of contented hens' belonging to the then Secretary, and many a time his Black Orpingtons would be taken home for the Sunday curry lunch, a colonial hangover. Club culture dies hard in Calcutta.

Peliti's and Firpo's are synonymous with 'the good old days'. 'By Appointment to the Viceroy of India, H. R. H. The Prince of Wales, H. R. H. The Duke of Connaught', Peliti's was the best appointed of the 'By Appointment' institutions of the time. It was to Peliti's that the business fraternity of Clive Street had been turning for the traditional Friday lunches since 1890. Chevalier Frederico Peliti was himself a great confectioner and won an award at the Calcutta International Exhibition for his twelve foot tall Eiffel Tower, 'a miniature marvel in sugar'. The building on Old Court House Street on the eastern side of B. B. D. Bagh, where the marble staircase leads up to a newspaper office, was once Peliti's.

Angelo Firpo opened a restaurant on Chowringhee after World War I. For the next half century, the glitterati of Calcutta entertained themselves and their friends at Firpo's. A lunch of minestrone soup, chicken vol au vent and vanilla ice cream topped with hot chocolate sauce and a wafer of biscotti was served for the princely sum of one rupee and eight annas only. A festive menu of the Fifties saved as a souvenir reads: Hors d'oeuvres varies—chilled asparagus, chilled artichoke bottoms, pâté de foie gras followed by Turtle Soup, Homard Thermidor, Roast Stuffed Turkey and Ham, Plum Pudding. The pudding was generously doused with brandy and set alight by Mr Firpo himself. A bottle of Scotch Whisky and a tin of Firpo's chocolates nestled among the paper hats, crackers and bugles set on immaculate white damask table linen. A good old Calcuttan remarks that when Firpo's closed its doors in the 1960s, it was goodbye to good eating in Calcutta.

Not so, as we shall see.

We met a little old lady in a cemetery, putting flowers on her grandfather's grave. Why did De Leemans, the lamp maker from Belgium, come here? 'Everyone came to Calcutta,' said Mrs Shea.

And so they did. The Portuguese came to Bengal by way of Bombay and left their indelible mark in the Bandel cheese made in their outpost on the Hooghly and converted the Bengali to sweetening curdled milk solids (which is the curd or chhana) and creating the hundreds of chhana sweets which Bengal is famous for. Other foods have blended with Indian tastes and we bring you some of the dishes which bear distorted Portuguese names, and may have originated in Portugal, but have now come to be identified as Goan food, Goa having been a Portuguese colony until 1961. Our friend Natalia Bieck helped us to choose the dishes which still have a little of Portugal in them. Goan friends in Calcutta have generously given us the recipes.

The Portuguese must have mixed all the spices of the Orient to make a buffath. On the south-west coast, there is a mixture of aromatic spices called buffath spice. Buffath is a beef and vegetable stew which looks innocuous but can be deceptively pungent. Buffath is also a part of Anglo-Indian fare.

Buffath may be made with leftover roast or steak, in which case the vegetables go in first and the meat is added with the spices. Our first recipe for buffath is an Anglo-Indian one and the second is a duck buffath which is Goan. No doubt both are of Portuguese extraction.

A recipe from Mona Benham's notebook.

Buffath - I

Beef and Vegetable Stew

Serves 6

Ingredients:
- **750 gms beef steak (cut into 2-inch cubes)**
- **5 large potatoes (thickly sliced)**
- **2 carrots (halved)**
- **2 radishes (halved)**
- **8 green onions with leeks (sliced)**
- **1 medium onion (sliced)**
- **1-inch piece ginger (ground)**
- **6 cloves garlic (ground)**
- **1 tsp turmeric powder**
- **6 dry red chillies (powdered)**
- **½ tsp mustard seeds (powdered)**
- **½ tsp cumin (powdered)**
- **2 tsp roasted coriander seeds (powdered)**
- **1 tbsp ghee or oil**
- **½ coffee-cup vinegar**
- **4 green chillies (split lengthways)**
- **salt to taste**

Method:
Mix the turmeric powder with the powdered dry red chillies, mustard seeds, cumin, roasted coriander seeds. Cover the meat with water and boil till half done in a pan. Add salt to taste, then add the vegetables and simmer gently for 5 minutes. Add the spices, green chillies and the vinegar. When the meat and vegetables are cooked, season with salt. Fry the sliced onion in the hot ghee or oil in another pan and 'stream (pour) the buffath on it.' Cover and cook a few minutes.

Buffath - II

Duck and Vegetable Stew

Serves 4

Ingredients:
- 1 duck (cleaned and jointed into 8 pieces)
- 250 gms medium potatoes (peeled, whole)
- 4 onions (peeled, whole)
- 1 large onion (sliced)
- 3 tbsp oil or ghee
- 4 cups water
- milk extracted from 1 coconut (see Chapter 2, page 66)
- 6 cloves
- 4 green cardamoms
- 2-inch stick cinnamon
- 1 tsp coriander powder
- 4 green chillies (sliced)
- 1 tbsp vinegar
- lime juice
- salt to taste

Method:
Heat the oil or ghee in a pan and fry the sliced onion till crisp. Take out half the onion and keep it aside. Put in the whole potatoes and brown slightly and then put in the whole onions. Fry for 4 minutes. Remove the potatoes and onions and set aside. Brown the duck lightly in the oil. Add the water and let the duck cook until it is almost done. Remove the duck from the pan and add the coconut milk. Add the whole potatoes and onions and the sliced browned onions and the cloves, green cardamoms, cinnamon and coriander powder, sliced green chillies and salt to taste. Let it cook for 10 minutes and add the duck and cover. When the potatoes are nearly ready, add the vinegar and cook down leaving 1 cup of gravy in the pan. Squeeze a few drops of lime juice over the buffath when eating. Serve with white rice or crusty rolls.

Temperado

Prawns Cooked in Coconut Milk

Serves 4

Ingredients:
- ½ kg prawns
- 1 tbsp oil
- ½ kg bottle gourd or young pumpkin (cut in ½-inch wedges)
- 2 tsps Kashmiri chilli powder
- milk extracted from 1½ coconuts (in two lots) (see Chapter 2, page 66)
- 2–3 green chillies (slit)
- 2 cloves
- 2 green cardamoms
- 2-inch stick cinnamon
- 1 tsp sugar
- salt to taste

Method:
Clean the prawns. Heat the oil in a pan and sauté the prawns till they turn red and keep aside. Add the bottle gourd or young pumpkin to the hot oil with the Kashmiri chilli powder. Stir fry for a minute and add one and a half cups of thin coconut milk. When the pumpkin has cooked add the prawns and green chillies, cloves, green cardamoms, cinnamon, sugar and salt to taste. Simmer for 5 minutes and add ½ cup of coconut cream. Cook gently until the surface of the temperado is red. Remove from fire and serve.

» A recipe from Mrs Lydia Fernandes and Mrs Caroline Fernandes.

Chicken Xacuti

Hot-and-Sour Chicken in Coconut Milk

Serves 4 - 6

Ingredients:
- 1.3 kg chicken
- milk extracted from 1 coconut (see Chapter 2, page 66)
- 1 large onion (sliced)
- 1 tbsp tamarind pulp (can be bought in the market)
- 200 gms oil
- salt to taste

For spices
- 1 coconut
- 8–10 green chillies
- ¼ nutmeg
- 1 large onion
- 5–6 cloves garlic
- 2½ tsp coriander
- ½ tsp cumin
- ½ tsp pepper
- 1 tsp aniseed
- 1 tsp poppy seeds
- 1 tbsp mustard seeds
- a pinch of fenugreek
- 1 green cardamom
- a pinch of caraway seeds (shahjeera)

For marinade:
- ¼ cup lime juice
- ½ inch piece ginger
- 3–4 cloves garlic
- 2–3 green chillies
- 2 tbsp coriander leaves

Method:

Clean and joint the chicken. Slice the onion. Extract the tamarind juice by soaking the pulp in half a cup of water and strain.

For spices

Grate the coconut, slice thinly the green chillies, grate the nutmeg, slice the onion, peel the garlic. Dry roast all the above on a griddle and grind to a powder with the coriander, cumin, pepper, aniseed, poppy seeds, mustard seeds, fenugreek, green cardamom, caraway seeds. Take care not to burn the onion.

For marinade

Grind together the ginger, garlic, green chillies, coriander leaves and mix it with the lime juice.

Marinate the chicken for half an hour in a dish. Heat the oil in a pan and brown the sliced onion. Add the chicken and sauté lightly. Cover, reduce heat and simmer for 7–10 minutes. Add the prepared spices and stir well. Add salt to taste. Cover and cook for another half hour. Add the coconut milk and tamarind juice. Mix well, cover, increase heat and cook for 10 minutes before taking it off the fire.

» Sorpotel is a typically Goan dish enjoyed on high days and holidays.

Sorpotel

Spiced Stew of Meats

Serves 15

Ingredients:

Stage 1
- 1 kg pork

- 1 pig's liver
- 2 pig's kidneys
- 1 ox tongue
- 1 beef heart
- 1 tsp turmeric
- 1 cup water
- salt to taste

Stage 2
- ¼ cup vinegar
- 2 large onions
- 12 cloves garlic
- 1-inch piece ginger
- 1 tsp cumin seeds
- 2 cloves
- 2 green cardamoms
- 2-inch piece cinnamon
- 10 peppercorns
- 10 dry red chillies

Stage 3
- 1 cup oil
- 2 onions (diced)
- 4 tbsp vinegar

Method:

Stage 1
Parboil in water with the turmeric and salt, the pork, pig's liver, pig's kidneys, ox tongue, beef heart in a large pan.

Stage 2
Grind in ¼ cup vinegar, the onions, garlic, ginger, cumin seeds, cloves, green cardamoms, cinnamon, peppercorns, dry red chillies.

Stage 3
Dice all the meat. Heat the oil to smoking in a large pan. Reduce heat a little and fry the meats until brown. Add diced onions, all the prepared spices and vinegar. Cook on a slow fire stirring occasionally till the oil comes to the top of the sorpotel.

» Vinegar is one of the constant ingredients in the Portuguese derived meat and poultry recipes. It may have been added both to tenderize and preserve the meat. Vindaloo is best made from pork, duck or beef. A recipe from Lt. Col. Hamilton.

Vindaloo

Pickled Pork

Serves 8

Ingredients:
- **1 kg pork (cubed)**

For marinade
- **½ cup good vinegar**
- **1 tbsp ginger (bruised)**
- **1 tbsp garlic (ground)**
- **2 tsp dried red chillies (ground)**
- **1 tsp coriander (roasted and ground)**
- **1 tsp cumin (roasted and ground)**
- **5 cloves (roasted and ground)**
- **5 green cardamoms (roasted and ground)**
- **6-inch piece cinnamon (roasted and ground)**
- **½ tsp salt**

For cooking
- **200 gms mustard oil**
- **3 bay leaves**
- **a few peppercorns**

Method:

To marinate
Steep the pork in the vinegar and salt together with the spices for the marinade. Marinate for 18 to 24 hours, turning once. Use a glass or ceramic utensil for marinating.

To cook

Heat the mustard oil in a deep stainless steel pan and put in the meat and the marinade. Add 3 bay leaves and a few peppercorns. Turn down the heat and simmer on a slow fire for two hours until the meat is tender. Serve hot with plain boiled rice.

Two teaspoons of ground black mustard seeds may be added to the marinade. Vindaloo keeps for a week in the refrigerator.

» One of the dishes our Portuguese friend recognized as having originated in her homeland is Bolo du Portugal. Bolo is Portuguese for cake. Goans use a lot of semolina in their sweets; we do not know whether this was a Portuguese flour substitute.

Bolo du Portugal

Portuguese Semolina Cake

Makes 8 slices

Ingredients:
- 1 cup semolina
- 1 cup ground sugar
- ½ cup butter
- 4 eggs
- 125 gms almonds
- 2 tsp rose water
- 1 tbsp brandy

Method:

Grind the almonds to a fine paste with the rose water. Add the semolina and mix in the ground sugar and butter. Beat until light and pale yellow. Add the yolks of the eggs, one at a time. Beat well each time. Add the brandy. Fold in the stiffly beaten whites of the eggs. Bake in a greased 9-inch cake tin in a moderate oven (350° F, 180° C) until the cake is set and a knife inserted in the middle comes out clean. All the grinding and beating processes may be done in a food processor.

» Europeans in India were great wine drinkers and celebrated every occasion with plenty of 'liquid refreshments'. The Goans carry on the tradition and more and more Indian wines are coming into the market, including a sparkling wine. It is not difficult to make perfectly potable wines at home, with the abundance and variety of Indian fruits.

Litchi Wine

10 - 12 litres

Ingredients:
- **3 kg litchies**
- **3½ kg sugar**
- **1 tbsp yeast**
- **6 litres boiling water**

Method:
Peel and stone the litchies. Place in a 10 litre plastic bucket and pour over them the boiling water. Stir well and cover the bucket with a cloth. Leave standing for 3 days stirring once daily. Leave for 1 week after that without stirring. Strain the liquid. Add the sugar and yeast. Stir well until the sugar dissolves. Leave for 7 days stirring twice daily.

Strain through a funnel lined with muslin into bottles. Cork loosely. Watch for bubbles of fermentation. When they settle, cork down firmly. Ready to drink in six months.

The bounty of summer fruits—mangoes, litchies,

pineapple and chickoo make wines for a merry Christmas.

» The Armenian church in Calcutta, in one of the oldest
   places of Christian worship and the small community
   of Armenians in the city still celebrates Christmas
   with a traditional lunch on 6 January. Rosie David
   who gave us these recipes caters the lunch at the
   Burra Club on Park Street (see Chapter 4, pg 150).

Samit Pilaff

Dill Pilaff

Serves 8 - 10

Ingredients:
• 1 kg small-grained sun-dried rice
• 150 gms oil
• 8 cups hot water
• 100 gms dill leaves (chopped)
• salt to taste

Method:
Wash the rice. Soak for half an hour if using old rice, and
drain. Heat the oil in a deep pan. Add rice and stir until
lumpy. Pour in the hot water. Add salt to taste and chopped
dill leaves. Cover and cook on slow fire until all the water
is absorbed and the rice is dry and fluffy.

Kuku

Spicy Spinach and Herb Omelette

Serves 4 - 6

Ingredients:
• 250 gms spinach
• 250 gms green coriander

- **250 gms spring onions**
- **4 eggs**
- **¼ tsp baking powder**
- **1 tsp curry powder**
- **1 tbsp flour**
- **2 tbsp oil**
- **salt to taste**

Method:
Chop the spinach, green coriander, spring onions with the tops. Wash, drain, add salt and leave for 1 hour.

Squeeze out all the water from the greens. Beat the eggs. Add the baking powder, curry powder, flour and salt to taste. Mix in the strained greens and beat well. Heat the oil in a frying pan and put in the egg mixture. Cook over medium heat until the eggs are set. To turn put a lightly greased dekchee lid under the eggs and flip over. Serve hot, cut in pieces.

» The Armenian dolma and the Jewish mahashas are the forerunners of the maachh potoler dorma (see Chapter 5). This recipe is the Armenian original of the Bengali version.

Potol Dolma

Stuffed Wax Gourd

Ingredients:
- **12 large wax gourds (potol)**
- **2 large onions**
- **2-inch piece ginger**
- **6 cloves garlic**
- **2 kg tomatoes**
- **100 gms sugar**
- **1 tbsp curry powder**
- **250 gms beef (minced)**
- **1 tbsp garam masala (powdered)**

- 1 tbsp raisins
- salt to taste

Method:
Cut one end off the wax gourd and scoop out the seeds, reserving the cut-off piece to lid it later.

Chop and brown the onions in a deep frying pan. Grind the ginger and garlic. Chop the tomatoes. Add these ingredients, the sugar, salt to taste and curry powder to the browned onions and cook till the tomatoes are thick and pulpy. Brown the minced beef. Add half the tomato mixture to the beef, add the powdered garam masala. Fill the wax gourd with the meat mixture. A few raisins may be added to the meat. Cover the wax gourd with the cut off end and secure with toothpicks. Place half the reserved tomato sauce in a deep pan and arrange the wax gourd over it. Cover with the remaining sauce and cook for 20 minutes or until the wax gourd is done, shaking the pan from time to time. A handful of chopped mint and dill may be added to the meat mixture.

Cabbage Dolma

Cabbage Leaves Stuffed with Meat

Serves 12

Ingredients:

- 4 kg cabbage

For filling
- 1 kg fatty beef
- 500 gms onions
- 2-inch piece ginger
- 8–10 cloves garlic
- 50 gms coriander leaves
- 50 gms mint leaves
- 50 gms fenugreek leaves

- **500 gms small-grained sun-dried rice**
- **4–6 green chillies (chopped)**
- **50 gms sugar**
- **salt to taste**
- **2 tbsp curry powder**
- **1 or 2 tbsp Dalda (saturated vegetable oil) or oil**

For assembling
- **2 kg tomatoes**
- **turmeric**
- **¼ cup vinegar**
- **200 gms sugar**
- **salt to taste**

Method:
Core the cabbage and plunge into a pan of boiling water for a few minutes to blanche. Take it out and let it cool.

Filling
Mince the fatty beef with the onions, ginger, garlic and coriander, mint and fenugreek leaves. Wash the rice and soak it for half an hour. Mix with the meat. Add the green chillies, sugar, salt to taste and curry powder. Mix in the Dalda or oil. Mix all the ingredients well and add a little water if the meat looks tough.

To assemble
Separate the cabbage leaves and lay them flat on a table. Put a spoonful of meat in each and roll them up. Chop the tomatoes fine.

Grease a large deep pan and arrange the dolmas and tomatoes in alternate layers starting and ending with tomatoes. Sprinkle each layer of tomatoes with a little turmeric. Cover it with a plate to weigh it down and cook slowly until the tomatoes are mushy and the meat is cooked, about 45 minutes. Uncover and cook over high heat to thicken the sauce. Add the vinegar, sugar and salt to taste. Cook for another 10–15 minutes.

» Calcutta must be one of the only cities in India where Jewish food is recognized as a separate cuisine. Thanks largely to Nahoum and Sons, cheese filled sambusak and cholla bread have become available to the New Market shopper. The few Jewish residents in Calcutta hold firmly on to their eating traditions. Reading through the recipes, the reader will find how much they influenced Bengali cooking, using local ingredients to make mahashas and anjooli and their unleavened bread and halek. It may be interesting to the reader to know that the hand-pulled rickshaw was introduced to Calcutta by a Jew, Salah Abraham Baqaal, who imported the two-wheeler from Singapore.

» Alu makallah is an accompaniment to murgh makallah, but is so identified with Calcutta's Jewish cooking that in our book it comes first. Potatoes were not grown in the Middle East and the Jews surely came across this vegetable in Calcutta. Perhaps an innovative Jewish housewife created it from the Bengali alu bhaja concept.

Alu Makallah

Whole Fried Potatoes

Serves 8 - 10

Ingredients:
- **20 medium old potatoes**
- **turmeric**
- **8 cups oil**
- **salt to taste**

Method:

Peel the potatoes and pare them down to the same size. Bring a pan of water to boil. Add salt and turmeric. Reduce heat and allow to cool. Add potatoes and bring to the boil again. Immediately drain in a colander and allow to cool.

Heat the oil in a deep wok or frying pan large enough to hold all the potatoes together. When the oil is smoking put in the potatoes and turn down the heat to a simmer. Cook potatoes till they form a light crust but are still yellow. Remove from the fire and allow to cool in the oil. When cool, pierce each potato 3 or 4 times and leave in the oil. Forty-five minutes before serving, put the pan back on the stove over a very low fire and brown potatoes evenly. As the potatoes start to brown, turn the heat high to brown and crisp the potatoes. When very crisp, drain and serve either on its own or with murgh makallah.

To keep the potatoes crisp, immerse the hot pan of potatoes in a basinful of cold water for a few seconds.

Murgh Makallah

Jewish Roast Chicken with Potatoes

Serves 4 - 6

Ingredients:

- 1¼ **kg chicken**
- 1 **small onion**
- 1 **tbsp onion paste**
- 1 **tbsp garlic paste**
- ½ **tsp turmeric**
- 1 **tsp black pepper (freshly ground)**
- 1 **cup water**
- 4 **cloves**
- 4 **cardamoms**
- 3-inch **piece cinnamon**
- ½ **cup oil**
- 1 **tsp salt**

Method:
Clean and joint the chicken. Chop the onion. Coat the chicken with the onion paste, garlic paste, turmeric, salt and freshly ground black pepper, mixed with the water.

Arrange the chicken in a large pan in a single layer and sprinkle over it the cloves, cardamoms, cinnamon and the chopped onion. Pour the oil over it and place the pan on high heat for a few minutes. Reduce heat to minimum, cover the pan and cook for half an hour or till all the water has been absorbed and the chicken is brown on one side. Cool slightly and turn over the pieces to brown on the other side and cook through.

» The classic relish served with murgh makallah is hilbeh, a chutney made of fenugreek.

Hilbeh

Fenugreek Chutney

Ingredients:
- 1 tbsp fenugreek seeds (soaked overnight and drained)
- 1 inch piece ginger
- 5 cloves garlic
- 5–6 green chillies
- a handful of green coriander leaves
- juice of 2 limes
- 1 tsp sugar
- ½ tsp salt

Method:
Grind together the fenugreek seeds, ginger, garlic, green chillies and green coriander leaves. Season with the salt and sugar. Moisten with the lime juice, and whisk the mixture. The consistency should be that of a thin batter. If it is to be eaten later, thin the chutney with a little more lime juice and water to get the correct consistency.

Bora Muslims make a similar fenugreek chutney which they call hulba and eat with paya (see Chapter 3) or if they are very partial to it, sip it as a drink.

Hilbeh can be made in a blender.

» Mahashas can be made with any vegetable that lends itself to being scooped out and stuffed. Some of the favourite vegetables are cucumbers, tomatoes, brinjals, red and green peppers, courgettes and wax gourd (potol). The vegetables should be fresh and firm and not too large.

Mahashas

Vegetables Stuffed with Meat and Rice

Serves 10 - 12

Ingredients:
* any one or a mixture of the above vegetables

For filling (makes 3½ cups filling)
* 500 gms mutton (minced)
* ½ cup long-grained Basmati rice
* 1 tsp garlic paste
* 1 tsp ginger paste
* ½ tsp turmeric
* 1 tsp black pepper
* 2 tbsp oil
* juice of 2 limes
* 2 tbsp mint leaves
* 1 tsp sugar
* 1 tsp salt

For assembling
* 2 tbsp oil
* 2 tsp thick tamarind paste
* ½ cup water

- 1 tsp sugar
- ½ tsp salt

Method:
Choose any one or a mixture of vegetables to be stuffed. Cut off a half inch piece of the stalk end of the vegetable. Reserve this end to use as a lid later. Scoop out the insides of the vegetables, taking care not to break the skin.

Filling
Wash the Basmati rice and soak in water, covered, for 1 hour.

Mix the garlic paste, ginger paste, turmeric, black pepper, oil, lime juice, salt, mint leaves and sugar with the minced mutton. Drain the rice and mix with the meat mixture.

Half fill the vegetables and cover them with the lids. Secure with toothpicks. Do not overstuff the vegetables as they will fill up as the rice expands with cooking.

Assembling
Heat the oil in a large flat pan and arrange the vegetables in it. Dissolve the salt, sugar, thick tamarind paste in the water and pour around the vegetables. Cook on a low fire until the vegetables are half done and brown on one side. Cool and carefully turn vegetables over and cook again and turn over. The mahashas may be cooked for 20 minutes in a moderate oven (350° F, 180° C).

Anjooli

Cold Dish of Fish in Coconut Milk

Serves 4 - 6

Ingredients:
- 600 gms white fish cut into 8 fillets
- a pinch of turmeric
- 2 large onions

* **1 medium brinjal**
* **6–8 green chillies**
* **25 gms coriander leaves**
* **juice of 1 large lime**
* **milk extracted from 1 large coconut (see Chapter 2, p 66)**
* **4 tbsp oil**
* **salt to taste**

Method:
Sprinkle the fish with salt and a pinch of turmeric and steam in a shallow pan for 10 minutes or until it flakes easily. Place in a 2-inch deep dish and refrigerate overnight. Slice the onions finely and sprinkle them with 1 teaspoon of salt. Leave it overnight. Slice the brinjal fairly thin, coat it with turmeric and sprinkle it with salt. Fry it in oil in a frying pan and leave aside. Chop the chillies and coriander leaves.

To assemble, drain the onions and place them over the fish to cover completely. Next arrange the slices of brinjal over the onions and pour the coconut milk over to cover completely.

Sprinkle thickly with the coriander and green chillies and dress with lime juice. Keep refrigerated. Serve cold.

» The recipe for stew fish taruball comes from a very old Calcutta Jewish cookbook. It uses ladies' fingers or bhindi, a very typical Middle Eastern ingredient. The proportions have been adjusted to suit modern requirements.

Stew Fish Taruball

Fish Stew with Ladies' Fingers

Serves 4 - 6

Ingredients:
* **500 gms white fish, bhetki or gurjali (the Indian salmon) recommended**

- **2 tbsp flour mixed with salt, pepper and mustard**
- **6 tbsp oil**
- **250 gms onions (thinly sliced)**
- **400 gms potatoes (peeled and sliced in ¼ inch thick rounds)**
- **400 gms ladies' fingers (bhindi) (topped and tailed)**
- **250 gms tomatoes (thinly sliced)**
- **4 cloves garlic (ground)**
- **4 green chillies (slit)**
- **1 tbsp flour**
- **2 cups water**
- **juice of 2 limes**
- **pepper**
- **salt**

Method:

Wash and dry the fish and cut it in steaks or fillets. Dredge the pieces with flour mixed with a little salt, pepper and mustard and keep aside.

Heat 4 tablespoons of oil to smoking in a deep frying pan. Reduce heat and sauté the fish till lightly browned. Remove from pan. In the same pan add 2 more tablespoons of oil. Fry half the onions till soft. Add the potatoes and fry for 5–7 minutes until the edges turn light brown. Add the okra (bhindi) and fry for another 5 minutes. Finally add tomatoes and cook for another 5 minutes. Lift out of pan and keep aside.

Add enough oil to that left in the pan to make it 2 tablespoons. Add the balance of the onions, the ground garlic and green chillies and fry for 5 minutes. Add the sautéed vegetables and sprinkle with the flour. Mix well and add the water. Cook for 10 minutes over moderate heat. Add salt and pepper and the fish. Cook gently for another 3–4 minutes. Add the lime juice and remove from fire. There should be some gravy left.

» The above dish can be eaten with chollah, a plaited bread strewn with nigella seeds.

Chollah

Jewish Plaited Bread

Serves 6

Ingredients:
- 3 cups flour mixed with ½ tsp salt and ½ tsp sugar
- 1 tsp yeast dissolved in 3 tbsp of hand hot (100° F, 36° C) water
- 1 tbsp butter and 2 tsp sugar melted in 1 cup warm water
- ½ beaten egg
- 1 tsp beaten egg mixed with 1 tsp water
- oil
- 1 tsp nigella seeds
- 1 tsp sugar

Method:
Mix the yeast mixture with the flour mixture in a bowl and rub well to distribute the yeast evenly. Mix the beaten egg with the dough and mix well. Add the water mixture a little at a time mixing it in to make a soft dough. Knead lightly until the dough leaves the fingers. Shape into a ball and leave to rise in a covered greased bowl, in a warm place.

When the dough has doubled its bulk (it should take one to one and a half hours) punch down and roll out on a floured board in a thick circle. Cut the circle into three strips of equal width. Starting from one end, plait the strips together into one long plait. Pinch ends to secure and place it on a greased baking tray to prove[*] for half an hour. Glaze with beaten egg mixed with water and a few drops of oil. Sprinkle the nigella seeds and sugar on the bread and bake in a pre-heated moderately hot oven (375° F, 200° C) for 20–25 minutes until the bread is nicely browned and there is a smell of baking bread from the oven.

The same dough can be used for making pizzas or breakfast rolls. For rolls divide the dough into 15

---

[*]   prove: baking term meaning the second rising of the dough

equal-sized balls and place in small cake tins for proving.
The baking time should be 15–20 minutes. You may or may
not glaze rolls or change the glaze according to your
preference.

» Friday visits to Nahoum and Sons in the New Market
always prove a treat. Cheese sambusaks, the
forerunner of the Indian samosa or singara, come in
fresh from the oven, as do other specialities.

Cheese Sambusak

Savoury Cheese Puffs

Makes 12 puffs

Ingredients:

For dough
- **250 gms flour**
- **100 gms margarine or butter**
- **water**

For filling
- **180 gms grated cottage cheese**
- **80 gms grated cooking cheese**
- **2 tbsp flour**
- **½ tsp baking powder**
- **2 eggs**
- **salt to taste**

Method:

Dough
Sift flour into a bowl. Cut the butter or margarine into pieces
and work into the flour until the mixture resembles
breadcrumbs. Gradually add enough water, working it into

the flour and butter mixture, to make a soft pliable dough. Knead gently until the dough leaves the fingers, for about 5 minutes.

Filling
Mix the cottage cheese, the cooking cheese, flour, baking powder, eggs, salt to taste, in a suitable china dish.

Assemble
Divide the dough into 12 equal-sized balls. On a pastry board or any clean, flat, even surface roll out each ball into a thin circle. Place a spoonful of filling on the centre of each circle and fold over to make a half moon. Seal the edges with water and press down with the tines of a fork. Place the prepared pastry on a baking sheet and bake in a pre-heated oven (350° F, 180° C) until the sambusaks are well risen and golden brown (about 15 minutes).

» The French have left one of the most enduring Western influences in India in pau roti, the common or garden loaf of bread.

Plain Loaf

Makes a 500 gm loaf

Ingredients:
- **2 cups flour**
- **1 tsp yeast dissolved in 3 tbsp of handhot water (100° F, 36° C) with ½ tsp sugar**
- **1 cup warm water mixed with 1 tsp salt and 1 tsp oil**

Method:
Wait for the yeast-water mixture to froth.

Sift the flour in a bowl and make a well in the middle and pour in the yeast-water mixture. With a spoon, carefully stir from the centre so that some of the flour from the sides falls to the middle, to make a thin batter. Cover this up thickly with flour from the sides and cover with a cloth. Leave in a warm temperature for 10–15 minutes until the batter has broken through the flour surface. Mix warm water mixture gradually into the flour. Mix well until you get a soft dough. Knead for 8 minutes until the dough leaves the fingers. Shape into a ball and leave covered in a greased bowl in a warm place to rise for one and a half to two hours. When the dough has doubled its bulk, punch down and shape into a loaf and place in a greased 500 grams bread tin, the dough to come three-fourths of the way up to the top of the tin. Cover and prove (let it rise) until the dough is well risen a little above the rim of the tin. Bake in a pre-heated moderately hot oven (375° F, 200° C) for 35–40 minutes until the top is brown and a skewer inserted into the middle of the loaf comes out clean. For a crisp crust brush the top with water and put back into the oven for a few minutes.

The crust rubbed with buttered paper improves the appearance. The same dough may be used to make Crusty Rolls in small tins baked for 20 minutes and French Bread shaped into a long roll and scored with a knife on the top.

» A much later contribution from the French was the soufflé. It was usual for Viceroys of India to bring in their entourage, an English butler, a French or English lady's maid and a French chef.

A team of Indian cooks worked in the Viceregal kitchens under the supervision of a French chef. More than one chef left service to set up on his own and open his own restaurant, serving to hoi polloi dishes that were prepared for the high table at Government House.

Lemon and Chocolate Souffle

Serves 8

Ingredients:
- **4 eggs**
- **2 tsp gelatine soaked in ½ cup water**
- **1 cup sugar (powdered)**
- **4 tbsp lemon juice**
- **1 tbsp lemon rind**
- **1½ cups cream**
- **60 gms bitter chocolate (grated)**

Method:
Separate the whites from the yolks. Beat the egg yolks with ½ cup powdered sugar till thick and yellow in a bowl and gradually add the lemon juice and lemon rind. Cook in a pan over low fire until the mixture coats the back of the spoon. Add the soaked gelatine in a stream, mixing it in thoroughly with a wooden spoon. Leave in refrigerator to set partially. Whip the egg whites in a bowl and when frothy, gradually add the remaining ½ cup sugar whipping all the time until it stands in peaks. Whip the cream in a bowl until it is thick and fluffy. Fold carefully into the egg white mixture and then fold it all into the cold lemon and egg mixture. Pour into a dish and leave to set in the refrigerator.

This soufflé is best made with the lemon called gandharaj lebu in Bengali. The recipe may be used to make soufflés with fruit purées substituting the lemon juice. We suggest ripe mango, cape gooseberry, Darjeeling orange (use the juice and add a tablespoon of brandy). Decorate the soufflé with piped cream and grated bitter chocolate.

This recipe is not for beginners.

» It was the Dutch who salted meat in a big way in Baranagar way back in the seventeenth century. Perhaps a little of the salt petre that was the cargo in the East Indiamen went into preserving meat and not for ammunition! Calcutta has kept the Dutch tradition and if the process given is too troublesome, the Calcuttan will go to his beef man in the New Market who will do a good job.

Salt Beef

Ingredients:
- 3 kg beef
- 50 gms coarse salt
- juice of 4 limes
- 1 cup dry broken up sugar cane molasses (gur)
- 1 tbsp salt petre (shora)

Method:
Wash and clean all the gristle from the beef. Keep the meat in one whole piece.

Place the meat in an earthenware or enamel bowl. A terracotta handi gives a special flavour to the meat. Rub into the meat the coarse salt, working it in well. Squeeze the lime juice on to the meat. Sprinkle the meat with dry broken up sugar cane molasses and salt petre. Cover the bowl with a piece of muslin or cheesecloth. Place in the refrigerator. In winter it is not necessary to refrigerate this dish. Turn the meat every day for 4–5 days and rub the brine into it very thoroughly. At the end of the salting time when the meat is nicely red, throw away the brine and wash the meat. Boil or roast in a deep pan for 30–45 minutes depending on the quality of the meat.

A piece of salted beef in the larder is an excellent stand-by for unexpected guests, packed lunch for office or with thin slices of marinated onions and cucumbers in salt in a mustardy sandwich.

» Somewhere between the Jewish mahashas, the
Armenian dolma and the Anglo-Indian alu chop,
tomato farci fitted into the kaleidoscope of Calcutta
cooking. Tomato farci may be made with freshly
minced meat or with leftover roasted or curried meat.
Fish and vegetables are also used to make farci.

Tomato Farci

Stuffèd Tomatoes

Serves 6

Ingredients:
• **6 large ripe tomatoes**

For filling
• **1 cup minced lamb or beef (cooked)**
• **1 tbsp oil**
• **2 medium onions (chopped)**
• **¼ tsp turmeric**
• **2 chillies (minced and seeded)**
• **1 tsp sugar**
• **salt to taste**
• **2 tsp parsley (chopped)**
• **water or gravy**
• **garam masala of 3 cloves (powdered), 2 green
cardamoms (powdered) and 1-inch stick cinnamon
(powdered)**

Method:

Filling
Heat the oil in a wok and brown half the onions. Add the
cooked minced lamb or beef, turmeric, sugar and salt. Cook
for 5 minutes and add the balance of the onions and chopped

parsley (the flat leafed parsley is available in Calcutta throughout the year and is used in most Anglo-Indian dishes calling for parsley). Cook for another 5 minutes. Add the gravy from the leftover roast if possible, otherwise a little water to moisten the mince. Add the garam masala powder and take off the fire.

To assemble
Cut a slice from the stem end of tomatoes. Scoop out the seeds and part of the pulp. Fill with the savoury meat filling. Grease a shallow oven proof dish or a baking tray and arrange the tomatoes on it. Place a small blob of butter on top of each tomato and bake in a medium hot (375° F, 200° C) oven for 15 minutes or until cooked but not mushy. Serve hot with boiled vegetables.

Although by boiled vegetables we generally mean 'English' vegetables like carrots, cauliflower, cabbage, peas and french beans, a number of 'Indian' vegetables are very successfully served as accompaniments to Western dishes.

Wax gourd (potol), ridged gourd, pumpkin, snake gourd, bottle gourd and onion greens to name a few, are excellent in a white sauce.

To Make White Sauce
Soften 1 chopped onion in 2 teaspoons of butter in a saucepan. Mix 1 tablespoon of flour in 2 cups of milk and add to the butter. Allow the mixture to thicken and add salt to taste and a teaspoon of white pepper.

Snake gourd (chichinga) and wax gourd (potol) are good cut in rounds and sautéed with a little butter and nigella seeds.

Ladies' fingers (bhindi) sautéed in butter with a chopped tomato and 3 cloves, thinly sliced garlic goes well with plain roasts and grills.

» Firpo's gave Calcutta a style of living which became part of the city's gracious ambience. Mr Firpo also

introduced Calcuttans to Italian food. We do not
aspire to those standards, but we feel he would have
given this recipe fair marks.

Lasagne

Italian Ribbon Noodles

Ingredients:
- **5 cups flour**
- **3 tbsp grated cheese**
- **2 eggs**
- **2 egg yolks**
- **2 tbsp water**
- **½ tsp salt**

Method:
To make the lasagne place the flour in a bowl and make a
well in the centre. In the well put the grated cheese, eggs
and egg yolks, water and salt. Work the flour in from the
sides of the bowl and mix with the other ingredients. Knead
into a firm dough. Divide dough into 4 parts and roll each
part paper thin. Place the sheets of dough on a clean
tablecloth and dry for 1 hour. Roll up the sheets and cut
them in ribbons one inch wide. Shake the ribbons loose. In
a large pan of boiling water add 4 tablespoons of salt and a
few drops oil. Drop in the lasagne and boil for 15–20
minutes.

Baked Lasagne

Serves 20 - 25

Ingredients:
- **500 gms beef or a mixture of beef and pork**
- **1 kg parmesan cheese**

- **500 gms mozzarella cheese**
- **300 gms ricotta cheese**
- **1 cup tomato purée**
- **1 medium onion**
- **2 tbsp oil**
- **1 clove garlic**
- **2 cups water**
- **1 tsp minced parsley**
- **2 tsp minced basil**
- **2 tsp minced oregano**
- **pepper**
- **salt**

Method:
Mince finely the beef or mixture of beef and pork. Chop the garlic and onion. Grate the parmesan cheese. Slice thinly the mozzarella cheese and ricotta cheese.

Heat the oil in a pan and fry the onion and garlic for a few minutes. Add the meat and brown well. Add the tomato purée, water, salt and pepper, parsley, basil and oregano. Simmer for one and a half hours. Add more water if the mixture is too dry. When ready it should be a thick sauce.

To assemble
Grease a deep fireproof dish and arrange in layers 1 portion cooked recipe lasagne cut in half, sauce, mozzarella cheese, ricotta cheese, until all the lasagne is used up, ending with ricotta cheese. Sprinkle the grated parmesan cheese on top. Bake in a pre-heated moderate oven (350° F, 180° C) for 20 minutes or until the cheese melts and the top is a light brown.

» There was an old house, painted green, on Shakespeare Sarani that could tell the tale of Christmas in Calcutta—soft-lit rooms heavy with Russian cigarette smoke, the band playing, 'Wish You Were Here', Maharajas, Boris, Viennese coffee and chicken à la Kiev—the 300 Club.

Chicken À La Kiev

Serves 4

Ingredients:
- **100 gms butter**
- **1 tsp parsley (chopped)**
- **1 tsp garlic (crushed)**
- **4 chicken breasts**
- **salt to taste**
- **1 tsp white pepper**
- **mustard**
- **1 beaten egg**
- **1 tbsp flour**
- **1 cup breadcrumbs**
- **1 cup oil**

Method:
Mix the parsley and garlic with the butter, divide it into 4 portions and mash the portions. Wrap in waxed paper and freeze individually, preferably overnight.

Clean and skin the chicken breasts, leaving the wing bone if possible. Put the wings between two sheets of grease-proof paper and bat them lightly to flatten, taking care not to break the flesh. Season with salt, pepper and mustard. Mix the beaten egg with the flour. Spread the breadcrumbs on a sheet of paper. Take the butter from the freezer, one piece at a time and make the cutlets one at a time, putting them back in the refrigerator as you shape them. Place the pat of butter on the point side of the wing and roll the meat over to make a closed cone. Tuck in the top end to secure. Dip in egg and flour and roll in the breadcrumbs. Refrigerate for 4–6 hours. Heat the oil in a deep pan and fry the cutlets one at a time. Serve at once. The butter will ooze out as the cutlets are cut. Serve with sautéed potatoes and a tossed salad.

Sautéed Potatoes

Serves 4 - 6

Ingredients:
- **4 large potatoes**
- **1 tbsp butter**
- **½ onion (minced)**
- **1 tbsp parsley (finely minced)**

Method:
Boil and skin the potatoes. Slice them in one-eighth inch thick rounds. Heat the butter in a frying pan and fry the onion till brown. Add the potatoes. Fry for 3 minutes on medium heat. Add the parsley. Toss it all for a minute in the pan and serve.

» Crumpets for tea under the trees at the Tollygunge Club is one of the joys of living in Calcutta. The recipe we give our readers is for drop scones, but baking powder substituted with yeast makes crumpets.

Drop Scones

Makes 8 - 10 scones

Ingredients:
- **1 cup flour**
- **2 tsp baking powder**
- **1 cup milk**
- **1 beaten egg**
- **1 tbsp oil**
- **1 tsp butter**
- **¼ tsp salt**

Method:

Make a batter with the flour sifted with the baking powder and salt. Mix in the milk, beaten egg and oil. Stir lightly to just mix. Heat the butter in a frying pan and swirl the pan to grease the whole surface. Heat to smoking, lower the heat and drop the batter in by the tablespoonful. It will spread into a circle. Wait until the surface bubbles and flip over. Cook for another 2 minutes. Lift out and put on a plate. Cook all the batter in this way. The quantity given should make 8–10 scones. Serve with butter and recipe liver pâté or grape jam.

To make crumpets dissolve 1 teaspoon yeast in 3 tbsp of hand hot (100° F, 36° C) water and wait for it to froth. Add to the batter to rise, covered, in a warm place for 1 hour. Stir down and use as in previous recipe.

» Coleslaw was one of the accompaniments to steak at the Golden Slipper Club during the war years (see text Chapter 8).

Coleslaw

Serves 4 - 6

Ingredients:
- 4 cups cabbage (shredded)
- 1·cup oil
- 1 tbsp vinegar
- 2 tbsp lemon juice
- 1 tsp ground onion
- 1 tsp ground garlic
- 1 tsp white pepper
- 1 tsp mustard
- 2 tsp sugar
- salt to taste
- ½ cup recipe mayonnaise (see pp 213–214 or pp 358–359)

Method:

Make a French dressing with the oil, vinegar, lemon juice, onion, garlic, white pepper, mustard, sugar, salt to taste. Toss the shredded cabbage in 3 tablespoons of this dressing and leave it to marinate for several hours. Just before serving, squeeze out the dressing from the cabbage and mix ½ cup mayonnaise.

Variations

- Add thinly sliced onions, capsicums and carrots.
- Add sliced apples or pineapple.
- Use a dressing of half mayonnaise and half plain yoghurt.
- Use a sour cream dressing: To make sour cream add 2 tablespoons of lime juice to 1 cup double cream and let it stand for 2 hours.

Chapter 5

Bawarcheekhana

Chicken
Curry,
Mulligatawny
Soup
and
Potato
Chop

Memsahibs, curries and chutneys
created a cuisine which the
bawarchee fused to perfection for
the burra sahib.

1802—'No European ever
dines without curry,' wrote
Hannah Marshman of the Baptist
Mission in Serampore, a Danish
settlement across the river from
Calcutta. Hannah managed the
mission housekeeping. Her
shopping was done in Calcutta
and sent by country boat for a
return fare of a rupee and four
annas. Her account book,
preserved in the William Carey
Museum of the Serampore
College, meticulously records her
bazaar hissab (accounts).

The Serampore Mission
dinner menu became the basis of
a meal planned by the memsahibs
of Calcutta and reads: ' . . . four
very large dishes of boiled rice
piled up in a heap; four dishes of

curry, three or four joints of meat, sometimes eight or nine
large fish, seven or eight dishes of vegetables from our own
garden . . .' The garden was the creation of William Carey,
as keen a botanist as he was a missionary. He planted some
of the vegetables in the college kitchen garden which have
become so much a part of our everyday lives that the fact
that they were imports has been forgotten. Cauliflower,
cabbage, broccoli, asparagus, French beans and peas had
arrived in the Calcutta markets by the early nineteenth
century.

Hannah goes on to say: 'Our victuals are always boiled
in earthen pots except when we have rump of beef. It is all
the English way except the curry. We have often puddings
and pies made by our own cook.'

Calcutta was growing up. From Fort and Factory, the
unplanned pattern of a town emerged. Theatres, balls,
banquets and funerals were a natural corollary. It was not
uncommon to dine with a friend and attend his funeral the
next morning. To a great extent, they asked for it, and
dressed, danced, dined and drank themselves to death.

Those were potable times. Bottles of claret and casks of
Madeira stored in the bottlekhana, as the pantry used to be
called, helped to wash down gargantuan meals. The ladies
did not lag behind—a bottle a day was deemed quite
appropriate. Some social order grew out of the early mess
life. Socializing, evening strolls and drives, theatres and a
bit of hard work pushed back the two o'clock dinner to seven
or eight o'clock in the nineteenth century. The tiffin
appeared at noon—the Anglo-Indian equivalent of
luncheon—and is still announced as tiffin by old-time 'koi
hai' retainers.

Instant devilry impregnated the starched British
kitchen with the invention of curry powder and devilled
eggs, kidneys and curry biscuits were born. Veeraswamy's
and Bolst's curry powders were the mainstay among the
condiments on the kitchen shelf at home and abroad. A
sprinkling would produce, in an instant, the highly
seasoned grills and stews. Perhaps a pinch went into a
particular favourite, Burdwan stew, 'made of flesh, fish and

fowl, a sort of Irish stew'. What is more, it was suggested that for the best results a silver saucepan be used!

Inevitably, Indianized dishes crept into the English kitchen. One such was the chicken country captain, locally known as the 'countree koptan'. 'This inviting and not unsubstantial whet for the palled and faded appetite of the old Bengalee, is made of a young fowl, or chicken, the Khansama calls it the chota moorghy . . . fried, partly curried with a soupçon of Imli, Tamarind acid, is truly a plate to be thankful for when you are sitting down to your Calcutta breakfast in the vapour-like steam heat of a Calcutta morning.'

Public Breakfasts were the fashion in 1786. The Hindoostany Tent on the Calcutta Race Course offered rice, snipe, teal, and a lot more for two gold mohurs per head for the January to March season. A century later, Sir Stuart Hogg Municipal Market, universally known as the New Market, was launched with a grand breakfast on the same style.

The popular curry was sometimes served at an Indo-Saxon breakfast preceded by chhota hazri in bed—also a grand affair when compared with the standard English breakfast the world over. Eggs and bacon, toast and marmalade and coffee had become the normal breakfast in many Calcutta homes. Some must have their bowl of porridge as well. This legacy of the Raj was a much more elaborate meal with a distinctly Indian flavour when the British breakfasted here. In the early days, there was kedgeree, an elaborate khichuri, and in season, topsi (mango) fish. Georgian sideboards in English country houses at breakfast time groaned under the nabob's addition of kedgeree, devilled eggs and fish cakes. We discovered that a choice of 'fried beckti and tartare sauce or fish cakes' was the breakfast menu of a club in Calcutta as late as 1940.

The English population also grew in Calcutta. Sahibs, no longer satisfied with a carefree bachelor life and the local girls, began to look back across the seas. And back home too, the parvenu nabobs returned to tell romantic tales of the

Orient. Their lavish living and bulging pockets tempted marriageable girls to board ships destined for Calcutta. Great was the reception awaiting the 'Fishing Fleets' when they sailed up the Hooghly. Sunday morning at St John's Church was a veritable marriage market. The Church compound was crowded with palkies and gharries bringing the chaperoned, rosy-cheeked new arrivals. In a week or so, the church bells would ring out and the organ play the Wedding March.

And the blushing bride found herself the mistress of a Palladian mansion, with a retinue of over twenty servants, a husband often old enough to be her father and no lingo. Of course there was the judge's lady who had been here 'forever' and the redoubtable Begum Johnson, who had buried four husbands and chose to live on in Calcutta till her death at the age of eighty plus. But by and large it was the memsahib and her cook who managed the kitchen. And the cook, if he was a classic Domingo, the archetype Dacca Christian cook, would ishtu (stew) the meat before putting it into the pie, thicken his custard with flour—saving the egg for his own dinner—and boil the mutton and serve it up as roast after doing 'leeteel brownee'.

To compound the problem, the cookhouse was removed from the main building and the memsahib. Food had to be carried some distance to the dining room in a large chest with four handles to protect it from the kites and crows. It was not uncommon for a silver serving spoon or fork to be carried off by a swooping kite, never to be recovered.

The bawarchee would rise to the occasion whenever there was a Burra Khana (banquet) and produce the finest pastry, the richest of game pâtés and the flakiest of tarts with a contrast of flavours and textures to match the greatest chef. His kitchen was Heath Robinson's workshop, equipped with bamboo and coconut shell ladles and chicken feathers as basting brushes.

Domingo has set a master menu for his successors:

Salary Soup
Fis

Heels fis fry
Madish
Russel Pups
Wormsil mole
Joint
Rost Bastard
Puddin
Billimunj. Ispunj roli
Toast Anchovy Poshteg

We have been able to decipher most of Domingo's esoteric menu except for Russel Pups—dogs were not eaten. Someone suggested Brussels Sprouts. So be it.

For those who are still left guessing here is a translation: Celery Soup, Fish, Hilsa Fish Fry, Main Dish, Vermicelli Mould, Joint, Roast Bustard, Pudding, Blancmange, Sponge Roll, Anchovy Toast, Poached Egg. The bustard, the Great Florican, was a prized game bird and alas, now almost extinct!

Help came from unexpected quarters in the form of cookbooks. In 1878, Col. Kenny Herbert published *Indian Cookery Book* under the pseudonym, Wyvern. His recommendations for the eight course meals he suggests came from newly opened provision stores. His three page discourse on the omelette is a measure of leisurely times, when country eggs were an anna a dozen and curly parsley grew in every garden.

Flora Annie Steele and Grace Gardiner acclaimed as 'Mrs Beetons of the Raj' wrote *The Indian Housekeeper and Cook* dedicated to

The English Girls
to whom
fate may assign the task of being
Housemothers
in
our Eastern Empire

Their book was young Isabella McNair's Bible as she

adventured through the jungles of housekeeping in the early twentieth century. The 'curry-bhat and gram-fed Ganga Din' who had been her husband's friend, philosopher and guide in his bachelor days, now turned to training his chhota memsahib into a burra mem who issued invitations to dinner at 8 for 8.15 P.M. The dinner was not just a matter of courses. Conversation to the right and to the left, seasoned hors d'oeuvres, two kinds of soup, a clear and a thick cream of almond, fish and shellfish, game, chicken, and red meats, interjected with sorbets and Russian cigarettes. Changing plates for every course hardly provided a breather for the khansama. Finally, the culmination of the cook's culinart was the sweety butty—transparent caramelized sugar baskets filled with fruit salad and cream.

We cannot resist a story about the sweety butty ending of a lunch hosted by a young Maharani for a senior Raja and his heir apparent. The guests of honour helped themselves to the two large sugar baskets while the other twenty guests looked down at their empty plates and the hapless Maharani at the butler, who with complete savoir faire organized jam omelettes.

Calcutta continued to grow. The adjutant birds, the unofficial scavengers, survived only on the crest of the Calcutta Municipal Corporation. In 1909, telephones were a convenience, motor cars more amusing than bullock carts and electric fans a joy.

But whatever the occasion and however diverse the menu, the hostess could not go wrong with mulligatawny soup, that rich golden liquid with all the spices of the East mingling to give its tantalizing flavour. Here is a ditty for mulligatawny overdone:

> First we had Mulligatawny soup
> Which made us all perspire
> For the cook, the obstinate nincompoop
> Had flavoured it hot as fire.

Underdone, it resembles dirty dish water and at its best is a dish fit for kings. The soup was served at one of the banquets on the occasion of the coronation of Queen Elizabeth II.

By the end of the nineteenth century, the mem had found her Calcutta feet. She hukumed (ordered) the cook to get a saklee (saddle) of mutton from Spence's and knew that the way to her husband's heart was via the coconut prawn curry she sent to the office in an ingeniously handy tiffin carrier—interlocking containers of equal diameter held together vertically by a detachable metal frame-cum-handle.

There was a personal rapport between the memsahib and the bawarchee. Appointment of a new incumbent was usually through chitties (written recommendations from previous employers). On scrutiny, she would often find that the last employer had left for England thirty years ago! These chitties used to go round the bazaar several times, for a price, of course.

The repertoire presented at such interviews was common to all three schools of Calcutta cooks. There was roast, bake, glacé and 'steam pudding' not to neglect the uninspired but perennial ishtu, brown or white. Through tact, praise and a small incentive given or taken, the cook would slowly produce at least a hundred preparations he had kept up his sleeve. The great artists of the Calcutta culinary corps—the Bihari Muslims, Dacca Christians and the Barua Mogs—rode the early morning 'cooks' tram to the New Market for daily fresh 'bazaring'. They are almost extinct as sons have chosen not to follow in their footsteps.

A few families who have old school cooks, hold on to them, tantrums and all. Tarakinkar Barua's masterpiece is smoked hilsa. He spends the entire day peering through his pebbled lens at the billion bones, separating them out, one by one to present the perfect boneless wonder. Mrs Mitter waits patiently for Ismael to return from his muluk (village) in Bihar to serve his out-of-this-world brandy snaps. Mrs Bhagat's guests look forward to her Domingo Gomes' chicken vol au vent, the result of many a box on the ear by his grandfather, cook to His Excellency, the Viceroy of India.

In the 1940s and 1950s, the mems returned from furlough and presented their bawarchees, already masters at decorating their dishes, with illustrated cookbooks. At the end of an excellent meal, a cake was offered to the guest of honour with THIS PUDDING IS VERY ECONOMICAL in candy pink icing right across it—flawlessly copied from the blurb in the book.

In the 1980s, Laura Sykes writes of her experience in dealing with her cook. Babu Lal's accounts show that Domingoism lives on—Potato Charps, Gussbary, Duck Kill Cilen, Fidar Dastar and an acunt book—to write the accounts in, of course.

Calcutta's catering schools have levelled out cooks and cooking through measuring cups and modern ovens discouraging the alimentary idiosyncrasies of the members of the Cooks' Clubs.

It was a hundred and fifty years ago that the Baruas, Ismaels and Domingos broke in the bawarcheekhana for the Indian sahib or brown sahib. The brown sahib was a product of new exchange economy, the carrier of a new and curious culture, and the liberal ideas of the West. Christian missionary activity, Rammohun Roy's (the founder of the Brahmo Samaj) socio-religious reforms and Lord Macaulay's Minute of 1835 recommending English as the medium of instruction, were mainly responsible for the change. Radicalism in England and the ideas of the French Revolution were in the air and caused ripples in Indian thinking.

Young men defied tradition and went abroad to study for the professions and services, hoping to squeeze through the chink in doors once tightly shut to them. A rebellious group of Hindu College students in Calcutta, fired by their teacher, the young, Anglo-Indian poet prodigy, Henry Vivian Louis De Rozio, indulged in socially forbidden food and drink by 'cutting their way through ham and beef and wading to liberalism through tumblers of beer', which rose to Burma teak tables made by C. Lazarus in enlightened Indian homes in Calcutta.

Married young, some demanded that their families accompany them abroad. To equip their hitherto sequestered wives for a very different lifestyle, husbands employed English governesses or asked the missionary ladies to visit the zenana (women's quarters) and teach the women the English language and etiquette.

While in England, the ladies coped admirably and cooked maachher jhole with Dover sole. Toru Dutt and her parents went to live in France for some time and in one of her letters she wrote that their French maid was quite adept at making cabbage dalna and ambole of eels.

The 'foren'-returned Bengalis were the butt of many a wisecrack and lampoon, but they survived to build a new 'Ingo-Bongo' society, giving Calcutta another dimension. They shook the foundations of the joint family system, sometimes for no fault of their own. The England-returned son set himself up in a separate establishment in a double-storeyed bungalow of Anglo-Indian architecture. In the westernization process, the master's family retainer, so long affectionately called by his first name, became the impersonal 'bearer'.

The additions to the staff were 'boy' who served at the table and khansama in charge of the sahibi part of the house and bawarchee assisted by masalchi, ostensibly the scullion but in fact the dogsbody. He ran errands and carried the bawarchee's daily bazaar, walking a respectful two steps behind. If he was ambitious and had a flair he might one day walk into his guru's shoes. Designations stuck fast, often to the point of ludicrousness. An old retainer started off life as 'boy' and when we met him he was pushing ninety and on the verge of retirement, but was still referred to as 'boy'.

A unique feature in the brown sahib's household was two kitchens. One under the lady of the house for Bengali food, and the other in a far-away-as-possible outhouse. Here Mrs Crawley's bawarchee, after her return to England, reigned supreme.

Some of the aromas from the bawarcheekhana wafted into the ranna ghar. The resourceful Bengali housewife transformed plantains, green jack fruit and banana flower into savoury cutlets with a meaty texture. The method was strictly vegetarian and wholly acceptable to her widowed mother-in-law. Not egged and crumbed but dipped in a flour and water paste and rolled in poppy seeds. It was the rule that her husband would eat lunch in her kitchen and this was the time to produce her innovations. Many of the foreign frills entered the ranna ghar and became part and parcel of a Bengali meal. Maachh potoler dorma and the gingery fillets of fried fish were admitted to Bangla ranna.

Another small but distinctive cuisine emerged. The Anglo-Indian kitchen. Children of mixed marriages, the Anglo-Indian is the original Calcuttan. The majority live in Calcutta. Anglo-Indian food is a little bit of this and a little bit of that, a delightful fusion of Western and Eastern cuisines. Lunch is a rice and dal sauce and a 'fried-up' bhaji. Plenty of onion, ginger, garlic and turmeric, often called saffron, and lots of chilli powder were added to a beef curry or a really fiery charchari. Dinner is a three course 'English' meal—soup, a side dish, a bland macaroni and cheese tarted up with onion, and ending with a baked or boiled custard or Bombay Pudding, a simplified version of the Portuguese bolo, squares of cooked semolina soaked in sugar syrup.

The Anglo-Indian housewife is as efficient a secretary as she is clever with réchauffés. She makes tongue tingling jhal frazies with leftover roast, pantaras or pancakes with a filling of minced meat and the classic alu chop, a cousin of the English meat rissole.

Warm and hospitable, the Anglo-Indian home is open house and no guest leaves without having a boxwallah's curry puff or a slice of Gran's home baked eight-egg cake. Sundays are extra special. The lunch menu is yellow rice, prawn curry, chicken dumpoke or ball (kofta) curry. In the doolie (meat safe), there are prawn patties from the Imperial Bakery in the New Market for Maisie's friends who are coming over after Mass. If her boyfriend stays on after lunch, there is a lot of laughter but if he leaves immediately after the meal, young Derek is sure to grumble about 'his everyday coming and eating Mother's chingri curry and not a word of love to my sister'.

Christmas cake with Anglo-Indians and Goans is a matter of personal pride. Many kilograms of cake mixture according to an old family recipe are handed over to the local rotiwala (bread man) three weeks before Christmas. Baked in half pound bread tins, cakes are exchanged between family and friends. The ingredients: karamcha—the Calcutta cherry, a sour fruit, preserved and coloured a brilliant red—manufactured by the Kabuli dried fruit sellers in the New Market; petha, crystallized white pumpkin, another ingredient is now added liberally as it is the cheapest of the preserved fruits; green cardamoms are added to cinnamon and finally a generous measure of rum poured into the mix. The daily dousing of the cake with rum makes for a merry Christmas.

Preparations for Burra Din start months ahead with the bottling of kala jamun (Indian blackberry) wine, while other home-made wines are matured for the festive season. Mona Benham, a member of the community, says that no wedding in Park Circus, where she lives, is celebrated without a bottle of her raisin wine.

With Indian independence, there was an exodus of Jews, Armenians, Chinese and Anglo-Indians. Those who remain have retained their identity. From England and America, from Australia and Canada, they return regularly to the city of their birth. The younger generations come in search of their roots. They munch hot-gram and buy sticks of red and white barley sugar in the New Market to carry back. The kathi rolls from Nizam's next door have migrated to Australia, they say, but without the nostalgia.

'Soups,' wrote the nineteenth century cookery writer Flora Annie Steele, 'fall into five classes. Clear soups or consommé, plain stock soups or bouillon, thick vegetable soups or purée, thickened soups and soups without meat.'

Consommé

Clear Soup

Serves 6

Ingredients:

For stock
- 1 kg meat (diced into one-inch pieces)
- water
- 1 large onion stuck with cloves
- 1 whole carrot
- 1 whole turnip
- 1-inch piece ginger
- bunch of parsley
- celery leaves
- 1 tsp sugar
- 1 tsp salt

- a little raw minced meat or beaten white of one egg

Method:

For stock
Place the diced meat in a greased pot. Add 8 tablespoons of water. Boil down till the bottom of the pot is covered with a jelly glaze. Add cold water 3 times the volume of meat. Add flavouring of the onion stuck with cloves, carrot, turnip, ginger, parsley and celery leaves, sugar and salt. Do not let it boil. Simmer for 3 hours. Take the pot off the fire and cool.

To clear

Add either a little raw minced meat or the beaten white of an egg to the soup and allow it to boil up once stirring all the time. Skim, take it off the fire, cool a little and strain. Add water if the soup has cooked down too much.

With city gas back in Calcutta, it is possible to think of the luxury of a long cooking consommé.

Garnishes of boiled diced vegetables or tiny pasta or royal custard embellish this soup. Sometimes, a poached egg is gently slid into the bowl of soup to make it a light but substantial meal. A glass of sherry added at the end makes it a party consommé. To make royal custard, steam a beaten egg over hot water until just set and cut into small cubes. Add to the soup as a garnish.

» Mulligatawny is the soup of the "koi hai" colonel whose cook created it and who took it back with him to Cheltenham or Bath for a taste of the good old days in India on a grey English Sunday. It literally means pepper water, but requires a little more than just pepper and water!

Mulligatawny Soup

Serves 6

Ingredients:
- **450 gms chicken (skinned, taken off the bone and cut into small pieces**
- **1 tsp coriander seed (roasted and powdered)**
- **1 tsp cumin seed (roasted and powdered)**
- **paste of ½ onion, ½-inch piece ginger, 2 cloves garlic**
- **2 medium onions (thinly sliced)**
- **2 tbsp oil**
- **½ tsp turmeric**

- ¼ tsp chilli powder
- 8 cups stock made from chicken bones and skin
- cooked rice
- wedges of lime

Method:

In a large pan heat the oil and cook the sliced onion until soft and just brown. Add the turmeric, chilli powder, powdered coriander and cumin and the onion-ginger-garlic paste. Fry over a medium hot fire until the spices turn colour. Add the pieces of chicken and salt to taste. Continue to fry until the juices in the pan are nearly dry. Add the chicken stock. Bring to a boil and simmer gently until the meat is well cooked. The stock should have reduced to 6 cups. Add more water if needed to make 6 cups. To serve, add a tablespoon or a little more rice to a bowl and pour the soup over and add 3 tablespoons of chicken to each bowl. Serve with wedges of lime to be squeezed into the soup before eating.

Variations:

- Coconut milk is added to the stock. To make coconut milk, grate a coconut and soak the coconut meat in 2 cups of hot water for 15 minutes. Strain through a sieve or muslin. Add to the soup just before taking off the fire. Cook gently for 3 minutes to thicken. Add a few curry leaves at this stage. Hot rice and wedges of lime are passed around with the soup.

Coconut Soup

Serves 6

Ingredients:

- 1 small onion (chopped fine)
- ¼-inch piece ginger
- 4 cups chicken stock

- 2 cups hot water
- 2 or 3 pieces chicken wings or bones
- 2 egg yolks
- 1 tbsp flour
- milk extracted from one large coconut (see above)
- salt to taste
- ½ tsp black pepper (freshly ground)

Method:

Add the onion and ginger to the chicken stock in a pan, bring to the boil and simmer for 10 minutes. Add the hot water and chicken wings or bones. Boil for another 30 minutes and take off the fire. Pass the contents of the pan through a sieve, pressing down so that all the liquid from the chicken goes into the soup. Whisk together the egg yolks with the flour and add slowly to the soup to thicken, stirring all the time. Add the coconut milk and stir gently. To serve heat through without boiling, check for seasoning, add salt to taste and black pepper.

Vegetarian Tomato Soup

Serves 6

Ingredients:

- 1 tsp butter
- 1 carrot (sliced)
- ½ small onion (sliced)
- 2 pieces celery (sliced)
- ½-inch piece ginger (ground)
- 1 tbsp flour or cornflour
- 500 gms tomatoes (cut in quarters)
- 4 cups hot water
- 2 tsp sugar
- 1 tsp pepper (ground)
- 1 bay leaf
- salt to taste
- 1 cup milk

• **sprigs of parsley for garnishing**

Method:
Heat the butter in a saucepan and gently sauté the carrots,
onion, celery and ginger until the onions turn a light brown.
Add the flour or cornflour and sauté for another two
minutes. Add the tomatoes and salt to taste. Mix well.
Reduce to a gentle simmer. Cover and cook for 10 minutes.
Add the hot water, sugar, pepper, bay leaf and salt.
Continue to simmer for 10–15 minutes. Remove from heat
and mix well mashing the vegetables with the back of a
wooden spoon, or putting it in the blender for a minute. Pass
through a sieve. Adjust seasoning. Before serving add the
milk and heat through without boiling. To serve garnish
with a sprig of parsley in each bowl.

» Fish Moulee is a delicately flavoured dish, much
   favoured at 'Ladies' Luncheons', fifty years ago.

Fish Moulee

Fillets of Fish in Coconut Sauce

Serves 6

Ingredients:
• ¼ tsp turmeric powder
• 2 tbsp oil
• 500 gms filleted fish cut in 1-inch by 2-inch pieces
• 2 cups milk extracted from 1 large coconut (see page 66)
• 1 medium onion (halved and sliced fine)
• 1-inch piece fresh ginger (sliced fine)
• 2 green chillies (cut in fine rounds)
• ½ tbsp flour

Method:
Sprinkle the turmeric powder over the filleted fish. Heat the

oil in a large heavy frying pan. On medium heat sauté the
fish 2–3 minutes turning once. Add the coconut milk. Let it
come to the boil, adjust heat to a brisk simmer. Add the
sliced onions, ginger, green chillies and salt to taste.
Simmer briskly until the liquid is reduced to almost half.
Alternatively, take a little coconut milk from the pan, cool
and add the flour, mix well and return to pan. Simmer for
10 minutes and remove from heat. The alternative is a safe
method, as it prevents the coconut milk from curdling.

» What the French call mayonnaise was not always
used in British India. What went for mayonnaise was
more a mustard sauce, akin to an English 'Butler's
Dressing', and not an emulsion of oil and egg yolks,
but a combination of various ingredients including
milk.

Here is a recipe for 'Mayonnaise Sauce' which
Minakshie's mother and many ladies before her used
in making fish mayonnaise.

Calcutta Fish or Prawn Mayonnaise

Serves 4

Ingredients:

For mayonnaise
• **4 hardboiled eggs**
• **1 tbsp dry mustard**
• **2 tbsp vinegar**
• **salt to taste**
• **2 tsp white pepper**
• **juice of one lime**
• **2 tbsp oil**
• **4 tsp sugar**

- **4 tbsp milk**
- **500 gms any white fish (bhekti) or 500 gms prawns**
- **½ onion (chopped)**
- **4 garlic cloves (crushed)**
- **½-inch piece ginger**
- **piece of fish skin (optional)**

To serve
- **a head of lettuce**
- **6 small cucumbers**
- **2 carrots**
- **1 medium onion**

Method:

The mayonnaise

Separate the whites and yolks of the hardboiled eggs. Place the yolks in a bowl. Add the dry mustard. Mix well until the yolks are completely broken up. Add the vinegar, salt to taste and white pepper. Mix well. Add the lime juice and continue to mix. Add 2 tablespoons of oil slowly, mixing all the time. Add the sugar and 2 tablespoons of milk. Mix thoroughly and taste to see the strength of the mustard. Add more if required. Add 2 more tablespoons of milk and oil. Mix thoroughly and use with boiled fish, prawns or vegetables.

To prepare the fish or prawn

Cut the fish in fillets or leave it in one piece; or, boil and peel the prawns and slit them along the back to halve. Poach the fish or prawns in a saucepan with the chopped onions, crushed garlic and ginger and a fishskin (if you can get a piece from the fishmonger) as this addition makes a rich stock. Boil the mixture in a small quantity of water. Strain and reserve the stock.

To serve

Wash the lettuce, separate the leaves and keep in iced water. Peel the cucumbers and cut them across in an inch and a half wide rounds; using a sharp knife, peel around the pieces in a continuous spiral until you reach the seeds. Discard the seeds and place the spirals in iced water. Roll each spiral into a tight roll and cut in thin round slices to make long strings. Keep in iced water. Peel the carrots and cut into long fine strips. Peel the onion and slice it in thin rounds. Separate the rings. Place the lettuce leaves in a flat dish. Pat dry the cucumber and carrots and place them with the onions neatly on the lettuce reserving a little for the garnish. Arrange the fish on the bed of vegetables. Mix half the sauce with 2 tablespoons of the reserved stock and spoon over the fish. Sprinkle a layer of cucumber strings and carrots on the fish and leave it in the refrigerator to set for about 8 hours. Before serving, spoon over the balance of the sauce.

» Smoked hilsa is a Calcutta speciality, probably born aboard a river steamer as it sailed up and down the Ganga carrying cargo to and from the up-country. The day's catch cooked over a charcoal fire in a temporary bucket stove became a boneless perfection in Calcutta's kitchens.

Other than the hilsa we use both the estuary and salt water bhetki, the other fish identified with Calcutta. In fact, these two fish were so popular, that two of the most sought after members of a Fishing Fleet acquired these epithets.

The best way to get a whole fillet of fish is to have it cut in the market. New Market fish stalls have the best filleters—of them, B. C. Ojha's men are the masters.

Smoked Fish

Serves 4

Ingredients:

- 1½ kg fillet of hilsa or bhetki
- 2 tsp salt
- 1 tsp freshly ground black pepper
- juice of 4 limes or 1½ lemons
- 1 tbsp oil (more if necessary)
- 1 tbsp dry mustard
- 1 tbsp molasses
- 2 tbsp anchovy sauce

Method:

Marinate the hilsa or bhetki in the salt, freshly ground black pepper, juice of limes or lemons, oil, dry mustard, molasses, anchovy sauce (an Indian variety is available).

Prepare the smoker

Smoking is best done over a charcoal fire with a half-inch coating of bran over which a cup of mudki (puffed rice coated with molasses) is scattered. Place the fish on a greased wire mesh, cover and smoke for 20 minutes, testing it for doneness.

If you are using an oven or top of a stove, use a large roasting pan. Cover the bottom with half an inch of sand and proceed as before. It is possible to get a wire toaster which will hold the fish in place and make it easy to turn over. This can be placed over the grill and covered. Hilsa is a bony fish, the fillets are in natural divisions which are taken apart to remove the bones and put together. A little of the marinade is reserved to pour over the fish before it is reheated for serving.

» There is a common belief that goat's meat is sold in

Calcutta as mutton. This is not so. There is a whole
mutton range in the New Market where the
wandering sheep are living evidence of dead mutton.
However, it is not of the best quality and has to be
treated before it is cooked.

Collar of Mutton

Serves 6

Ingredients:
- **1½ kg shoulder of mutton**

For filling
- **250 gms sausage meat**
- **1 onion (chopped)**
- **1-inch piece ginger (chopped)**
- **1 small bunch parsley (chopped)**
- **salt to taste**
- **½ tsp black pepper (freshly ground)**
- **½ beaten egg**
- **1 hard boiled egg**
- **4 tbsp oil**
- **1½ cups water**

Method:
Get your butcher to bone and flatten the shoulder of mutton.
Beat it flat again and put in the centre a filling of sausage
meat, seasoned with onion, ginger, parsley, a little salt and
black pepper. Moisten with half a beaten egg and spread
the mixture over the shoulder to an inch of the edge. In the
centre of the filling, place the hard boiled egg. Roll up the
shoulder like a sausage, tucking one end of the meat under
the filling. If you have a larding needle, sew it up with twine,
or tie it up securely with twine remembering that it will
shrink during cooking. Heat the oil in a pan. Coat and roll
the meat with salt and black pepper and brown over high

heat until evenly browned all over. Add the water, cover with a fitting lid and cook over a medium flame checking to see if the meat is tender. It should cook in one and a half hours. Collar can also be roasted in a pre-heated moderate (350° F, 180° C) oven for one and a half hours, basting frequently.

Good accompaniments are carrots with honey and ginger (see Chapter 5 pg 220) and sautéed potatoes.

» The 'saklee of mutton' ordered by the memsahib of yesteryear is no longer roastable and Spence's has closed its doors. We give a recipe for roast leg of mutton with mint sauce.

Always buy your meat a day or two before it is to be roasted and keep it in the lower part of your refrigerator. Tell your butcher to prepare it for roasting.

Roast Mutton

Serves 6

Ingredients:
- 2 kg leg of mutton
- 1 tbsp onion paste
- 1 tbsp ginger paste
- 1 tbsp garlic paste
- 3 tbsp Worcestershire sauce
- 1 cup (if the mutton is lean) ½ cup (if it is fatty) oil
- 1 tsp black pepper
- salt to taste
- 2 cups water
- 6 large potatoes (peeled)
- 1 tbsp flour

Method:

Pierce the leg of mutton all over with a skewer. Rub it all over with the onion paste, ginger paste and garlic paste mixed with Worcestershire sauce and oil, black pepper and salt to taste. Massage these ingredients into the meat as this helps to tenderize it.

Heat oil to smoking in a large deep pan, reduce to medium heat and brown the mutton well on all sides. Add the water to the pan, cover and simmer for two hours, checking to see if the meat is cooked, basting it with the juices that come out of it. Turn it once during cooking time. The meat will be reduced by a third after cooking and the joint at the leg bone will move easily. When pricked with a fork, the liquid that comes out will be a pale colour, not red. During the last 20 minutes of cooking, arrange the potatoes around the meat. Lift out the meat and potatoes when they are cooked and prepare the gravy.

Put the pan and all the juices back on to the fire and wait for the fat to bubble. Add the flour and brown before adding half a cup of water. Cook until the gravy thickens. Serve separately.

Mint Sauce is the classic accompaniment to roast mutton. To make it, mix half a cup of finely chopped mint in 1 cup of malt vinegar. Add 2 teaspoons of sugar and half a teaspoon of salt. Let it stand for at least 1 hour.

» Vegetables accompanying 'English' food in Calcutta are often an unrecognizable mess blanketed in a tasteless white sauce. With a little imagination the vast range of vegetables in the Calcutta market can not only be accompaniments but dishes in themselves.

Carrots with Honey and Ginger

Serves 6

Ingredients:
- **1 kg large red carrots (peeled and sliced into ⅛-inch rounds)**
- **2 tbsp mint leaves (chopped fine)**
- **juice extracted from 2 oranges**
- **1 tbsp orange peel (grated)**
- **4 tbsp butter**
- **1 tsp salt**
- **2 tbsp ginger paste**
- **1 tsp freshly ground black pepper**
- **3 tbsp honey**

Method:
Arrange the carrots evenly at the bottom of a pan and just cover them with water. Add 2 tablespoons of butter, salt and place on a medium flame. When the water comes to the boil, reduce heat, cover the pan and cook until the water is absorbed. Before serving, melt 2 tablespoons of butter in a shallow pan. Add the carrots, stir once, then add the orange juice, ginger paste, black pepper and honey. Cook over high heat until the liquid has dried and there is a glaze on the carrots.

Shake the pan at this stage of cooking to prevent the carrots from sticking. Add the mint leaves and orange peel, mix well and serve immediately.

» New peas and mint are the perfect accompaniment to roast mutton.

Boiled Peas with Mint

Serves 4

Ingredients:
- **1 kg new peas**
- **water**
- **½ tsp salt**
- **2 tsp butter**
- **handful of chopped mint**
- **1 tsp black pepper (ground)**

Method:
Shell the new peas. Put them in a pan with just enough
water to moisten them, about 3 tablespoons, the salt and
butter. Cook over gentle heat until peas are tender. Add a
handful of chopped mint and a teaspoon of black pepper.
There should be just enough liquid in the pan to be absorbed
during reheating. The discarded shells can be used in
khosha charchari (Chapter 2, pp 47–48).

Hint: a pinch of cooking soda added to green vegetables
while they are cooking help to retain the colour. A little
sugar added to the pan brings out the flavour.

» Flora Annie Steele, who wrote *The Indian
Housekeeper and Cook* in the nineteenth century,
says, 'Potatoes should always start cooking in cold
water and after the first boil simmer slowly. Then,
they need an hour to dry after being drained.' For
mashed potatoes always peel potatoes before boiling.
Cook in the above method.

» Nowhere does dal soup taste as good as in an Anglo-Indian home where it is a standard starter to a meal. We normally make dal soup with masoor dal. The Anglo-Indian soup includes a good beef stock or half a kilogram soup bones. The soup can be either vegetarian or with a chicken or mutton stock.

We give a vegetarian recipe.

Dal Soup

Serves 4

Ingredients:
- 5 cups water
- 1 cup masoor dal (split dried red lentils)
- 1 onion (finely sliced)
- 1 tbsp butter
- ¼ tsp turmeric
- 1 tsp black pepper (ground)
- salt to taste

Method:
Bring the water to the boil in a saucepan and add the dal. Cover and cook until the dal is mushy. In another pan fry the finely sliced onion in the butter until brown. Pour into the pan of dal and add the turmeric, black pepper and salt. Cover and simmer for another 10 minutes. Remove from heat, cool and strain through a sieve.

To serve, garnish with (a) crisply fried small croutons of bread called 'sippits' (b) bread croutons crisped in the oven without any oil. Serve wedges of lime with the soup.

For non-vegetarians crisply fried and crumbled bacon may be added as a garnish.

Serve chilled or reheat before serving.

» One of the imports from India into Georgian England
  was kedgeree which appeared in covered silver dishes
  on the sideboard for breakfast in country houses. At
  home, kedgeree makes a good light luncheon or
  Sunday supper dish.

Kedgeree

Serves 8

Ingredients:

For court bouillon
- ½ large onion
- 2 bay leaves
- 6 peppercorns
- a few leaves of parsley
- a twist of lemon peel

- 500 gms firm white fish fillet
- 2 tbsp butter
- ½ large onion (sliced)
- 2 cups rice
- 1 tbsp curry powder
- 1 tsp black pepper (ground)
- salt to taste
- juice of 1 lemon
- 2 hard boiled eggs (sliced)
- sprigs of parsley

Method:
Make a court bouillon by boiling the onion, bay leaves,
peppercorns, parsley and a twist of lemon peel in a saucepan
of water. Strain.

     Poach in 6 cups of this liquid the firm white fillet of fish.
We recommend bhetki or gurjali, the Indian salmon. Cook
for 10 minutes and lift out the fish. Strain the stock and
reserve. Flake the fish.

Heat the butter and brown the sliced onion in a large saucepan or wok. Add the rice and stir fry for 5 minutes. Add 4 cups of the reserved stock. Let it come to the boil, cover the pan and simmer for 15 minutes or until the rice has absorbed the liquid and the grains are cooked but separate. Add the flaked fish, curry powder, ground black pepper and salt. Mix well with a fork and cook for another 5 minutes and stir in the lemon juice.

Place in a flat dish and garnish with the sliced hard boiled eggs and a few sprigs of parsley.

» How this recipe was contrived we have no idea. It appears to fall somewhere between a Bengali khichuri and the English kedgeree. It was a favourite for nursery meals and served to invalids. The basic ingredients are chicken, rice and milk.

Pish Pash

Serves 6

Ingredients:
- 1 kg chicken (cut into 12 pieces)
- 1 cup rice
- 3 cups water
- 2 bay leaves
- 6–8 peppercorns
- 1 medium onion (cut in half and sliced)
- ½ inch piece ginger (thinly sliced)
- salt to taste
- 1 tbsp butter
- 1 cup milk

Method:
Set the chicken to boil with the water in a saucepan. Add

the bay leaves, peppercorns, onion and ginger. Add salt to taste and the rice. Simmer gently. When the water is reduced to half, add the butter and milk. Continue to cook until the rice is soft and pappy.

» Anything cooked with spices became a 'curry' to the sahib. For the folks 'back home' to enjoy a curry and to simplify cooking it, the curry powder was evolved. No Indian, nor in fact any Britisher really interested in Indian food, uses curry powder.

Curry powder is a mixture of several spices ground together and is available commercially all over the world today. A good curry powder includes turmeric, coriander, cumin, fenugreek, mustard seeds, aniseed, cinnamon, cloves, cardamoms and peppercorns. It may also include powdered ginger, garlic, nutmeg and bay leaf.

Packaged masalas are now sold in nearly all grocery stores, specially mixed for making different dishes. The shopkeeper will also mix spices to specification and required strength, making it much easier to cook a good curry without tears!

Chicken curry is surely the common denominator for special occasion eating in non-vegetarian homes in Calcutta. Whatever else there may be on the table, a good chicken curry is a sure winner.

While looking for recipes, we were inundated with the most exciting versions of chicken curry and found it difficult to choose. The two we give here are an old English one (as the sahibs improvised on the bawarchee curry) and a newer Calcutta curry (from Mrs Sita Pasricha's notebook, courtesy Mrs Tara Sinha).

Chicken Curry - I

Serves 4–6

Ingredients:
- **1 kg chicken (cleaned and jointed)**
- **a little flour**
- **turmeric powder**
- **3 tbsp oil**
- **1 large onion (sliced fine)**
- **1 medium onion (ground)**
- **1-inch piece ginger (ground)**
- **5 cloves garlic (ground)**
- **1 large cooking apple (chopped)**
- **1½ tbsp curry powder**
- **2½ cups water**
- **a few raisins**
- **salt to taste**

Method:
Coat the chicken with a little flour and turmeric. Heat the oil in a saucepan and fry the sliced onion till it is light brown. Add the ground spices, the apple and curry powder. Fry over gentle heat for 3 minutes. Add the chicken and fry for another 5 minutes, taking care not to burn the spices. Add salt to taste. Add the water and raisins. Simmer and cook until the chicken is tender. Serve with rice, 'dall' and mango chutney (see pg 88).

Chicken Curry - II

Serves 4–6

Ingredients:
- **1 kg chicken (cleaned and jointed)**
- **2 tbsp oil**

- **2 onions (sliced)**
- **1-inch piece ginger (ground)**
- **3 cloves garlic (chopped)**
- **1 tomato (sliced)**
- **1 tsp turmeric**
- **2 tsp coriander (powdered)**
- **2 tsp cumin (powdered)**
- **¼ tsp chilli (powdered)**
- **salt to taste**
- **½ cup yoghurt**
- **2 cups hot water**

Method:
Heat the oil and brown the onions in a deep pan. Add ginger and garlic and the chicken and brown. Stir all the time to prevent burning. Add the turmeric, coriander, cumin and chilli powders. Add salt to taste. Cook for 2 minutes and add the tomato. Cook for another 2 minutes and add the yoghurt and hot water. Simmer gently until the chicken is tender. This is a light curry, and tastes very good with rice or chapatti.

» The next recipe comes from Mona Benham and we reproduce it more or less as it was written in her book. The language is as descriptive as the koormah (sic) is tasty. An interesting feature of this recipe is that it has no onions, ginger or garlic.

Fowl Curry Koormah

Serves 4–6

Ingredients:
- **1 kg chicken (cleaned and jointed)**
- **1 dessert spoon [1 tablespoon] khus khus (poppy seeds)**
- **1 tbsp coriander (roasted and husked)**

- 1 slice coconut
- 1 dessert spoon [1 tablespoon] jeera (cumin)
- turmeric
- red chillies
- 2–3 tbsp sour curd (yoghurt)
- salt to taste
- 3 tbsp ghee

Method:
Grind the khus khus, coriander, coconut, jeera, turmeric and red chillies, and mix it with the sour curd. Lather it on the cut up fowl. Add salt to taste. Heat the ghee in a pan and cook the fowl on a gentle fire.

Mona belongs to the day when dessert spoons were in use as opposed to tablespoons. We now use the word tablespoon for dessert spoon, and large tablespoon for what Mona calls just a tablespoon. Curd we have called yoghurt and khus khus, poppy seed.

» Bread and Butter Pudding is an item which will always be found on the menus of cheap cafeterias and diners in Calcutta. The waiter comes across and tells you what is going for the day. He yells across the room to the person taking orders. When it comes to pudding, you will hear the call 'once piece pudding!'

Bread and Butter Pudding

Serves 6

Ingredients:
- 3 cups milk
- 2 eggs
- 3 tbsp sugar
- ½ tsp vanilla essence
- a day old loaf of bread

- **butter**
- **1½ tbsp raisins (cleaned and washed)**

Method:

Boil the milk down to make one and a half cups. Cool. Separate the whites from the yolks of the eggs. Whisk the yolks with the sugar in a bowl until thick. Pour into the milk. Whip the egg whites in another bowl till thick and frothy. Fold into the milk mixture. Add the vanilla essence. Cut off the crust of the day old loaf of bread and slice the remaining loaf into one-fourth inch slices and butter them. Cut each slice into one by two-inch pieces. Grease a rectangular baking dish and arrange a layer of bread pieces on it. Spoon enough custard over it to cover, sprinkle raisins over it. Cover with another layer of bread, custard and raisins and leave to soak for 1 hour. Bake in a medium hot oven (375° F, 200° C) for 20–25 minutes when the top should be nicely browned and a toothpick inserted in the pudding should come out clean.

A layer of jam between the layers instead of the raisins makes a nice change.

» Summer brings a bounty of fruits to the Calcutta markets. Fruit purées or fools made with fruit and custard make a refreshing end to a summer meal.

Tepari Fool

Cape Gooseberry Fool

Serves 6

Ingredients:
- **1 cup gooseberry (teparis)**
- **½ cup water**
- **2 tbsp sugar**

- **2 cups milk**
- **2 tbsp double cream**

Method:
Stew the gooseberries in a small saucepan with the water and sugar. Sieve and cool the thin purée. Thicken the milk in another saucepan till it is two-thirds its original quantity. Cool and mix the purée with the thickened milk and refrigerate for at least two hours. Stir in the double cream before serving. A thin custard may be used instead of the thickened milk. Make half the quantity of custard made according to recipe for bread and butter pudding (pp 228–229). Cool. Mix fruit purée.

Green Mango Fool may be made the same way. Check the purée for acidity before adding the milk and add more sugar if required. A pinch of salt reduces the acidity.

The same recipes put into ice trays and frozen make very acceptable ice creams.

» Come winter and date palm molasses (gur) floods the market. Men carrying basketfuls of earthenware pots of gur come to the city from the nearby districts where the gur is made. Three Palm Pudding was created as if only to use this delicious sweet.

Three Palm Pudding

Serves 4

Ingredients:
- **cream and milk extracted from 1 coconut**
- **100 gms large-grained sago**
- **gur**

Method:
Extract cream and milk from 1 coconut (see Chapter 2 pg 66). Boil the large-grained sago in a small saucepan and set

in small glass dishes. Serve with a small jug of the coconut milk and cream mixed together and another jug of heated molasses. Pour over the sago and mix and eat it.

» Lunchtime conversation between husband and wife in an 'enlightened' late nineteenth-century Bengali household, was the start of many an innovation in the ranna ghar. Jewish, Armenian and other Europeans entertained their Bengali business associates and the England-returned professionals to dolmas, fowl curries and mahashas. 'What did you eat last night?' from a young wife brought answers which inspired her to experiment in her kitchen. And the newly appointed bawarchee in the kitchen outhouse allowed some of the aromas from his creations to waft and be adapted into eggless and even uncrumbed chops and cutlets acceptable to the ladies of the house.

Wax gourd (potol) is one of the quiet constants of Bengali cuisine. Elegantly oval shaped with a dark and pale green pinstriped skin it is usually peeled in alternate stripes. Wax gourd not only appears in jhal, jhole and charchari, but is also delicious when lightly grilled in butter or covered with a light white sauce as an accompaniment to grilled fish and meat. Maachh potoler dorma, an Armenian adaptation, is the Bengali cook's brainwave.

Maachh Potoler Dorma

Wax Gourd Stuffed with Fish

Serves 4

Ingredients:
- **6 large wax gourds (potol)**

For filling
- **200 gms boneless white fish**
- **1 tsp turmeric**
- **½ tsp salt**
- **2 tsp ghee or mustard oil or a half-and-half combination**
- **1 large onion (chopped)**
- **1-inch piece ginger (ground)**
- **1 tsp sugar**
- **salt to taste**
- **2 green chillies**
- **2 cloves (powdered)**
- **2 green cardamoms (powdered)**
- **1-inch piece cinnamon (powdered)**

- **1 cup mustard oil**

Method:
Cut off one end of the wax gourds and hollow them out with a salt spoon or hair pin, reserving the cut bits for a lid. Take care not to break the skin. Scrape the skin gently.

The filling
Boil the fish in a small pan with the turmeric and salt. Drain, flake and keep aside. Heat the ghee and/or mustard oil in a wok. Fry the onions till they are lightly browned. Add the ginger and fry for another 30 seconds. Add the fish and brown lightly. Add 1 teaspoon sugar and salt to taste, the green chillies and the garam masala powder of cloves, green cardamoms and cinnamon and fry for another minute. Take it off the fire before the mixture gets too dry.

Cool and mash the filling with your fingers and carefully fill the wax gourd cases. Secure the lid with toothpicks. Put a very light coat of turmeric on the wax gourds and fry them in the hot mustard oil in a wok over a medium flame until the wax gourds are soft. The frying must be done in a shallow pan. To serve re-fry until heated through.

» Many of the newly created 'dry' as they were called,

were offered to wedding guests who could not stay for the main meal. A plate of 'dry' would consist of a fish or meat filled potato 'chop', a savoury fillet of not fried fish but fish fry with a teaspoon of thinly mixed mustard and a salad of thinly chopped lettuce, beetroot and onions, or if the occasion was particularly special, a prawn cutlet. For vegetarians the chop would be filled with chhana, mocha or enchor and rolled in poppy seeds. There may be a pea kachori or radhaballabi and alur dom.

A recipe from the members of Nari Seva Sangha.

Matarshutir Kachori

Green Pea Kachori

Makes 20 Kachoris

Ingredients:

For pastry
- 2 tbsp oil
- 500 gms flour
- 1 tsp sugar
- pinch of salt

For filling
- 1 tbsp oil
- 1 kg green peas (shelled and ground with 2 green chillies)
- 1 tbsp sugar
- 2 tsp ginger paste
- 1 tsp aniseed (roasted and powdered)

For assembling
- 2 cups oil

Method:

To make pastry
Rub the oil into the flour and add the sugar and a pinch of salt. Add enough water to make a stiff dough, cover and let it rest.

To make filling
Heat the oil in a wok. Add the peas, sugar, ginger paste, roasted and powdered aniseed. Fry a little, take off the fire and keep aside.

To assemble
Divide the dough into 40 portions and roll them out into fairly thin circles. Put 2 large tablespoons of the filling on 20 circles of dough. Cover each with another circle of dough. Brush water on the edges and seal. Twist the edges to give a plaited effect and make the sealing more effective. Heat the oil to smoking in a wok. Reduce heat. Fry kachoris a few at a time to a golden brown.

Fish Fry

Fried Fillets of Fish

Makes 4 pieces of Fish Fry

Ingredients:

For marinade
* ½-inch piece ginger
* 1 medium onion
* 2 cloves garlic
* 2 minced green chillies
* 2 tbsp good vinegar or juice of 2 limes
* 1 tsp white pepper
* salt to taste

* 4 fillets of white fish (2-inch wide, 4-inch long, ½-inch thick)

- **2 cups breadcrumbs**
- **2 eggs (beaten with 2 tbsp flour)**
- **1 cup oil**

Method:

To make marinade

Grind together the ginger, onion, garlic. Mix into the ground spices the minced green chillies, vinegar or the lime juice, white pepper and salt to taste.

Spread the breadcrumbs on a piece of waxed paper or brown paper. Place the fillets of white fish in the marinade for at least half an hour, turning the fish once or twice. Before frying dip into the egg and flour mixture and coat with breadcrumbs.

Heat the oil in a frying pan. Fry the fillets 2 at a time to a golden brown. Serve immediately.

The fish may be egged and crumbed ahead of cooking time and refrigerated. The best fish for frying is bhetki, but any white fleshed flaky fish may be used. Pomfret, haddock, and the Indian salmon are very good fried in this way.

Chingri Cutlet

Prawn Cutlet

Makes 4 large cutlets

Ingredients:
For marinade, batter, coating (see Fish Fry above)
- **8 large bagda prawns**

Method:
Make the marinade, the batter and the crumbs exactly the same way as for Fish Fry.

To prepare:
Remove the shells and the head, but leave the tail on. Split

the flesh down the middle and remove the black thread. Flatten the prawn with the back of a knife and proceed as for fish fry. Take care to keep the cutlets flat by pressing them down with a spatula while frying. Since bagda prawns are prohibitively expensive, food shops prepare their very popular prawn cutlets by mixing 300 grams of shelled minced shrimps with the marinade, shaping the cutlets into flat ovals and frying them in the same way as in Fish Fry.

Chicken cutlets are made in the same way and were a favourite 'train food' when travel by long distance train was a holiday in itself.

» We have said in the text that chingri maaccher chiney kebab is the ultimate in style (Chapter II). Here is a recipe which may be worth the expense and effort.

Chingri Maachher Chiney Kebab

Stuffed Crayfish 'Chinese' style

Serves 6–8

Ingredients:
- 1 kg crayfish (6–8)
- large pot of water
- 3 tsp turmeric
- 2 onions (finely chopped)
- 4 cloves garlic (finely chopped)
- 1-inch piece ginger (finely chopped)
- 2 cloves (powdered)
- 2-inch piece cinnamon (powdered)
- 1 black cardamom (peeled and ground)
- 6 peppercorns (powdered)
- 6 allspice berries (kebab chini) (powdered)
- a blade of mace (powdered)
- a grating of nutmeg
- 3 tbsp ghee
- 2 tbsp yoghurt

- **2 tbsp dehydrated milk (khoa)**
- **salt to taste**

Method:

Wash the crayfish thoroughly. Bring to the boil a large pot of water with the turmeric. Drop the crayfish in the shell, claws and all into the water and boil for 10 minutes.

Remove from water and cool. Now comes the tricky part. Make a cut in the shell between the head and tail to scrape out all the flesh from the tail and the coral from the head, leaving the shells intact. Chop the meat and mix with the coral.

Heat the ghee in a wok and fry the onions till lightly browned. Add the ginger and garlic and fry for another 3 minutes. Add the crayfish meat and all the other spices and turn it over in the ghee until it is well coated and the spices are fragrant. Add the yoghurt and dehydrated milk, salt to taste. Mix well into a not too dry consistency.

With a small spoon fill each shell with the mixture and secure the head and tail with toothpicks. Add a little more ghee to the pan in which the stuffing cooked and grill the whole fish in it. This gives a nice shine to the shell. If the filling is too little to fill all the shells, 100 grams of shelled minced shrimps may be added to the fish mixture while frying. Spices may be adjusted according to taste.

» S.K. Mitra, a resident of North Calcutta cooks as a hobby. He creates his own version of foods he has enjoyed. He shared with us a recipe of a fish cutlet he tasted at Chachar Dokan, an eating place in North Calcutta, a haunt of theatre lovers.

Chachar Cutlet

Chacha's Cutlet

Makes 15 large or 20 small cutlets

Ingredients:
- 1 kg white fish (boiled, skinned and boned)
- 7 slices bread
- 1½ cups water
- 4 eggs
- 2 cups breadcrumbs
- 1 tsp melted butter
- 2 tsp black pepper powder
- 2 tsp garam masala powder of green cardamoms, cloves and cinnamon
- 1 cup ghee or 1½ cups oil
- salt to taste

Method:
Soak the bread in the water for ten minutes and squeeze out the water. Mash the fish. Beat the eggs lightly with a fork. In a large bowl, mix the fish with the bread, butter, salt, pepper and garam masala. Mix in the eggs, keeping about a fourth aside to coat the cutlets. Mix well. The mixture should be easy to handle. Shape into oval shapes or croquettes with your hands. Place the remaining beaten egg in a shallow pan. Spread the breadcrumbs on a sheet of paper. Dip the cutlets into the beaten egg and coat with breadcrumbs. They are now ready to fry. Place them on a large platter. Heat the ghee or oil to smoking in a large frying pan. Lower the heat and fry the cutlets a few at a time turning them once until they are golden brown. Garnish with thinly sliced onions, cucumber and boiled beetroots. Serve with freshly-made mustard sauce.

» Basanta Panda, a professional Oriya thakur rolled

out radhaballabis to feed 500 as he dictated the recipe
for this Calcutta special.

Radhaballabi

Fried Bread with a Filling of Lentil Paste

Makes 20

Ingredients:

For the dough:
- **500 gms flour**
- **100 gms ghee**
- **water**
- **½ tsp baking powder**
- **1 tsp salt**

For the filling:
- **125 gms kalai dal (split black lentils)**
- **a large pinch asafoetida (1 gm)**
- **1-inch piece ginger**
- **1 tsp dry ginger powder**
- **1 tsp red chilli powder**
- **1 tsp aniseed roasted and powdered**
- **1 tsp sugar**
- **1 tbsp dehydrated milk**
- **½ tsp powdered mace**
- **salt to taste**

To fry
- **400 gms ghee**

Method:

The dough
Sift the flour with the salt and baking powder. Mix in the
ghee with the tips of your fingers until the mixture
resembles breadcrumbs. Add the water gradually until you
have a stiff but pliable dough. Knead well for 8 minutes.

Form into a ball and leave covered for 2 hours.

The filling

Soak the dal for 2 hours, drain and grind to paste with the ginger and the asafoetida. Mix in the ginger, chilli and aniseed powders, sugar and salt. Heat the ghee in a shallow pan or wok and fry the mixture lightly for 5 minutes. Take the pan off the fire and mix in the mace and dehydrated milk.

To make up and fry

Divide the dough into 20 equal-sized balls. Flatten each ball in the palm of your hand to form a cup. Fill with half a teaspoon of filling and reshape into a ball. Flatten each ball slightly and roll it out into a circle on a floured surface, taking care that the filling does not break through the dough. Heat ghee in a wok to smoking and quickly lower heat because if the ghee burns it will discolour the radhaballabis. Fry the radhaballabis one or more at a time, depending on the size of the wok. Press down the sides to make them puff up. Turn once. It is advisable to fry these one at a time, because they often split and the filling comes out.

Radhaballabis may be eaten hot, but are generally served at room temperature.

» Devilry wandered from the bawarcheekhana to the ranna ghar and resulted in dimer devil and chhanar devil, inside-out versions of Scotch eggs.

Dimer Devil

Calcutta-style Devilled Eggs

Serves 6 - 8

Ingredients:
• **6 eggs**

- **2 tbsp filling (see above Maachh Potoler Dorma pp 231–232)**
- **1 tbsp flour mixed in ¼ cup water**
- **breadcrumbs**
- **1 cup oil**

Method:

Hard boil the eggs and halve them lengthwise. Scoop out the yolks and mash them with the filling. Put the two halves together and dip the eggs in the flour and water batter. Roll in the breadcrumbs and fry in hot oil in a wok over medium heat until golden brown. The eggs need not be crumbed, in which case, the batter should be a little thicker, enough to make a thin coating on the egg.

Chhanar Chop

Potato Chops filled with Cottage Cheese

Makes 8 chops

Ingredients:

For filling
- **1 medium onion (chopped)**
- **1-inch piece ginger (chopped)**
- **2 green chillies (seeded and chopped)**
- **300 gms fresh cottage cheese (chhana)**
- **1 tbsp raisins**
- **1 tbsp oil**
- **¼ tsp turmeric powder**
- **½ tsp chilli powder**
- **1 tsp sugar**
- **salt to taste**

For casing
- **8–10 large potatoes**

To assemble
- **2 eggs (beaten) with 1 tbsp flour**

- ½ cup oil
- browned breadcrumbs

Method:

Filling
Break up the chhana with your hands. Sauté the raisins in oil. Heat the oil in a wok and fry the onions till just turning brown. Add the turmeric powder, chilli powder, the ginger and green chillies and stir fry over medium heat sprinkling with water until the spices turn colour. Add chhana and mix well. Add the sugar and salt. Add the raisins. Cook for 5 minutes and remove from fire.

Casing
Boil the potatoes in their jackets. Peel and mash them well and divide into 8 equal portions.

Assemble
Shape a mashed potato portion into a cup in the palm of your hand and three-quarter fill with the chhana filling. Close up the cup and shape into a flattened egg shaped cutlet or into a bolster shaped croquette. Coat in a mixture of eggs beaten with the flour and roll in browned breadcrumbs. Leave to rest for at least half an hour before frying. Heat the oil in a frying pan to smoking. Reduce heat and fry the chops to a golden brown, turning once.

Mochar Chop

Potato Chops with Banana Flower Filling

Makes 8 chops

Ingredients:

For filling
- 1 large spadix of banana
- 1 tsp turmeric

- a little salt
- 1 tbsp ground ginger
- 1 tsp cumin (powdered)
- 1 tsp black pepper (powdered)
- 1 tsp garam masala powder of green cardamoms, cloves and cinnamon
- 1 tsp chilli powder
- 1 crushed bay leaf
- 2 tsp sugar
- salt to taste
- 1½ tbsp ghee

For casing
- 8 large potatoes

To assemble
- 1 tbsp flour mixed in ¼ cup water
- 100 gms poppy seeds
- ½ cup oil

Method:

Filling
Prepare the flowers from a large spadix of banana in the way described in Chapter 2 (pp 81–82). In a pan boil the flowers with the turmeric and a little salt. Drain and mix well with ginger, cumin and black pepper, garam masala, chilli powder, bay leaf, sugar and salt to taste. Fry in the ghee over medium heat in a wok until the mixture is still moist and there is a fragrance of spices. Remove from fire and cool.

Casing
Make the casings in the same way as for Chhanar Chop (pp 241–242). Fill and shape into croquettes. Dip each into a thin paste of flour mixed in water. Roll in poppy seeds and fry in the hot oil over medium heat.

Green jack fruit (enchor) and plantain (kanch kala) can be treated this way. For potato chops, the potatoes should be boiled in their jackets and peeled after boiling.

» Those members of our family who say they are not
hungry when there is stew for dinner, eat happily
when ishtu is served. This is a Bengali variation of
stew derived from the Anglo-Indian kitchen. We call
it ishtu because it is the common pronunciation in
Bengali.

Ishtu

Stew

Serves 8

Ingredients:
- 1 kg mutton or goat's meat (cut in 1-inch cubes)
- 500 gms small white onions (peeled)
- 2 medium onions (ground)
- ½-inch piece ginger (ground)
- 1 kg potatoes (peeled and cut in 1-inch pieces)
- 2 tbsp oil or ghee
- 1 tbsp coriander powder
- 1 tbsp black pepper (freshly ground)
- 1 tsp garam masala powder of green cardamoms, cloves
  and cinnamon
- 1 tbsp Worcestershire sauce
- 1 tsp vinegar
- 1 tsp sugar
- salt to taste

Method:
Boil the meat in water in a large pan. When it is
three-fourths done, add the small white onions and potatoes
and more hot water if you feel the water is insufficient.
Remove from fire when the meat and vegetables are cooked.
Heat the oil or ghee in a large pan and add the onion and
ginger paste, coriander powder and black pepper. Fry for 5
minutes and add the meat and vegetables and the broth in
which they were cooked. Bring to the boil, reduce heat and

simmer for 5 minutes. Add the garam masala powder, Worcestershire sauce, vinegar, sugar and salt to taste. Simmer for 5 minutes and remove from fire.

While going through Anglo-Indian recipe books, Minakshie found several references to 'sauce' and vinegar used for the best part to 'finish' a dish. Insofar as we know, 'sauce' in a Bengali kitchen was Worcestershire sauce. It holds its own even today, and has been joined by tomato ketchup.

» An old resident of Calcutta described a pudding he often had as a child when he visited relatives in north Calcutta, who had a bawarchee. Since there was no written recipe, we have tried to recreate the taste which lingered for over eighty years.

Chhanar Pudding

Cottage Cheese Pudding

Serves 4

Ingredients:
- **300 gms cottage cheese (chhana) (grated)**
- **10 gms dehydrated milk (khoa) (grated)**
- **2 tbsp butter**
- **2 eggs (beaten till light and frothy)**
- **200 gms sugar (ground)**
- **50 gms raisins (cleaned and chopped)**
- **50 gms almonds or cashew nuts (cleaned and chopped)**
- **1 piece orange peel (cleaned and chopped)**
- **½ tsp lemon rind (grated)**
- **1 tbsp flour**

Method:
Beat the butter into the cottage cheese and dehydrated

milk. Gradually beat in the eggs and the sugar alternately.
Add the prepared fruit and the lemon rind. Place in a
greased and lined 8-inch cake tin. Bake on medium heat
(350° F, 180° C) in an oven for 20 minutes or until the
pudding is set. Be careful not to overcook as it will curdle.
To avoid a disaster add the flour to the mixture after you
have folded in the fruit.

» Anglo-Indian cuisine is a most interesting culinary
  episode because of the many tastes which have gone
  into it. The plain English roast leg of mutton is laced
  with some spices and results in a highly palatable
  dish. The leftovers, if there are any, are used up in a
  dozen different delectable ways.

Minced Meat for Filling

Filling for 8 potato chops

Ingredients:
- 1 cup minced lamb or beef (from leftover roast or curry)
- 1 tbsp oil
- 2 medium onions (chopped)
- ¼ tsp turmeric
- 2 chillies (seeded and minced)
- 1 tsp sugar
- salt to taste
- 2 tsp parsley (chopped)
- water or gravy
- 3 cloves (powdered)
- 2 green cardamoms (powdered)
- 1-inch stick cinnamon (powdered)

Method:
Heat the oil in a wok or frying pan and brown half the
onions. Add the cooked minced lamb or beef, turmeric,

chillies, sugar and salt. Cook for 5 minutes and add the balance of the onions and chopped parsley (the flat leafed parsley is available in Calcutta throughout the year and is used in most Anglo-Indian dishes calling for parsley). Cook for another 5 minutes. Add the gravy from the leftover dish if available, or a little water to moisten the mince. Add the garam masala powder of cloves, green cardamoms and cinnamon and take off the fire.

» Alu chop is one of the stalwarts of the Anglo-Indian kitchen and with pantaras and jhal frazee makes up a trio of réchauffés regular on the Anglo-Indian menu.

Alu Chop

Meat and Potato Chop

Makes 8 chops

Ingredients:
- 8–10 potatoes
- 2 eggs beaten with 1 tbsp flour
- 2 cups browned breadcrumbs
- 1 portion recipe filling (see pp 246–247)
- 6 tbsp oil

Method:
Boil, skin and mash the potatoes. On a sheet of paper, spread the browned breadcrumbs evenly. Make the filling. Divide the potatoes into 8 portions. Shape each portion into a cup in the palm of your hand and place a tablespoon of filling in it. Roll it together and pat to make secure. Shape into ovals. Dip the chops in the flour and egg batter, roll it in the breadcrumbs and fry in the hot oil in a wok or frying pan till golden brown.

Pantaras

Pan Rolls

Makes 14 rolls

Ingredients:
- 2 eggs
- 1 cup milk
- 1 cup flour
- a pinch of baking powder
- filling (see pg 246–247)
- 2 eggs beaten with 1 tbsp flour
- oil

Method:
In a bowl whisk together the eggs, milk and flour. Add a pinch of baking powder. Grease a frying pan and heat it. When drops of water sprinkled on the pan bounce off it turn down heat and add 2 tablespoons of the batter and swirl the batter to spread it evenly over the pan. When bubbles appear on the batter turn over and cook for another 3 minutes. Lift the pancake carefully and continue to cook the rest of the pancakes in the same way, greasing the pan each time.

To fill
Place a pancake on a flat board. Spoon a portion of filling over it along one end, leaving a bare edge on all sides. First fold the edge nearest the mince over the mince. Then fold the top and bottom edges over the mince and roll over to the other end. Seal with egg and flour mixture by dipping each pantaras into it, roll in breadcrumbs and fry in hot oil until golden brown.

Jhal Frazee

Meat Fried with Onions and Chillies

Serves 4

Ingredients:
- 3 tbsp oil
- 1 onion (cut in quarters)
- 1-inch piece ginger (sliced)
- 2 dry red chillies (broken or cut into neat pieces)
- 2 cups leftover mutton or beef (cut into 1½-inch strips)
- salt to taste
- 2 potatoes (cubed and coated with turmeric)

Method:
Leftover beef or mutton makes the best jhal frazee. Heat 2
tablespoons of oil in a wok or frying pan and fry the onion
and ginger until they are soft. Add the chillies. Fry a little
and add the meat. Fry quickly until the meat is well mixed
with the spices, add salt to taste and set aside. Add 1
tablespoon of oil and heat and fry the potatoes till they are
soft. Mix with the meat. Heat through and serve. Take care
not to make the meat dry by over frying.

Fresh meat may also be used to make jhal frazee, but
it must then be cut, boiled with turmeric and fried as before.

A well-liked accompaniment to jhal frazee is pepper
water, the recipe for which will be found in Chapter 7
(pp 336–337).

» Bhoonie means a fry, and this fried meat has the unusual flavour of dill.

Bhoonie

Fried Meat and Dill

Serves 2

Ingredients:
- **300 gms beef or pork**
- **a handful of dill greens (sowa saag)**
- **2 tbsp oil**
- **1 onion (sliced)**
- **5 green chillies (sliced)**

Method:
Dice the beef or pork and coat it with turmeric, cook in a pan in salted water and oil till almost dry. Put in the sliced onion, sliced green chillies and dill. Stir fry until the water is dry and the oil comes to the top. The meat should be a nice brown.

» Sunday lunch after church in an Anglo-Indian home is a very special affair. The menu may consist of a variety of courses but 'always there will be' a yellow rice and a minced meat preparation. The Sunday mince is freshly cooked and not a made up dish.

Kofta Curry and Yellow Rice are a Sunday special in the Rodrigues home. Peter Rodrigues runs a catering service and shared these favourite recipes with us.

Kofta Curry

Serves 8

Ingredients:

- **1 kg beef (minced)**
- **2 tsp ginger (chopped)**
- **2 tsp garlic (chopped)**
- **5 green chillies (chopped)**
- **1 tsp parsley (chopped)**
- **½ tsp turmeric**
- **2 tbsp flour and extra flour to roll the koftas in**
- **salt to taste**

For gravy

- **3 large onions (ground)**
- **1-inch piece ginger (ground)**
- **6 cloves garlic (ground)**
- **2 green cardamoms (ground)**
- **3 cloves (ground)**
- **2-inch piece cinnamon (ground)**
- **3 dry red chillies (ground)**
- **1 tsp turmeric**
- **4 tbsp oil**
- **2 bay leaves**
- **2 cloves**
- **2 green cardamoms**
- **1-inch piece cinnamon**
- **1 cup water**
- **salt to taste**

Method:

To prepare the koftas:

To the minced beef add 2 tablespoons flour, ginger, garlic, minced green chillies, chopped parsley, turmeric and salt to taste. Take small portions of the mince and make into balls. Roll the balls in flour and keep aside.

Heat the oil to smoking in a pan, reduce heat and fry

the koftas to a nice brown. Lift out of the pan and keep aside.

To make the gravy
In the same oil add the ground spices and fry for 5 minutes.
Add the bay leaves and cloves, green cardamoms, cinnamon.
Fry for another 5 minutes or until the spices look brown and
the oil comes to the top. Add the water and the koftas and
salt to taste. Simmer covered for 15 minutes. Take off the
fire.

The koftas need not be fried before being put into the
gravy, in which case cook them for 2 minutes in the gravy.

Yellow Rice

Serves 8

Ingredients:
- **1 kg fine rice**
- **50 gms ghee**
- **½ tsp turmeric**
- **1 cup coconut milk extracted from 1 coconut (pg 66)**
- **2 bay leaves**
- **1 cup water**
- **salt to taste**

Method:
Wash and dry the rice. Heat the ghee in a pan and put in
the rice and turmeric. Fry for 5 minutes, or until the rice
looks transparent. Add the coconut milk, bay leaves, the
water and salt to taste. Cook until the rice is done, the grains
separate and fluffy. Add more water during cooking time if
necessary. Turn the rice with a fork from time to time.

Ball Fry

Fried Meat Balls

Serves 4–6

Ingredients:
- **500 gms pork (minced)**
- **4 onions (chopped)**
- **6–8 green chillies (chopped)**
- **2 tbsp mint (chopped)**
- **parsley (chopped)**
- **1 tsp pepper (ground)**
- **salt to taste**
- **2 cups oil**

Method:

Mix the onions, green chillies, mint and parsley with the minced pork, and add the pepper and salt to taste. Roll into balls. Heat the oil to smoking in a wok. Reduce heat and fry the meat balls (koftas) till well browned. Fry over a medium. flame, fairly slowly as the koftas must be cooked through.

Tamarind Dal

Split Red Lentils with Tamarind

Serves 8

Ingredients:
- **500 gms masoor dal (split dried red lentils)**
- **3 cups water**
- **1 onion (chopped)**
- **2 cloves garlic (chopped)**
- **1 tbsp tamarind paste (made by soaking 1 tbsp tamarind pulp in 4 tbsp water)**
- **1 tbsp oil**
- **¼ tsp turmeric**
- **2 dried red chillies**

• **salt to taste**

Method:
Boil the water in a large pan and add the masoor dal. Take off the scum as it rises, turn down the heat, cover and cook until done. Keep aside.

Mix the tamarind paste into the dal. Add salt to taste. Heat the oil to smoking in a pan. Reduce heat to medium and add the onion, garlic and dried red chillies. Fry for two minutes. Add the dal and tamarind mixture with the turmeric. Cover and simmer for 5 minutes, mix well to break the dal. Take off the fire.

Liver and Heart Dopiaza

Sheep's Liver and Heart with Onions

Serves 6

Ingredients:
• **1 full sheep's liver and 1 full sheep's heart**
• **2 onions (chopped)**
• **2 cloves garlic (chopped)**
• **1-inch piece ginger (chopped)**
• **2 tsp coriander (roasted and powdered)**
• **2 tsp cumin (roasted and powdered)**
• **3 dry red chillies (roasted and powdered)**
• **4 tbsp oil**
• **3 tsp turmeric**
• **salt to taste**

Method:
Boil water in a large pan and put in the full sheep's liver and heart. Throw away the water and clean and cube them.

Heat the oil in a pan and brown the onions, set half of them aside. Add to the onions in the pan all the prepared spices and the turmeric. Do not add the cumin and coriander at this stage. Fry the spices over medium heat for 3–4 minutes. Add the meats and let them cook till done. Add the browned onions and the cumin and coriander and salt. Stir well, cook for another 5 minutes and remove from fire.

» A curry meal in any language is not complete without a good mango chutney. 'Hotted' or sweetened in varying degrees, children as much as colonels enjoy the Colonel's Sweet and Hot Mango Chutney.

Colonel's Sweet and Hot Mango Chutney

Makes 3 - 4 kg

Ingredients:
- **50 medium green mangoes**
- **1 tbsp slaked lime (chuna)**
- **120 gms ginger**
- **120 gms garlic**
- **50 gms dry red chillies**
- **4 large cooking apples**
- **500 gms raisins**
- **200 gms almonds**
- **2½ kg sugar**
- **1 bottle malt vinegar**

Method:
Peel, cut and seed the green mangoes. Soak in cold water for half an hour. Drain and cut in chips. Soak overnight in a stainless steel bowl in enough water to cover in which the lime (the kind eaten with betel) has been added. Drain and sun for 1 day.

Grind the ginger, garlic and dry red chillies in half a cup of vinegar. Peel, core and slice the cooking apples, clean the raisins, soak, skin and sliver the almonds.

Bring the sugar slowly to the boil in the remaining malt

vinegar in a large stainless steel pan. Cook to a thin syrup.
Add the ground ingredients. When mixed, add the mangoes
and apples. Bring to the boil and if the liquid is insufficient,
add more sugar and vinegar, in proportion.

Cook the chutney till it is thick and add raisins and
almonds. Cook for another 10 minutes, cool and bottle.

The apples, raisins and almonds may be omitted, but
make a great difference if they are added.

To Sterilize Jars for Bottling:

Use wide mouthed glass jars for jams and glass bottles for
sauces.

Wash the jars or bottles thoroughly and place in a cold
oven. Turn the oven to hot and leave the bottles for 10
minutes. Pour hot jam or sauce into the prepared jars or
bottles. If your bottles have metal caps, they can go into the
oven but plastic caps will melt.

» When the seedless black grapes from the south came
   to the Calcutta market at an affordable price,
   Sohinder Grewal's husband insisted that she make
   jam out of them. Many friends benefited from his
   management and her labour. We give Sohinder's
   recipe for her delicious grape jam.

Grape Jam

Makes 1 kg

Ingredients:
- 1 kg black grapes
- 125 ml water
- 1 kg sugar
- 2 tsp citric acid to preserve

Method:
Stew the black grapes in the water in a heavy stainless steel pan on a slow fire for 15–20 minutes. Add the sugar. Mix well to dissolve sugar completely and bring to the boil, remove scum and simmer until setting point is reached. Add the citric acid. A little drop of jam in a teaspoon of water will jell when the jam is ready to take off the fire. A drop of jam on the edge of a saucer will crinkle and set when it is ready. Bottle in hot sterlized jars.

» Cape gooseberries (tepari) have a short season in Calcutta. With a longer growing period and the success of cold storage, it keeps coming to the market through February and March.

Cape Gooseberry Jam

Makes 1 kg

Ingredients:
- **1 kg decaped gooseberries**
- **½ cup water**
- **750 gms or 1 kg sugar**
- **¼ tsp potassium metabisulphide to preserve**

Method:
Boil the decaped gooseberries in the water for 15–20 minutes in a stainless steel pan. Add the sugar depending on taste and stir well until the sugar has dissolved completely. Bring to the boil and remove scum. Simmer and keep removing the scum as it rises. Test for setting by putting a little hot jam in a teaspoon of cold water. If the jam jells, it is ready to bottle. Add the potassium metabisulphide and let it come to the boil once more. Bottle in hot sterilized jars.

» The very English marmalade has become a breakfast
regular in some Calcutta homes. It was the memsahib
who introduced jams and jellies into a world of achars
and chutneys. While her cook would do the tedious
preparations, it was usually the memsahib herself
who made the jams and preserves.

The Darjeeling orange gives body to the delicious
flavour of the kumquat in the marmalade we have
chosen. Kumquats grow in pots and gardens, on
terraces and in verandas. They are too few to make
marmalade for the year, but if a few are left after they
go into the kumquat orange marmalade, they can be
very happily preserved in brandy.

Kumquat Marmalade

Makes 500 - 750 gms

Ingredients:
- **500 gms kumquats**
- **3 thin-skinned oranges**
- **750 gms or 1 kg sugar**
- **juice of 1 lemon**
- **¼ tsp potassium metabisulphide to preserve**

Method:
Cut the kumquats into small pieces. Peel the thin-skinned
oranges. Soak the peel in water and scrape off the inner
white pith. Cut into thin strips 1-inch long. Remove the pulp
from the oranges and set aside. Put the orange pips in a
muslin bag. Soak the peel, pulp, pips and the kumquats
overnight in 2 pints of water in a ceramic bowl. Boil in a
stainless steel pan and reduce to half its quantity. Remove
pips. Add the sugar and stir well to dissolve sugar. Add the
lemon juice. Bring to the boil and remove scum. Simmer,

removing scum as it comes up and testing to see if the
marmalade is set. Test for setting by putting a little
marmalade in a teaspoon of water. If the marmalade jells,
it is ready to bottle. Add potassium metabisulphide and
bring to the boil once more.

Susan Lewis gave us a recipe which follows the above
method using a mixture of orange and sweet lime peels.

To make Kumquat Brandy
Sterilize a wide mouthed glass jar. Place in it 1 cup
kumquats washed and pricked all over with a fork, 1 cup
sugar and 1 pint (500 ml) brandy. Screw on the top of the
bottle and leave for three months before drinking. Use the
fruit for cakes and puddings.

» An accompaniment to roast mutton is guava jelly
which is also delicious eaten with bread.

Guava Jelly

Makes 500 gms

Ingredients:
- 1 kg guava
- 10 cups water
- 4 cups sugar
- ¼ tsp potassium metabisulphide to preserve

Method:
Wash and cut the guava into large cubes. Boil in the water
until the fruit is quite soft. Strain through a nylon sieve or
muslin and measure the juice. If it is very thin, then reduce
it to measure 5 cups. Add the sugar and stir to dissolve.
Bring to the boil and skim off the scum. Simmer until setting
point is reached. To test for setting put a little jelly in a

teaspoon of cold water. If it sets, the jelly is ready to bottle. Add potassium metabisulphide and bring to the boil once more.

» Karamcha (*Carissa caranda*, Calcutta cherry) makes a more tart jelly and is excellent with roast meats. Proceed the same way as guava jelly only leave the fruit whole. All fruit for jams and jellies must be ripe and of the best quality to get the best results.

Chapter 6

Oodles of Noodles

There was a time when Calcutta, a city of many firsts, was the only one with Chinese restaurants. In fact, it was one of the few cities in the world with a China Town. Visitors who came for work or play made time for at least one Chinese meal.

Chinese travellers, tradesmen and Buddhist monks had come to India through the centuries. Yong Atchew was the first to settle here two hundred years ago. The Chinese community of Calcutta make an annual pilgrimage at their New Year in February to his scarlet horseshoe shaped tomb in Achipur, named after Atchew, twenty-four kilometres south of Calcutta. Around 1780, Governor-General Warren Hastings granted him land for a sugar plantation and a group of about 150 Chinese men came to

Chop Chop Chow, Chiney Charchari and Chhurpi

work for Atchew. When he died in 1783, his compatriots moved to Calcutta. Their numbers swelled when they were joined by a band of Chinese sailors who deserted their ship, the *Macao*.

Seventy-five years later, a small group of Chinese shoemakers set up their shops in Kosaitola on Bentinck Street and skilfully fashioned good, inexpensive, 'English-style' footwear for the Calcuttan. By the mid-nineteenth century, they had established themselves and had earned the reputation of being 'industrious, sober, honest and above all clean people'. Their foibles were opium and gambling. At the time, the opium trade was flourishing and clippers to China were loaded with the insiduous cargo at nearby Burrabazar's Aphing Chowrasta or Opium Junction. Though the river and the opium trade have since receded, the name remains and innocuous yellow laddus (round sweetmeat balls) are the merchandise at Aphing Chowrasta today.

A steady migration of carpenters, cabinet-makers, shoemakers, dentists and launderers arrived in Calcutta during the turbulent days of the Kuomintang rule followed by World War II and Mao's Revolution. And so the continued renewal of their cultural ties have helped to preserve the identity of the single largest group of Chinese in India today who live in Calcutta.

The majority are Hakka, tanners and shoemakers by profession. The Cantonese took to carpentery and restaurant keeping. Cantonese is the style served in Chinese restaurants all over the world. They made their home in the heart of the city where the Armenians and Jews lived. This made way for Calcutta's China Town. Good Luck flags fluttered over doorways and recreated a mini China in the maze of lanes and bylanes not far from the commercial hub of Dalhousie Square, now B. B. D. Bagh. Cheek by jowl with opium and gambling dens, eating houses mushroomed. Many were actually in Chinese homes. The menu for the day was a steaming soup, rice or noodles and two other dishes. Office-going Bengali gourmets, always on the prowl for the 'authentic thing', soon discovered the best ones.

Forty years ago, an evening in China Town for Calcutta's élite was a much talked about adventure. A convoy of Buicks and Minervas wound their way through Chattawalla Gully and Blackburn Lane, past pokey smoke-filled rooms screening huddles of Chinamen passing the pipe and playing Mahjong. 'Those were the days,' says a very respected nonagenarian, nostalgically recalling her salad days, 'when the Police Commissioner—an Englishman no doubt—accompanied our party to one of those dens of iniquity before baked crab at Nanking restaurant.' The original China Town has been bulldozed to widen the roads and multi-storeyed office buildings have risen from the rubble.

Nanking is no more. Once it not only served the acme of Chinese food in Calcutta, but was also a travellers' inn. The Chapel on the first floor, with its ceremonial red lap chok (candle) and smoke rising from the Siang joss sticks were the offerings of travellers to the Safe Travel God.

The fondness for Chinese food is shown in the medley of buyers crowding the market on Sun Yat Sen Street in the early hours of the morning. Broad in the beam and soft in the bosom, Mao-suited Chinese mamas hang up spicy red and white sausages over rows of mustard greens and squares of bean curd. The large Chinese grocery sells dried Shitakai mushrooms, sea cucumbers, prawn wafers, dried fish, star anise and noodles. Soya and chilli sauces, locally made, are in great demand. Sauce and noodle making is a big cottage industry in Calcutta and its products find their way to other Indian towns and cities.

Cooking Chinese food at home has become so popular that Calcutta housewives make long journeys to the market to stock up their Chinese larders. Buyers and sellers eat a hearty breakfast—steamed and fried dumplings, smoked spare ribs, fresh noodles and a hot meat ball soup—straight off a roadside charcoal fire. Night shift journalists from the newspaper offices in the vicinity, sup off spicy pigs' trotters on Chattawalla Gully. We wonder whether shopping is only the excuse and the breakfast the real reason for getting husbands out of bed at that ungodly hour of the morning!

China Town has moved to Tangra in East Calcutta. Hakka tanners have been drying hides on the ramparts of their fortress-like homes built here over the last few decades. As a result, many eating houses have sprung up undaunted by the smells wafting on Calcutta's southerly winds from the garbage dump and the tanneries around. The boom in business has eaten into the family living space. More rooms are now made over for eating. There are some regular restaurants with air-conditioned sections.

An amalgamation of the flavours from China—Canton, Peking, Hakka, Shantung and recently Schezwan—has emerged as Calcutta's very own Chinese cuisine called 'Tangra type'. Tangra is where Calcuttans now go and take their friends to chow. We have another example of the city's ability to give and take and absorb the culinary culture of all its peoples.

Confucius said, 'There is no one who does not eat and drink. But few there are who can appreciate taste', and the joy of eating Chinese food is the taste.

Good cooking is making the best use of eating material, only changing the natural taste of the ingredients but not taking its place. For the essence of Chinese cooking is in the traditional insistence that what is cooked must have a taste or flavour even though, as in Bengali cooking, the materials used may be the humble potato peel or the cheapest fish. The palatability must not depend only on the use of seasonings.

Chinese, huo buo, which literally means 'fire-timing' is what counts in all good cooking. Cooking time may take a hundred years like the egg or a hundred seconds as in the stir fries. Animal fats add taste but have been almost completely replaced by bean and peanut oils. The most important seasoning of Chinese food is soya bean sauce.

Vegetables are cooked without either waste or water. The emphasis on non-starchy vegetables and small portions of meat or fish commend a Chinese meal to diabetics and older people.

A Chinese meal has no set courses and has been described as a sharing of a little of several different dishes. As in most Eastern cuisines, Chinese dishes accompany the staple, rice or noodles, whereas in the Western eating system, the cereal complements the dish.

In the Chinese seating arrangement, the host sits near the kitchen door and the guest of honour is farthest from his host. Food is not generally offered and dishes are not passed around. The guests reach out with their chopsticks. At a birthday party, noodles instead of cake very appropriately offer long life to the birthday person.

We are often asked, 'Do you get real Chinese food in a Chinese restaurant?' We answer, 'You can if you ask for it.' Restauranteurs try to cater to the tastes of the people of the place and a tradition of American-Chinese or Calcutta-Chinese food has grown up which is interesting though not Chinese-Chinese.

A guide to eating out Chinese style cannot be exhaustive. Park Street offers a variety of cuisines. While many of the air-conditioned restaurants serve a multi-cuisine, there are exclusively Chinese restaurants, now ironically owned mainly by non-Chinese though the head chefs are Chinese. At Waldrof, Bar-b-que and Golden Dragon, Bengalified Cantonese has been created and has spilled out on to roadside barrows. In fact, Chinese chilli sauce even goes into the roadside kathi roll and chow often has a liberal interlacing of tomato and chilli sauces. Chimney Soup comes bubbling to the table and is the speciality of How Hua just off Park Street. Along Chittaranjan Avenue, where the Metro tunnels its way northwards, Chung Wah is one of Calcutta's oldest Chinese restaurants. It is indicative of the food pulse of the city that it is still going strong. The dapper Aus were prominent citizens. Their interests included horse and pigeon racing. Peter at Nanking restaurant and Henry at Chung Wah entertained their high society friends at Chinese banquets.

Over the years, Calcutta has shown, not only a catholic but a discerning palate. The fastidious Calcuttan prefers the smaller restaurants with a particular style. For him Chinese food is not just the anchor dishes of fried rice, chowmein or sweet and sour fish or pork. He looks for Hakka and Schezwan styles of cooking. Schezwan cooking appeals to the Calcuttan being a fine balance of flavours with hot pepper freely added during cooking or when the dishes are served. The city's five-star hotels have Chinese kitchens which turn out exotic dishes with baby corn, Shitakai mushrooms and jumbo prawns at jumbo prices. Clubs too, have Chinese kitchens and the Bengal Club has added foods from South East Asia.

Ta Fa Shun was another restaurant with old China Town regulars who still talk of great dinners served in their private dining rooms. Winter melon soup was served in a large gourd filled with tiny pink shrimps, dried mushrooms, bamboo shoots, transparent noodles, small pieces of chicken and pork, chunks of the gourd flesh cooked in a light chicken broth. It was covered and steamed and brought in its delicious entirety to the table. When the Dalai Lama was given asylum in India, his followers in Calcutta found the Chinese food served at Ta Fa Shun most suited to their palates. The Dalai Lama's Trust bought over the restaurant in the early Sixties and renamed it Kunga. Some cooks from His Holiness's personal service worked here and turned their hands to old favourites like mandarin fish and hot-and-acrid soup.

There is a similarity between Chinese and Tibetan food both in philosophy and in preparation. Both cuisines are thrifty and very little is thrown away. Food is stir fried, braised or boiled. The presentation is an exquisite combination of shapes and colours. Meat and vegetables are dried when available and preserved for the piercingly cold winter months when the Tibetan, possessed of the wanderlust, returns to his fireside.

The arrival of winter is announced in many Indian towns by the appearance of Tibetans with armfuls of woollen garments, rather like the Kabuliwalas with their dried fruits from Afghanistan and John Chinamen from Shantung who came with bundles of delicate Chinese embroidery on lingerie and linens.

Tibetans make a picnic out of any outing. It is not an uncommon sight at any fair or exhibition to see a group of contented chhurpi-chewing (dried cheese) Tibetans sitting on woollen carpets with flasks of butter tea and baskets of food, happy to spend the day wherever they are.

Calcutta knows Tibetan food as momos, meat or cheese dumplings, steamed or fried and thukpa, a meal-in-a-dish of noodle soup with pieces of meat and vegetables, although in many Tibetan homes, the meat and vegetables are stir fried and served separately. The taste for momos was acquired by the children who went away to boarding school in the Darjeeling hills and spent all their pocket money on the dumplings. When they came home for the long winter vacation, home cooking was good but they sometimes longed for momos which were not to be had for love or money until an enterprising couple from Darjeeling opened their living room on Suburban Hospital Road in Bhowanipore to momo fans. Here on scrubbed tables, momos come straight from the moktu (steamer) accompanied by bowls of hot soup and home-made chilli sauce that sends the unsuspecting through the ceiling. Momos are always served with at least one, and in homes, an assortment of chutneys.

Like their fellow Tibetans, this elderly couple migrate temporarily to the cool hills in summer and momo enthusiasts are no longer disappointed to see the padlock on their front door as Momo Hut and at least a dozen others in different parts of the city keep the momo steaming throughout the year. There are a few multi-cuisine restaurants which now have momos on their menu.

Pemayangtse in Park Circus follows the tradition of Tibetan eating houses in a front room of the home of a Tibetan lady married to a Bengali gentleman. She has introduced shabhaley, meat filled fried bread, shapta, pork or chicken in a sweet and sour sauce and other dishes with

Shangri-La-like names and a delicate taste.

Tibetans are not great sweet eaters but at New Year which coincides with that of the Chinese calendar, and other festivals, khapsey and sangabhaley, in dainty covered baskets accompany greetings to friends and relatives. Khapsey are rice flour batter cookies prettily shaped and fried but the taste is bland and they are difficult to make. Sangabhaley is interesting as it is yet another variation of the rolled and fried delight of dough in delicate layers, very subtly sweetened with powdered sugar which also makes an appearance as khaja, baclava, and empress gaja in other cuisines.

Nepalese and Bhutanese from the Himalayan kingdoms have market garden and business links with Calcutta. Though their cuisine is not yet readily available, friends invited to their homes enjoy their cooking and ask for the recipes like alu achar from Nepal and cheese with dried red chillies from Bhutan, to be tried out in their kitchens and eaten with a gift of red rice from a Bhutanese host.

Thai cuisine, popular in other metropolitan cities has made its debut in a few restaurants. It appears to be a craze with residents returning from tours to the Far East to experiment with Thai recipes, using some easily available ingredients like galingale (aam ada) from the bazaar and lemon grass grown in pots. With a touch of Calcutta, excellent tom yam soup, Thai golden rice and chicken and peanuts delights family and friends.

Pastas, green and white, have joined the instant noodle clan on shop shelves. Calcuttans, young and old, have taken to chow in a big way so much so that one noodle-surfeited seven-year-old was heard sorrowfully to say, 'Chop chop chow is the worst thing that was ever invented!'

Much has been written about the eloquence of Chinese cuisine, of the highly developed methods of cooking, serving and eating. In Calcutta, Chinese food means fun eating, an outing with friends or family and a shared meal. From the bowl of soup to the foo yong—all is shared. Each person orders one dish and everyone dips into everything. Soup after a show is often on the cards and a Chinese soup can be a meal-in-a-dish. Calcutta was introduced to hot-and-acrid soup at Ta Fa Shun.

Hot-and-Acrid Soup

Serves 10

Ingredients:
- **200 gms soya bean curd**
- **1 cup boiled chicken**
- **1 cup small shrimps**
- **4 spring onions**
- **2-inch piece ginger**
- **6-8 cloves garlic**
- **a few dried mushrooms**
- **100 gms button mushrooms**
- **4-5 cups strong chicken broth**
- **1-2 tbsp soya bean sauce**
- **4 tbsp malt vinegar**
- **1 tsp sugar**
- **salt to taste**
- **3 tsp black pepper (ground)**
- **2 tbsp cornflour mixed in half cup water**
- **a handful of beansprouts (chopped)**
- **1 tsp black pepper**
- **a few green onions (chopped)**

Method:
Cut the soya bean curd into small cubes. Dice the boiled

chicken. Boil the small shrimps. Chop the spring onions with some of the greens. Grate the ginger and garlic. Soak a few dried mushrooms and slice the button mushrooms and braise them lightly in oil.

Bring the chicken broth to the boil with 4 cups water in a large pan. Add the soya bean sauce, malt vinegar, sugar, salt to taste and 2 teaspoons of black pepper. Boil for 1 minute and add all other ingredients. Cook for 5 minutes and add the cornflour mixed in water and thicken. Add a handful of chopped beansprouts and another teaspoon black pepper, a few chopped green onions and serve immediately.

» An all-time favourite is chicken corn soup made with tinned sweet corn.

Chicken Corn Soup

Serves 6

Ingredients:
- 1 cup tinned sweet corn
- 5 cups chicken broth
- ½ cup shredded chicken
- salt to taste
- 1 tsp soya sauce
- 1 beaten egg
- green onions (finely chopped)

Method:
Cook the sweet corn in the chicken broth until it is creamy and smooth in a large pan. Add the shredded chicken and cook for another 10 minutes. Add salt to taste and soya sauce. For this soup we use the light soya sauce, sold as Soya Sauce A. Just before serving, heat soup to the boiling point and stir in the beaten egg with a fork. The soup may be

garnished with a little cooked shredded chicken and very finely chopped green onions.

» Baked crab, a speciality of the old Nanking Restaurant has caused more than one embarrassing moment thanks to its upside down presentation. The uninitiated have tried to pierce the shell with a fork and caused more au fait fellow guests to comment on their gaucheness. However, the delicacy of the dish made up for the awkward situation. Though named baked crab, the crab in this recipe needs no baking.

Baked Crab

Serves 4

Ingredients:
- **8 live crabs**
- **1 tsp garlic (very finely chopped)**
- **1 tsp ginger (very finely chopped)**
- **1 tsp green chilli (very finely chopped)**
- **a slice of bread soaked in water (optional)**
- **1 egg white**
- **3 tbsp oil**
- **cucumber salad**
- **chilli vinegar**
- **soya bean sauce**
- **green chillies (chopped)**

Method:
Clean and shell the live crabs. The claws should be broken. The spongy stomach should be discarded and the shells scrubbed thoroughly. This is of vital importance as any contamination in the shell can cause salmonella poisoning.

    Scrape all the meat out of the body and claws and mix

with the garlic, ginger and green chilli. To add to the bulk, a slice of bread soaked in water may be added to the meat. Add the egg white to bind the mixture and stuff it into 4 cleaned crab shells. Heat the oil in a fairly deep frying pan and fry the crabs, shell side up, until the stuffing has set. Turn over and fry and watch the blue-grey shell turn red as it cooks. Serve shell side up on a bed of cucumber salad. Dress at the table with chilli vinegar and soya bean sauce with chopped green chillies.

» Henry Au, the owner of Chung Wah restaurant, would serve mandarin fish when he entertained his friends. That is how good the dish is.

Mandarin Fish

Serves 4

Ingredients:
- **750 gms whole fish**
- **2 tbsp onion, ginger and garlic (ground together)**
- **salt to taste**

For sweet and sour sauce
- **1 tbsp carrot (in julienne strips)**
- **1 tbsp capsicum (in julienne strips)**
- **1 tbsp onion (in julienne strips)**
- **2 tbsp soya bean sauce**
- **2 tbsp malt vinegar**
- **2 tbsp brown sugar**
- **2 tbsp tomato ketchup**
- **2 tbsp cornflour**
- **2 cups water**

Method:
Clean and scale the fish. We choose a variety of bhetki called

bhola bhetki which has one central bone and firm white flesh. Score the fish on both sides. Marinate in the mixture of onion, ginger and garlic and salt to taste. Steam the fish for 15 minutes over hot water in a large pan and keep aside. Or you may coat the marinated fish with a light batter of 1 egg beaten with 1 tablespoon of flour and 2 tablespoons of water, and fry whole in a large pan, just before serving.

Make sweet and sour sauce:
Boil together the soya bean sauce, malt vinegar, brown sugar, tomato ketchup in 2 cups water mixed with 2 tablespoon cornflour in a small steel pan. Cook until thick and translucent. Put in the vegetables and cook a further minute. Arrange the fish on a flat dish and pour the sauce over it.

If the fish is to be fried, it must be crisp and hot.

Prawns with Capsicum and Pineapple

Serves 6

Ingredients:
- **1 can pineapple**
- **1 kg medium sized prawns**
- **1½ cups large capsicum**
- **5 medium onions**
- **2 tbsp oil**
- **1-inch piece ginger (chopped)**
- **8-10 cloves garlic (chopped)**
- **1 cup chicken stock**
- **2 tbsp soya bean sauce**
- **3-4 tbsp malt vinegar**
- **a dash of black pepper**
- **salt to taste**

Method:
Drain the can of pineapple, and cut enough slices to make one and a half cups of chunks. Reserve the liquid. Clean and de-vein the prawns. Cut to match in size the large capsicum.

Peel and cut the onions lengthwise in six pieces. Heat the oil in a wok or deep frying pan and fry the ginger and garlic. Add the reserved pineapple juice and chicken stock. Let it come to the boil and add onions. Cook for a minute and add the prawns, capsicum and pineapple chunks. Add the soya bean sauce, malt vinegar, black pepper and salt to taste if necessary. Cook for about 5 minutes. The vegetables should be crunchy. If there is too much gravy, add 2 tablespoons of cornflour mixed in half a cup of water to the gravy to thicken.

Variation
- 1-inch cubes of pork fried in an egg and cornflour batter may be cooked in this way instead of prawns.

» Five Spice Powder is used to flavour dry, fried and roasted foods in Tibet and China. A mixture of equal parts of cinnamon, red pepper, black pepper, star anise and allspice is slightly roasted and powdered.

Quick Fried Chilli Chicken

Serves 4-6

Ingredients:
- 2 cups chicken winglets, back and neck
- five spice powder
- cornflour
- 1 cup oil
- salt

Method:
Cut the chicken winglets, back and neck into bite-sized pieces. Coat with a mixture of salt, five spice powder and cornflour. Heat oil to smoking in a wok and fry the chicken pieces quickly till they are crisp. Serve with soya bean sauce

and vinegar with chopped green chillies.

» With many a new exotica entering the Chinese kitchen, an old timer, the egg foo yong or Chinese omelette, as our children called it, has gone out of fashion. We still enjoy the great, big flat, yellow circle of egg and vegetables, cut into as many slices as there are eaters. Our recipe with a little green mango has the Calcutta touch.

Egg Foo Yong

Chinese Omelette

Serves 4

Ingredients:
- **6 eggs**
- **1 tbsp water**
- **2 tsp onion greens (chopped)**
- **3 green chillies (chopped)**
- **2 tsp flat chives (chopped)**
- **2 tsp grated green mango**
- **2 tbsp oil**
- **salt to taste**

Method:
Beat the eggs with the water until they are thick and yellow. Add the onion greens, green chillies, flat chives and green mango. Add salt to taste—be careful not to add too much. Heat the oil in a large frying pan and pour in the egg mixture. Fry over medium heat for 3 minutes. Slide a greased dekchi lid under the omelette and flip it over. Cook for another 3 minutes. The omelette should not be overcooked.

Variation:
- Prepare the eggs the same way. Leave out the mango and add 1 teaspoon of light soya bean sauce. Place in a large bowl and put a handful of peas in the mixture. Set it in a covered pot of simmering water and cook for 10 minutes, or until the eggs are just set.

Gold Coin Prawns

Makes 12 pieces

Ingredients:
- **6 slices of bread**
- **200 gms shrimps (coarsely chopped)**
- **1 tsp chopped onion, ginger and garlic**
- **salt to taste**
- **4 tbsp oil**
- **1 tbsp cornflour**

Method:
From the slices of bread cut 12 small circles.

Mix the shrimps, onion, ginger, garlic and salt to taste. Heat the oil in a small frying pan. Mix the cornflour with the prawn mixture and press a little onto each circle of bread. Fry till golden brown.

Variations:
- Cut the bread into squares and sprinkle the prawn mixture with sesame seeds before frying.
- Serve with mustard made with 1 tablespoon mustard powder, 1 tablespoon vinegar, ¼ teaspoon salt, ½ teaspoon sugar.

» The Chinese say noodles are a symbol of long life and they celebrate birthdays with noodles.

Chiney Charchari

Calcutta Stir Fried Vegetables and Noodles

Serves 4

Ingredients:
- 2 tbsp oil
- 1 tbsp spring onions (sliced fine)
- 1-inch piece ginger (sliced fine)
- 4 cloves garlic (sliced fine)
- 1 tbsp carrots (sliced fine on the slant)
- 1 tbsp capsicum (seeded and sliced fine)
- 125 gms button mushrooms (sliced fine) (if dried mushrooms are being used they should be soaked in water for an hour)
- 1 tbsp malt vinegar
- 1 tbsp light soya bean sauce
- 4 cups egg noodles (boiled and drained)

Method:
Heat the oil in a wok or frying pan and add the onion, ginger and garlic. Cook for 30 seconds. Add the other ingredients and cook for 2 minutes stirring constantly with a spatula. Add the malt vinegar and light soya bean sauce. Cook for 1 minute.

Mix in the boiled and drained egg noodles quickly. Check the salt. If a very savoury noodle is preferred, 1/4 teaspoon of turmeric and 1 teaspoon of chilli powder may be added with the noodles.

» Eating momos has become the 'in' thing in Calcutta. In fact, this is a simple traveller's dish. No Tibetan travels without his moktu and the inns all along the trade route from Lhasa to India served hot soup and steaming momos to weary travellers.

Momos

Meat Dumplings

Makes 40 momos

Ingredients:
- **500 gms flour**

For filling
- **300 gms fat pork or beef (coarsely chopped)**
- **1 tsp onion (chopped)**
- **1 tsp garlic (chopped)**
- **500 gms soup bones**

For chutney
- **1 tomato**
- **2 tsp chilli powder**
- **6 cloves garlic**
- **salt to taste**
- **chopped green onions and coriander for garnishing**

Method:
Mix the flour into a stiff dough with water. Knead well, form into a ball and let it rest. Mix the fat pork or beef with chopped onion and garlic.

Roll the dough into small rounds and put a teaspoon of filling in each. Fold over to make a semicircle and pinch the edges together with water to seal. Pleat the edges and place the momos in a greased steamer. Boil the soup bones in a large pot of water. Set the momo dish over this and let them steam for 30 minutes.

Chutney
Char the tomato and grind it with the chilli powder, garlic and salt to taste. This can be made in seconds in the blender. Serve the momos in the steamer and the strained soup in large bowls. Garnish with chopped green onions and coriander.

» Thukpa is a bowl of noodles in soup with meat and/or vegetables served on top to make it a meal-in-a-dish.

In some homes the soup with noodles is served separately and a variety of stir fried vegetables and meats are served as accompaniments.

Thukpa

Noodles in Broth

Serves 8

Ingredients:

For Soup
- **4 cups cooked noodles**
- **8 cups strong salted broth**

For Stir Fries

I
- **½ cup thin slivers of beef undercut**
- **½ cup celery cut to match beef slivers**
- **1 tsp light soya sauce**
- **2 tsp oil**
- **¼ tsp sugar**

II
- **½ cup thin 1-inch squares of pork tenderloin**
- **1 quartered onion**
- **½ cup cooked bamboo shoots cut to match the pork**
- **½ cup sliced fresh mushrooms (if dried mushrooms are used, they must be soaked in water for an hour)**
- **2 tsp oil**
- **salt to taste**

III
- **½ cup shredded chicken**
- **½ cup French beans, finely cut on the slant**
- **2 tsps oil**
- **salt to taste**

For Chutneys

I
- 1 cup cottage cheese
- 8 cloves garlic
- 2 tsp chilli powder
- salt to taste

II
- 50 gms roasted sesame seeds
- 8 cloves garlic
- 2 tsp chilli powder
- salt to taste

III
- 2 large tomatoes
- 8 cloves garlic
- 4 green chillies
- 1 small bunch green coriander
- ¼ tsp sugar
- salt to taste

Method

Soup
Just before serving, heat broth to boiling and put in the noodles. Or you may boil the uncooked noodles in soup, in which case the amount will depend on the size of the packet of noodles you have.

Stir Fries

I
Heat oil to smoking in a wok. Reduce heat and fry the beef for 30 seconds. Put in the celery and fry for another 30 seconds. Add soya sauce and sugar. Mix thoroughly and serve at once.

II
Heat oil to smoking in a wok and reduce heat. Fry the pork for 3 minutes. Add the vegetables and fry for another minute. Add salt, mix thoroughly and serve at once.

III

Heat oil to smoking in a wok. Reduce heat and fry the chicken for 2 minutes. Add the beans and fry for another minute. Add salt, mix well. Serve at once.

Chutneys

I

Grind together all the ingredients, or place them in a blender and blend at medium speed for 15 seconds.

II

Grind together all the ingredients, or place them in a blender and blend at medium speed 15 seconds.

III

Char the tomatoes and skin them. Chop the chillies, coriander and garlic. Grind all the ingredients together, or place them in a blender and blend them at medium speed for 15-20 seconds.

» A good ice-breaker at a party is the chimney pot soup, gyako. This can be as simple or as elaborate as one wishes. There are no hard and fast rules about what goes into a gyako, and we present a selection of meats and winter vegetables—the cold weather is the only time a gyako is welcome in Calcutta.

Gyako

Chimney Pot Soup

Serves 10

Ingredients:
- **meat or chicken stock**
- **100 gms beef undercut (thin slices)**
- **soya bean sauce**
- **vinegar**

- **2 chicken breasts**
- **100 gms white fish**
- **100 gms fat pork**
- **salt to taste**
- **10 gms dried mushrooms (soaked in water and chopped)**
- **2 carrots (cut in large thin circles)**
- **100 gms peas (shelled)**
- **2 stalks celery (threaded and cut into 2-inch lengths)**
- **100 gms cabbage (cut in large squares)**
- **100 gms soya bean curd**
- **25 gms glass noodles (soaked in water for ½ hour)**

Method:

Marinate the thin slices of beef undercut in soya bean sauce and vinegar. Shred the breasts of chicken. Mince together the white fish and fat pork very finely. Add salt and make them into balls. Take a ball in the palm of your hand and make a dent in it. Place a little chopped mushroom. Cover it up and roll into a ball.

Prepare the soup pot while the stock boils separately.

Place the meats in alternate layers at the bottom of the pot. Place the carrots, celery and cabbage over that in alternate sections. Place the peas and mushrooms over that. The glass noodles and bean curd come right on top. Pour the stock over all this, add salt to taste and cover the pot. Set it over the prepared charcoal brazier. The coals should be glowing. The soup is ready when the pot starts bubbling. Uncover, ladle out and serve with plain boiled rice.

» These three relishes are served with gyako. Additions and subtractions are of individual choice.

Sauces for Gyako

I

Ingredients:

- **5 cloves garlic**
- **5 green chillies**
- **1-inch piece ginger**

* **juice of 5 limes**

Method:
Chop the garlic, green chillies and ginger fine. Put all these in the lime juice.

II
Ingredients:
* **2 tbsp chilli powder**
* **5 cloves garlic**
* **1 tbsp vinegar**
* **salt to taste**
* **1 tbsp oil**

Method:
Grind the chilli powder with the garlic, vinegar and salt to taste. Heat the oil and fry the chilli garlic paste for 2 minutes.

III
Ingredients:
* **10 green chillies**
* **½ cup dark soya bean sauce**

Method:
Chop the green chillies and put them into the dark soya bean sauce.

» Glass noodles or phing make a refreshing salad.

Phing Salad

Glass Noodle Salad

Serves 8

Ingredients:
* **50 gms glass noodles (phing)**

- **2 small cucumbers (shredded)**
- **1 chicken breast (cooked and shredded)**
- **2 carrots (cut in julienne strips)**
- **1 tsp sesame seeds**
- **½ tsp chilli powder**
- **juice of 2 limes**
- **a few drops of oil**
- **salt to taste**

Method:
Soak the glass noodles in water for 15 minutes. Drain and boil them for 5 minutes. Drain and cool. Mix cucumbers, chicken and carrots together with the glass noodles.

Roast and grind the sesame seeds with the chilli powder. Toss into the salad. Just before serving, add the lime juice, oil and salt to taste. Toss and serve.

Variation:
- Fifty grams of soaked, boiled and drained phing, stir fried with 4 Chinese sausages cut in 1-inch pieces and a handful of chopped mustard greens, sprinkled with soya bean sauce, make a tasty hot dish. The greens must go in last, after the other ingredients have cooked for 3 minutes. No salt should be added to this dish as the sausages are salted and the greens have their own salt.

» All ingredients for Chinese and Tibetan cooking are available at the Chinese market on Sun Yat Sen Street in Calcutta. It is best to go early as the fresh food stalls close down by noon.

» Apples, asparagus, avocado, strawberries and peaches from Bhutan have added an extra zip to Calcutta's cuisine.

What the Calcuttan has not savoured are the delicious red rice, cheese and chilli ema dashi cooked in Bhutanese homes in the city. The original recipe calls for the fiery Bhutan chilli and high cottage cheese, but Calcutta neighbours object to wafting aromas and so the ingredients have been tempered down.

Ema Dashi

Chilli Cheese

Serves 6

Ingredients:
- **100 gms Kashmiri chillies**
- **200 gms onions (chopped)**
- **2 cups water**
- **2 tbsp butter or ghee**
- **1 cup diced cooking cheese**

Method:
Seed and soak the Kashmiri chillies in water. Chop the onions. Drain and cut the chillies in small pieces and boil them in a pan with the onions in the water. Cook until the onions are soft but not mushy. Add the butter or ghee. Stir well and add the diced cooking cheese. Use a cheese that melts easily.

Cook over a low fire without stirring for 10 minutes.

Stir, check for salt and take off fire.

» So many of us have early memories of Darjeeling, of the laughing people, of pony rides and lullabies sung to us by Dhanmaya or Jethi Didi. And of the inimitable taste of their alu or rambera (tomato) achar smuggled in to us if we were good.

We asked Nepali friends for recipes, and the one we give here is how Mashima in Hazra Road made it.

Alu Achar

Potatoes with Sesame Seed

Serves 6

Ingredients:
- **500 gms medium potatoes (boiled, skinned and cut in quarters)**
- **50 gms white sesame seeds (roasted and dry ground)**
- **1 tsp chilli powder**
- **¼ tsp ground allspice**
- **¼ tsp lemon peel (grated)**
- **salt to taste**
- **2 tbsp mustard oil**
- **1 tsp panch phoron (whole five spice)**
- **2 dry red chillies**
- **4–5 green chillies (slit)**
- **juice of 1 lemon (gandharaj lebu)**

Method:
Mix in the white sesame seeds with the potatoes. Add the chilli powder, allspice, lemon peel and salt to taste.

Heat the mustard oil to smoking and add the panch phoron, dry red chillies and slit green chillies. Let it sputter and the red chillies smoke. Pour onto the potatoes and mix like a salad dressing, coating the potatoes well. Add the lemon juice and mix well. Serve at room temperature.

Mashima's daughter adds 2 tablespoons of yoghurt with the sesame seeds before mixing them with the potatoes.

» Thai food is as yet little known in Calcutta. The easily available ingredients and the similarity to the well-liked Chinese food are sure to make Thai food a 'table topper'. The following recipe was given to us by Rakhi Das Gupta, Minakshie's younger daughter, who caters Thai food in Delhi.

Tom Yum Goong

Shrimp and Mushroom Soup

Serves 8

Ingredients:
- **250 gms prawns or shrimps**
- **1 cup button mushrooms (sliced)**
- **5–6 green chillies (chopped fine)**
- **1–2 leaves of lemon grass or 2 pieces of lemon peel (chopped fine)**
- **50 gms coriander leaves (chopped fine)**
- **8 cups chicken stock**
- **2½ tbsp fish sauce**
- **2–3 tbsp lemon juice**
- **½ tsp chilli powder**

Method:
Clean the prawns or shrimps.

Bring the chicken stock to the boil in a pan. Add the shrimp and the lemon grass/peel. Simmer for 2–3 minutes. Add the mushrooms and green chillies and half the coriander. Simmer for another 2 minutes. Remove from fire and season with the fish sauce.

Add the lemon juice and chilli powder. Garnish with coriander. Serve at once.

» Who would have thought that the mundane raw papaya (kancha pepey) would enter the world of international cuisine? The Thais did it.

Raw Papaya Salad

Serves 8

Ingredients:

For dressing
- 3–4 tbsp soya bean sauce
- 1 tbsp fish sauce
- 2–3 tbsp lime juice
- 1 tsp sugar
- 10–12 green chillies (finely chopped)
- ½-inch piece ginger (finely chopped)
- ½-inch piece galingale (aam ada) (finely chopped)
- 2–3 pods garlic (roasted and powdered)
- 1 medium onion (roasted and powdered)
- 1 small piece dried fish (powdered) (optional)

For salad
- 1 medium raw papaya (peeled and cut fine)
- 2–3 radishes (peeled and cut fine)
- 1–2 cucumbers (peeled and cut fine)
- 10 spring onions (cut fine)
- 500 gms french beans (stringed, boiled and cut fine)
- 2–3 tomatoes (finely sliced)

For garnishing
- a handful of chopped coriander leaves
- a handful of peanuts (roasted and crushed)

Method:
This salad may use a bit of dried fish in the dressing.

Mix the dressing:
To the soya bean sauce add the fish sauce, lime juice, sugar,

chillies, ginger, galingale (aam ada), garlic, onion, and dried fish (optional). Mix well and refrigerate overnight.

Put all the vegetables in a bowl and add the dressing. Garnish with the coriander leaves and peanuts.

Chapter 7

A Cosmopolitan Jigsaw

Dalbati, Dosa and Sarso Saag

Calcutta belongs to everybody and nobody. Anyone who feels at home in the city of confounded chaos and confusion is a Calcuttan. In a jampacked bus stuck in the perennial traffic jam, the ordeal is often made bearable by a spontaneous and piquant Bengali humour along with the bonhomie of fellow travellers. They have come from Kanya Kumari in the south, the Himalayas in the north, distant Dwarka in the west and the North Eastern States. In time they have woven the fabric of Calcutta's economic and cultural life.

The menfolk came to work and when settled, brought their families. People from a particular village made a niche for themselves in a particular trade or occupation. There was, and still

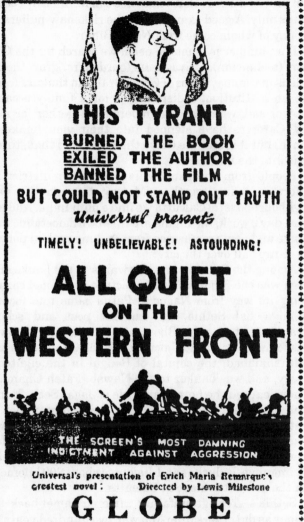

THIS TYRANT

BURNED THE BOOK
EXILED THE AUTHOR
BANNED THE FILM

BUT COULD NOT STAMP OUT TRUTH

Universal presents

TIMELY! UNBELIEVABLE! ASTOUNDING!

ALL QUIET
ON THE
WESTERN FRONT

THE SCREEN'S MOST DAMNING
INDICTMENT AGAINST AGGRESSION

Universal's presentation of Erich Maria Remarque's
greatest novel: Directed by Lewis Milestone

GLOBE

DAILY AT 3, 6 & 9-30 P.M.

Book in Advance 'Phone. Cal 1171

"The screen's most damning indictment against
aggression" March 11, 1940.

is, an unwritten code that vacancies can be filled by country cousins only. A good example are the rickshaw-pullers, the majority of whom come from North Bihar.

If a plumber is what we need, we search for the Oriya mistri (technician). Oriya malis (gardeners) grow the best gardens in the city. Clubs of Oriya Brahmin thakurs (cooks) were an institution, indispensable for a family occasion, happy or sad, when large numbers ate together for many days. Caterers have stepped into their vien (makeshift kitchen) but it is still the Oriya thakur's hand that stirs the magic into the masala.

People from the same village, town or district find comfort in living together. Moving through the paras (neighbourhoods) of Calcutta we find a mini India. And after a hard day's work, the nights are filled with nostalgic songs of home and new aromas rise from cooking pots on portable bucket-fires all over the city.

Among the first to come eastwards to the banks of the Ganga was the Rajasthani. The picture of a camel caravan picking its way from Nagor to Patna came into focus as Kanhaiya Lal Sethia, an eminent poet and scholar, narrated the story at his Bhowanipore residence of how the Jains found their way to Calcutta. Manek Chand Seth came to Murshidabad, the capital of Bengal in the eighteenth century, and was banker to the Nawab. Fateh Chand, his nephew, earned the hereditary title of Jagat Seth, 'Banker of the Universe', and this became the family name. The Jagat Seths controlled the fortunes of Bengal. They were indeed at one time the Rothschilds of India. Other Jains followed and prospered around the court at Murshidabad, in Azimgunge, Baluchar and Jiagunge about 200 kilometres from the new settlement at Calcutta.

Sethia's great-grandfather came on camel-back from Bikaner as did others from Marwar two hundred years ago. His ancestors obtained an agency for Manchester cotton and later jute. Cotton piece-goods[*] and jute were the realms in

---

*   Piece-good: fabrics, especially Lancashire cottons, woven in standard
        lengths.

which the Rajasthanis ruled, and by the end of the nineteenth century they also held the monopoly over the hundi—the indigenous banking system—in Calcutta.

The frugal Rajasthani, with his lota kambal (metal water pot, blanket) bedded down under the skies in Sutanati, the cottonopolis of Burrabazaar. It is to his credit that from such meagre beginnings he raised the richest marketplace where pearls and papad amid a myriad other things and crores of rupees change hands a thousand times a day. The amount defies computation.

The Rajasthanis of Calcutta are followers of Jainism and Hindu Vaisnavism. Both are vegetarian but there is a difference in the choice of vegetables. The Oswal Jains, who first came to Calcutta, were mainly gem merchants and bankers. To uphold their first and foremost vow 'not to kill', the Jains have developed a self-disciplinary food philosophy both discriminative and ascetic. They prefer dried vegetables to fresh, and some refrain from eating tubers which they recognize as being full of reproductive cells. In the case of dried vegetables there is no question of propagation and therefore no destruction.

Over the years, Bengali culture brushed off on some families, among them the Nahars and the Kolays who came to Calcutta soon after the fall of Murshidabad in 1757. Though they strictly follow the tenets of Mahavir, they are indistinguishable from the Bengali in language, dress, choice of and preparation of vegetarian food.

A second group, the Agarwals, came to Calcutta later in the century. They came mainly from Marwar and Mewar and Marwari became the generic name for Rajasthanis. And once the rail tracks reached Rajasthan, they came by the train load.

Food on their arduous journeys was dalbati, now cooked on a gas stove on wet monsoon days, an ideal meal for picnics. Bati is made of wheat flour kneaded with ghee and looks like a dinner roll. The dough is roasted over embers after the dal is boiled. Sweetened and crumbled, the same dough is called churma and keeps for several weeks.

In Rajasthan there is a saying that ghee is easier to come by than water and so ghee and water reverse roles in the cooking methodology of the Thar desert dwellers.

Some prominent ladies of the Rajasthani community in Calcutta have given us a wonderful insight into the food culture of this single largest migrant group. Their diet reflects a tough and tenacious people weathered by harsh geographic conditions. Strict vegetarians, their staple was bajra (a millet) and moth (dewgram). Their sweets are called laddus and are generally made of gram flour and sugar.

The circumspect Rajasthani woman did not have much to choose from in the way of cereals or greens in the arid conditions in which she lived. She had to save on water and fuel. She put fogla, keria and sangar, typical of Rajasthan and whatever else was available and edible into the pot. Vegetables are called saag and are few and far between. Fresh beans, berries and the edible leaves and fruits of hardy creepers in season are cooked with a great deal of ingenuity. What is not eaten is saved, dried in the shade and prudently stored for the whole year. Fenugreek and mint leaves are dried and used extensively—probably for their medicinal properties. Sangar ka phali, a favourite, is also preserved in oil. Gawarphali (cluster bean) grows well in the dry climate and is said to be good for diabetes. Bhey (lotus stem) is sliced and dried. It tastes good cooked with sangar and kher, and spiced with coriander, turmeric, red mustard seed, chilli and soured with amchur (dried mango powder). This dish keeps for a week.

Lentils are the main source of protein. The popular ingredients in a Rajasthani meal are papad and bori. Lentils—chana and toor dals—are washed and soaked overnight and ground manually to form a thick paste which is shaped and sun-dried. Winter is papad- and bori-making time for the whole year for the household with some to spare for friends and relations. Papad, known as poppadams, fried or roasted, is familiar to most readers as part of a meal anywhere in India. A Marwari meal is not complete without roasted papad. Papad bori ka patolia is a delicious mutation of papad and bori, two items always in readiness in the larder.

At weddings, dal ka seera, a halwa of roasted moong dal and dehydrated milk, badam ka seera, a similar preparation with almonds, are served. Malpura, an all-India sweet, is a thickened milk-and-flour pancake. The special sweet is made from gond, resin from acacia trees.

Sweets of at least four varieties are offered first and only when the guests can eat no more, come kachori (fried whole wheat bread with seasoned dry dal filling) and gatta (fried lentil pasta curry), pakora (vegetables fried in lentil batter), dahi vada (fried lentil cakes in yogurt), papad and stir fried vegetables.

Some old Agarwal Marwari families living in the city for three generations read and speak Bengali. They eat rice and enjoy West Bengal's bounty of green vegetables. They cook Bengali vegetarian dishes and have made the sandesh and rosogolla their very own. The meteoric rise of the rosogolla has been attributed, in part, to a Marwari businessman, one Mr Bagla. The story goes that tired and thirsty after his work in Baghbazaar, he stopped at a sweet shop and asked for water. The owner, as it happened, was the king of sweetmeat makers, Nobin Chandra Das who in keeping with tradition offered Bagla his latest invention with a glass of water. Bagla was bewitched by this fluffy confection and soon by word of mouth the rosogolla was on its way to fame and we believe, the Das's fortunes.

On the other hand, the younger generation have travelled far and wide and have acquired a taste for salads, eggless cakes and au gratin dishes. Exotic vegetables like asparagus and broccoli have reappeared. Bottled and fresh baby corn and strawberries and cream appear on buffet tables beside the traditional dilkhusal, a delicious sweet made from dehydrated milk or cottage cheese, gram flour and dried fruits and nuts.

For an authentic Rajasthani meal, not always cooked in Marwari homes in Calcutta, we were invited to the

Rajasthani Guest House on Zakaria Street.

In Calcutta's heyday, rajas big and small gravitated to the city in the winter 'season'. Rajput princes lent sportive glamour as golfers and polo players. While Burrabazaar was strictly vegetarian, shikar meats like pickled wild boar and venison appeared only on their tables at posh addresses referred to as 'Camp Calcutta'.

Gujaratis, another growing business community of Calcutta from the west, are also vegetarian. Their snacky eat-from-the-hand farsan, mostly savoury, soon captured the city's taste and the enterprising Gujarati bania (trader) has opened numerous shoplets selling dhokla (steamed savoury lentil, rice or semolina sponge), khandvi (gram flour rolled pasta) and ganthia (gram flour fried pasta) served with raw papaya chutney, a favourite breakfast food. 'Kitty Party' goers and card players of Calcutta serve unconventional fillings of cheese, chutney and ketchup sandwiched between unconventional 'breads' like dhokla. Large glass faced tins of different types of dalmot (fried grams, pressed rice and peanuts) in a variety of colours, shapes and sizes are mixed hot, hotter or hottest, according to the customer's choice. Once you start munching a mixture, it is addictive. Many a bowl of dalmot punctuates conversation and heightens conviviality at cocktail parties.

To add to the mosaic of Calcutta, the pale complexioned, hook-nosed handsome Parsee dressed in long black coat and pheta, already established in the China trade, sailed in from Bombay. Dadabhai Behramji Banaji, a shipping magnate, was the first to come to this boom town in 1767. Rustomjee Cowasjee Banaji followed in 1812. Twenty-five years later, his family joined him and in no time at all Calcutta welcomed the best known Parsee dish, dhansak (meat cooked with lentils) and prawn patia (prawn curry). There was a time when a Parsee would request a Bombaywalla for dhansak masala (spices). The demand for dhansak with the growing community and the favour it found among friends, encouraged some ladies to compound it in their Calcutta homes.

A small and singularly distinguished group, the Parsees of Calcutta have endeared themselves to the people of this city by their uprightness, hospitality and generosity. What they hold supreme is the Zoroastrian religion. And Zoroaster preached the veneration of all the elements, plant and animal life. Parsees do not eat meat for one month in the year which prompted a Parsee friend to say, 'Zoroaster was a great conservationist.' They have no food taboos. Some do not eat beef in deference to a promise made when they sought asylum in a Hindu kingdom in western India over a thousand years ago. Their love of food sees them entertain lavishly in their homes furnished with the best of camphor chests, carved Chinese whatnots and polished period tables and chairs.

The Parsee sense of humour is unmatched, as is their ability to laugh at themselves. They are great egg buffs; acuri and many of their preparations are wholly, partially or at least egg topped. On Dhanteras, a Parsee friend quips, 'We also do achhoo michhoo or what you might call puja, on our car, circling it with eggs and then cracking them on it.' At a Navjote ceremony and on festive occasions, browned vermicelli in syrup with raisins is served. Sweet yogurt set at home, hard boiled eggs and bananas are auspicious foods.

An old-fashioned Parsee kitchen contains enormous copper patilas. They prefer copper to any other metal for their cooking vessels. On certain days, the kitchen is cleaned and decorated with powdered rice designs and torans (garlands) of roses and tuberoses.

A Parsee lady is never happier than when talking about food. Shireen Tata has lived in Calcutta for over forty years. She speaks authoritatively about their eating customs. A standard Sunday lunch includes dhansak, brown rice, keema kebab (minced meat kebab) and kachumbar (minced onion and cucumber, fresh coriander and green chillies with a squeeze of lemon). True, recipes everywhere vary from family to family. Dhansak, cooked in many a Calcutta home, is never served at a Parsee marriage for it is traditionally eaten on the fourth day of mourning.

Mithoo Vatcha's eyes light up as she describes a wedding menu she has been asked to plan. Vatcha is the only Parsee caterer in Calcutta and much in demand. At a Parsee-Bengali wedding, Vatcha served salina murghi (chicken with potato straws), a Parsee meat polau, achar with dried fruits, kachumbar and masala dal. The meal ended with a typical Parsee custard, a very rich caramel custard cooked slowly so that the milk browns while thickening.

Most Parsee foods are simmered on a slow fire after the first burst of heat seals the juices in the meat. Fish is preferred whole. Rawas, the hilsa of the Arabian Sea, full of tasty roe during the monsoons, is preserved in salt. The fish in patrani machhi is often pomfret stuffed with coconut chutney and wrapped in banana leaves. Traditionally, the wrapped fish placed in a basket and baked in a pit has a special flavour which the modern oven cannot create. Bengali guests are thrilled to find the similarity with their maachh paturi, while Calcutta Parsees have taken to alur dom in a big way. They use panch phoron in their version of chhenchki which goes by the same name. Whereas foods and eating habits generally have a rural base, this is not so with the Parsee diet brought from Pars in Iran.

As we have observed, with the expansion of the railway network, travel became quicker, cheaper and less hazardous and so entrepreneurs from the north, the south and the west converged on the City of Opportunity. The tolerant, hard-working Sindhi from the Indus Valley traded his way to this eastern port and by the mid-nineteenth century, Karachi and Calcutta, 1500 kilometres apart, drew closer together.

The Sindhi amils were mainly in government service, though many excelled in the fields of banking and finance. India's independence lost for them forever their homeland and the 1947 exodus brought the bhai bandh traders. They set up shops in and around the New Market area where a few of the oldest and biggest shops selling saris, jewellery and watches were already owned by Sindhis. Perhaps this may be a reason why most people connect the Sindhis with good salesmanship and excellent shop manners, and as a young Sindhi lady wrote, earned for the Sindhis the epithet 'a nation of shopkeepers more than the British'. They found digs close to their workplace and Sindhi eating houses contributed to Calcutta's cooking pots.

The Sindhi not only shares the Bengali's passion for fish, he also relishes the roe or ani, which is the Sindhi word meaning children and is understandably a common ending to many of their surnames.

In our search for authenticity, we have met some brilliant oral historians and the most innovative cooks. The Lalwanis were both. While Chandra Lalwani entertained us with coffee, she told us how she has taught her Bengali maid to cook kok palla (whole fish seasoned with green herbs). Her husband, Chatu, told us about life in Sind and his boyhood obsession with Rabindranath Tagore's translations in Sindhi. He has lived in Calcutta most of his working life and has chosen to stay on in retirement. Among the migrants, it is the Sindhis of Calcutta who know of no other place that they can call their own.

The South Indian is yet another piece in the cosmopolitan jigsaw. But in his case the connection goes back a long time to when Bengal was Vanga. The links with the Deccan plateau are very strong and outside the pale of Aryandom. Bengal became a part of the Magadha Empire in the days of the Mauryas. In AD 1023, the princes of Bengal were attacked by Rajendra Chola I of what is now Tamil Nadu and the illustrious Sena dynasty of Bengal in the twelfth century originated in South India.

The reason for turning historical is that many writers on Bengali cooking sometimes forget the strong ties with the Deccan in the daily tempering of their dals. Sambhara is as important in South Indian cooking as is the phoron in Bengali cooking. A delicate blending of spices gives a distinct taste and aroma to each dish. A good South Indian and Bengali cook is one who has mastered the art of the sambhara.

Then there is the banana bond which unites southern
and eastern India in their love for the green banana, its red
flower and milk white stem. Green banana kofta appeared
on the Raj Bhavan menu when C. Rajagopalachari from
Madras took up residence as Governor.

Coconut palms are typical of the South Indian coastal
landscape and the coconut is an important ingredient used
in many imaginative ways. Coconut and tamarind
flavoured fish and prawn curries from Andhra Pradesh and
Kerala are demanded from friends who use local substitutes
for sea fish.

'Curry' deserves a paragraph. Kari is a South Indian
word. For the world curry is Indian food per se. The British
made it a part of the colonial vocabulary to describe any
yellow gravy coloured with turmeric, euphemistically
misnamed as saffron. Professor N. Vishwanathan explains
in a nutshell that for the Brahmin, kari denotes a dry
vegetable preparation, and in a non-Brahmin household,
kari was a meat dish, and the Professor broke into a song
of maan kari (venison curry). He went on to tell us about
the karvaypillai or curry leaf, which translated, means the
leaf used in cooking, an essential South Indian seasoning.

In modern times, the first to settle from the four states
of southern India were the Chettiars, the captains of
industry from Tamil Nadu. They are non-vegetarians.
Chettinad food can be eaten at Nagarathar Viduthi or
Chettiar House, the oldest South Indian den in Ezra Street
or when the five-star hotels bring chefs from the south to
stir up a Chettinad chicken.

The South Indian is a rice-eater and a meal usually has
three courses—rice with sambhar (lentils), rasam (pepper
water) and curd accompanied with vegetable poriyal and
kootu. South Indian vegetarian cooking is simple,
nutritious and has a rich variety. In poriyal, the vegetables
are sautéed and then pressure cooked or lightly cooked in
their own juices. Kootu has a gravy. Salads, pickles and
poppadams complete the meal.

Idli (fermented lentil and rice cakes), dosa (lentil and

rice pancakes) and vada (fried lentil cakes) are popular
Calcutta Sunday breakfast or a complete meal, downed with
filter coffee at Prema Vilas near the Kalighat Metro station.
Generally no drink other than water is offered with an
Indian meal. There are, however, sherbats made from
seasonal fruits served as refreshments and jeera pani is
served as an appetizer in the north.

Punjabification of Indian food is worldwide and has
perhaps made the greatest single contribution to
contemporary Calcutta kitchens. Northern India took the
'love apple' to heart and the Punjabi's zest for the tomato
encouraged the cautious Bengali to embellish his jhal, jhole
and ambole with its tang and colour.

Let us go back to the time when the Grand Trunk Road,
India's oldest highway, built by Sher Shah Suri connected
Punjab and Bengal. Through the quirks of history, the two
states had many things in common of which the partition
of the subcontinent was the most significant.

A line of dhabas, that began as eating places on the
Grand Trunk Road, later grew into open-air motels on the
National Highways. The food follows a basic pattern of roti
and tarka dal, always fresh and wholesome, and cool lassi.
These dhabas cater to truck drivers who on their long hauls
between major cities cannot afford to be sick or sorry. Garib
ka Hotel (the Poor Man's Hotel) in Bhowanipore, is the
oldest dhaba. It served the pioneer Punjabi who had come
to the city. By public demand, the Ballygunge Phari Dhaba
has air-conditioned its dining space upstairs for its
increasing clientele who come from all over the city for
matar panir, gajar ka halwa and a glass of refrigerated
lassi.

Bachan Singh Saral, the editor of the Punjabi
newspaper, *Desh Darpan* in Calcutta, told us that the
Punjabis are one of the largest communities which have
made Calcutta their second home. The Punjabi's height and
the Sikh's headgear singles them out anywhere. In Calcutta
they have been associated with buses, trucks and taxis.
They held the monopoly of the motorized public transport

system till 1957. They were also into textiles, coal mines and industry. After Independence, a large number of Punjabis from West Punjab near the North-West frontier (now in Pakistan) made Calcutta their new home. Several went into the hotel and restaurant business and are very successful. It was the Khullars who emphasized and elaborated on Punjabi cooking and it is to their Amber, Sagar and Zaranj restaurants in central Calcutta that the connoisseur goes for tandoori chicken and naan (leavened bread), tangri kebab (chicken leg) and kulfi. Amber's chefs have applied the tandoori treatment to fish and prawns. So much so, that tandoori preparations are often a part of a Bengali marriage feast.

Defying anatomy, a Punjabi's heart is bigger than his stomach and it is this dimension which extends to his truck, his tractor and his table. The warmth of a Punjabi host is greater than the hot phulka or alu ka paratha (potato filled fried bread) that keeps dropping on to the guest's stainless steel thali.

We called on a Sikh family and found that the Singh Grewals from Kila Raipur in Ludhiana had just finished lunch—doi maachh, typically Bengali, and phulkas, typically Punjabi. Like many others, they enjoy the finesse of Bengali cooking. 'Punjabi food,' says Sohinder Grewal, 'is simple, wholesome and nutritious without any frills. There are few courses but plenty of each.'

Lalo Puri, a doyenne of the Punjabis in Calcutta, insisted that we taste her kari chawal while she savoured in her conversation the joys of saag simmering on an earthen fire in the good old days. It is now made in a jiffy in a pressure cooker. 'It's not quite the same,' say the white-haired ladies in a truck garage as they roll out their memories of recipes of sarso saag and makai ki roti the way they made it in their village.

Contrary to the general impression, Punjabis are by far and large vegetarian. The women, we are told, cooked a meat curry for their menfolk occasionally but did not always eat it themselves.

Changes are bound to take place with changed circumstances but like Chinese food, Punjabi cuisine can be tasted in small pockets from California to Calcutta.

In this great shambles of a mega city, agencies for distributing free food to the hungry are many. But in the Sikh gurdwaras, rich and poor sit together at a langar and share a sustenance which is an embodiment of their philosophy of the Fatherhood of God and the Brotherhood of Man. We are reminded of Guru Govind Singh riding out after a meal made of equal portions of whole wheat, sugar and ghee cooked in four times the amount of water, which sustained him and his men through the battle-long day. The same delicious karah prasad is cooked and served in gurdwaras the world over.

Yet another facet of Calcutta's truly cosmopolitan character are its polyglot bazaars. They have a flavour and colour given by all the peoples who live in the metropolis. Regional food specialities are an everyday feature in markets in particular areas of the city where people from different states have settled and created their own ambience.

Rajasthani homes replenish their larders from Burrabazaar, though some have moved to other residential areas. Moat ki dal, dried leaves of sangar, gawarphali beans and the best of fruits and spices are displayed in the narrow cobbled lanes of the city's richest bazaar. Provisions and health food stores in central and south Calcutta and in posh Park Street follow the pulse of the city, stocking broccoli and baby corn, the best of papads, hajmis and churans (digestives) and paan masala (betel flavourings). A recent arrival from Bikaner, Haldiram Bhujiawala's name appears in neon lights over air-conditioned glass and chrome shops—a snacker's delight.

For the Punjabi, the very Bengali Jadu Babur Bazaar, in short Jaggu Bazaar, is where they get everything from jhatka meat (slaughter of sheep and goats by a single stroke of the chopper) to shakkar (unrefined sugar) in winter. A bottle of pickle bought from a venerable Sikh gives a touch of 'back home' Jalandhar to makai ki roti. Vegetables from the Punjab and the rest of India—tinda, arbi and kundri—have sprouted into the markets. West Bengal's fertile soil takes kindly to any new implant to give Calcutta's cosmopolitan residents a feeling of home.

Lake Market in south Calcutta accommodates the residents from south of the Vindhya mountains. Outside the main market, mounds of fragrant flowers are sold for the luxuriant black plaits of hair, the pride of the South Indian woman. The aroma of freshly ground coffee beans from Komola Vilas makes known their prefered beverage. Tier upon tier of stainless steel utensils, without which a South Indian cook cannot function, rise from pavement stalls around the market. On the open doors of tiny grocery shops hang bunches of outsized red bananas from Kerala. Giant corms of ole sit roundly on the counter. Jars of baby green mango pickle, sambhar masala and potato papads tumble out of open shelves to satisfy the samayalkaran from Palghat—the land of the best cooks.

The dining room sideboard in a Calcutta home catches the eye. On its polished, crowded surface stand bottles of tomato and chilli sauces, marmalade, packets of dalmot from the north and mudduku (savoury crisps) from the south, gobi salgam achar (cauliflower and turnip pickle) from the Punjab, Britannia biscuits, a box of Nahoum's cheese cakes and the ever handy packet of instant noodles with a tastemaker from the multinationals. Here is a true manifestation of Calcutta's gastronomic give and take.

The camel caravan that picked its way to Bengal from Rajasthan carried, in its load, the ingredients to make dal bati the traveller's journey food (see text Chapter 6).

Dal

Serves 6

Ingredients:
- **50 gms arhar dal (red gram)**
- **50 gms chana dal (split dried Bengal gram)**
- **50 gms moong dal (dried moong beans)**
- **25 gms urad dal (split dried black gram lentils)**
- **100 gms whole moong dal (whole moong beans)**
- **1½ tsp salt**
- **½ tsp turmeric**
- **2 tsp chilli powder**
- **1 tsp sugar**
- **4 tbsp ghee**
- **2 tsp garam masala powder**
- **5 cloves**
- **5 green cardamoms**
- **4 bay leaves**
- **1-inch piece ginger (sliced finely)**
- **1 tsp black mustard**
- **¼ tsp fenugreek**
- **½ tsp cumin seeds**
- **¼ tsp asafoetida**
- **chopped coriander leaves**

Method:
Wash the dals. Boil water in a pot and put in the dals. Lower heat and let the dals simmer. Add salt, turmeric, chilli powder, sugar and 1 tablespoon ghee while cooking. When the dal is cooked, stir well and add garam masala powder. Heat 3 tablespoons ghee to smoking. Reduce heat and fry

the cloves, green cardamoms, bay leaves, finely sliced ginger, black mustard, fenugreek, cumin seeds and asafoetida. Add to the dal. Add chopped coriander leaves.

Bati

Steamed and Roasted Whole Wheat Cakes

Makes 20 batis

Ingredients:
- **750 gms whole wheat flour (atta)**
- **5 tbsp ghee**
- **2 tsp salt**
- **1 tsp sugar**
- **1 tsp sodium bicarbonate**
- **1 glass (250 ml) hot water**
- **1 cup hot ghee**

Method:
Mix the whole wheat flour with the ghee, salt, sugar and sodium bicarbonate. Knead into a stiff dough with the hot water. Knead well and leave to rest for an hour. Break off pieces the size of a lime and roll into balls. Flatten each ball a little and fold it in from the sides in pleats like a topknot.

Boil water in a pan, cover it and place the pieces in a single layer on the lid. Cover them and let them steam for 20 minutes. Take them off the fire and spread them out.

Roast them over an open flame, a coal fire if possible, otherwise a gas fire will do. Rub off the ashes and soak in a cup of hot ghee for 7 minutes. Serve with dal.

» Gawarphali or cluster beans are one of the few vegetables that grow in arid Rajasthan. They have appeared by demand in the Calcutta markets.

Gawarphali Curry

Cluster Bean Curry

Serves 4

Ingredients:
- **200 gms cluster beans**
- **6 tbsp oil**
- **½ tsp cumin**
- **a pinch of asafoetida**
- **½ tsp turmeric**
- **1 tbsp chilli powder**
- **2½ tbsp coriander powder**
- **1 tsp salt (or to taste)**
- **1 cup water**
- **½ tbsp dried mango powder (amchur)**

Method:
Top and tail the cluster beans to remove the strings. Boil the beans in a pan and drain them. Heat the oil in a wok or frying pan and fry the cumin and asafoetida. Add the beans and sauté for 2 minutes.

Add the turmeric, chilli powder and coriander powder.

Add the salt and the water and let the beans cook a few minutes. Add the dried mango powder (amchur). Let it cook for a few minutes and take it off the fire.

50 grams dried beans can be cooked the same way.

» Lentils and dried vegetables make up a large part of the Rajasthani diet. Bori and papad are cooked into curries and lentil based sweets are served on auspicious occasions. A recipe from Mrs Manjula Duggar.

Papad Bori Ka Patolia

A Papad Bori Mix

Serves 4

Ingredients:
- 1½ cups water
- 100 gms large spiced bori (broken up)
- 4 pieces papad (cut in quarters)
- 1 tsp ghee
- a pinch of asafoetida
- ¼ tsp cumin seeds
- 1 tsp black pepper (ground)
- salt to taste

Method:
Boil the water and add the bori. When these are cooked, add the papad. Cook a minute, take off the fire and drain. Heat the ghee and fry the asafoetida and cumin seeds. When they are fragrant, add the bori and papad, black pepper and salt to taste. Mix well and serve.

This dish may be part of a meal or a snack.

» Another recipe from Mrs Manjula Duggar.

Dil Khushal

A Lentil-based Wedding Sweet

Serves 6

Ingredients:
- 60 gms split dried Bengal gram semolina (chana dal sooji)
- ghee
- ½ tsp water

- **100 gms dehydrated milk (khoa)**
- **¼ cup water**
- **60 gms sugar**
- **saffron soaked in rose water**
- **¼ tsp ground green cardamom**

Method:

Mix the chana dal sooji with ¼ teaspoon ghee and the water. Let it rest for an hour. Rub the dehydrated milk through a sieve.

In a pan heat 1½ tablespoons of ghee. Add the sooji and cook over slow heat until golden. Take off fire and mix in the dehydrated milk thoroughly. Re-heat the mixture, mixing well all the time. Cool and spread on a plate.

Boil the water and add the sugar. Cook to a fairly heavy syrup. It will form a thread when dropped from a spoon. Add a few threads of saffron soaked in rose water and the green cardamom. Mix in the cooled sooji. Spread the hot mixture on a greased plate and cut into 1-inch cubes. Serve at room temperature.

» Mrs Mithoo Vatcha, who caters for many Parsee weddings and other big occasions, generously gave us these recipes.

While we listened, three other Parsee ladies, also redoubtable cooks, nodded in approval.

Dhansak Dal

A Stew of Lentils, Vegetables and Meat

Serves 16

Ingredients:
- **1 kg arhar dal (split red peas)**
- **½ kg masoor dal (split red lentils)**

- ¼ kg chana dal (split Bengal gram)
- ¼ kg moong dal
- 200 gms white pumpkin (chaal kumro) (cut in 2-inch cubes)
- 200 gms red pumpkin (cut in 2-inch cubes)
- 1 brinjal (cut in 2-inch cubes)
- 1 onion (cut in 2-inch cubes)
- 1 potato (cut in 2-inch cubes)
- 1 tsp coriander, 1 tsp cumin, 2-inch piece ginger, 5 cloves garlic, 3 dry red chillies, ½ tsp black mustard, 1 tsp fenugreek - ground together to form a paste
- 1 tsp turmeric
- 2 tbsp packaged sambhar powder
- 1 tbsp packaged chana masala
- salt to taste
- 4 tbsp oil

Method:

Wash the dals. Heat water in a large pan and put in the dals with 2 inches of water above them. Allow to boil up and remove the scum. Cook for 10 minutes and add the vegetables, turmeric and salt. Reduce flame and cook on slow fire till done. Strain the dal.

Heat the oil in a small pan and fry the prepared spices till they turn colour. At this stage Mrs Vatcha adds 2 tablespoons of packaged sambhar powder and 1 tablespoon of packaged chana masala. Fry all together and pour over cooked dal. Thicken dal and taste for salt.

For Mutton Dhansak, add pieces of boiled mutton to the dal before you add the spices. The longer you cook this dal the better the taste.

» Bengalis are thrilled to find that someone besides them cooks fish in banana leaves.

Patrani Macchhi

Fish Wrapped in Banana Leaves

Serves 8

Ingredients:
- 4 banana leaves (cut in quarters to make 16 pieces)
- 1 kg fish (cut in 8 large fillets)
- 1 grated coconut, 6 green chillies, 50 gms green coriander, 2 tsp cumin seeds, 2 tsp sugar, 6 cloves garlic - ground together
- salt to taste
- juice of 3 limes

Method:
Cut the banana leaves and make 16 pieces out of them. Cut the fish into 8 large fillets. Bhetki is the best for this dish as it is bone free. Parsees prefer pomfret.

Add the lime juice to the mixture of ground spices, herbs, sugar and salt. Coat the fish well with this paste. Place the banana leaves in crosses, making 8 crosses, 1 for each fillet of fish. Place a fillet in the centre of a cross and fold over to make an envelope. Tie the envelope with string. Repeat the process for the remaining 7 fillets. Place the fillets in a small wire or bamboo basket. Boil water in a large pot. Cover the basket with a cloth and lower it over the boiling water. Steam for 10 minutes. The envelopes can be put in a greased fire-proof dish and baked in a moderate (350° F, 180° C) oven for 10 minutes. They can also be steamed in a steamer.

» Parsees are great egg eaters and this way of baking

eggs makes a nice light supper or lunch.

Papeta Par Eeda

Eggs on Potatoes

Serves 2

Ingredients:
- **4 medium potatoes (peeled and thinly sliced)**
- **4 tbsp oil**
- **1 tsp garlic paste**
- **1 tsp ginger paste**
- **4 chopped green chillies**
- **4 eggs**

Method:
Fry the potatoes in the oil in a wok or frying pan until they are three-quarters cooked. Add the garlic paste, ginger paste and green chillies and mix well.

Place in a shallow greased oven-proof dish and break the eggs over them. Cook under a grill until the eggs are set. You may cook in a moderate (350° F, 180° C) oven. The eggs can be cooked this way over ladies' fingers which have to be finely sliced and fried before putting the eggs on them.

» Tarka Dal, Makai Roti and Sarso Saag in winter, are, to the Bengali, the epitome of Punjabi dhaba food and he will drive miles to get it. Contrary to what the Punjabi may say, the Bengali knows the whole black lentil dressed with a variety of seasonings as Tarka Dal. The following four recipes are from Sohinder Grewal.

Tarka Dal

Whole Black Lentils with Seasonings

Serves 4

Ingredients:
- **200 gms either whole moong dal (whole moong beans) or sabut urad (whole black lentils)**
- **6 cups water**
- **1 tsp turmeric**
- **2 tsp chilli powder**
- **1 large tbsp garlic and ginger paste**
- **salt to taste**
- **1 tbsp ghee**
- **3 tbsp chopped onions**

Method:
Pressure cook the dal in the water with the turmeric, chilli powder, garlic and ginger paste and salt.

Cook for 30 minutes for moong and 45 minutes for urad dal.

Stir well. The dal must be thick and creamy.

Heat the ghee to smoking in a small pan or ladle. Reduce heat and fry the chopped onions till golden, add to dal and cover.

Calcutta's preference: Heat ghee, fry onions as before, with the addition of a handful of green coriander, 4 green chillies and a tomato all chopped together. Add 2 tablespoons of butter or cream before serving.

» This is a winter dish Calcutta looks forward to when the fresh mustard greens and spinach come in from the villages.

Bathu is a seed sown with the mustard and the leaves give their own flavour to the dish. Chalai is another edible leaf for which we have no English name. Sohinder insists that all five saags must be included.

Sarso Saag

Mustard and Other Greens

Serves 8

Ingredients:
- 1 kg mustard greens (chopped)
- 500 gms spinach (chopped)
- 250 gms fenugreek greens (chopped)
- 250 gms bathu (chopped)
- 250 gms chalai (chopped)
- 15–20 green chillies (chopped)
- 250 gms onions (chopped)
- 50 gms ginger, 2 large pods garlic - ground to a paste
- 50 gms maize flour (makai atta), 50 gms gram powder (besan) - mixed together
- salt to taste
- 8 cups water
- 100 gms ghee

Method:
Wash the greens thoroughly. Put all the greens with the garlic and ginger paste, green chillies, salt to taste in a pressure cooker with 8 cups water and cook under pressure for at least 1 hour. Take off the fire and let it cool. (The pressure must be released on its own before you open the cooker.)

Mash the greens completely with a wooden churner used to churn dal. While mashing the greens, add the flour mixture gradually mixing it in thoroughly so that there are no lumps. Return the pan to the fire and cook over a slow flame for 10 minutes, stirring all the time, until the saags are a creamy consistency.

Heat the ghee and fry the onions till golden brown. Add the saag and mix lightly. Check for seasoning.

Serve with Makai Roti.

Makai Roti

Maize Flour Bread

Makes 8 rotis

Ingredients:
* **1 cup hot water**
* **250 gms maize flour (makai atta) (sieved)**
* **ghee**

Method:
Sprinkle 1 cup hot water on the maize flour. Mix well. The mixture should be moist but not pasty.

Cover with a cloth. Take enough dough for one roti at a time and knead under the heel of the hand till it is smooth and holds together. Dampen hands from time to time. Flatten the dough between the palms and pat it into a circle ⅛-inch thick. Take care that the roti does not break. Cook on a hot griddle for two minutes on each side till well browned. Spread with ghee and keep covered.

Gajar Halwa

Carrot Pudding

Serves 12

Ingredients:
* **1 kg large red carrots (grated)**
* **16 cups milk**
* **2 tbsp ghee**
* **a handful of raisins (washed and soaked)**
* **200 gms sugar**
* **slivers of almonds**

Method:
Boil the milk in a large pan and reduce it to measure 12 cups. Cook the carrots and the milk on a low fire until they are a thick mass. Add the ghee and cook the carrots until they leave the sides of the pan. The raisins may be added at this time. Add the sugar and cook slowly until the pudding has a shiny caramelized look. Take off the fire and decorate with slivers of almonds.

» The above four dishes cannot be cooked in a hurry, they require stirring and watching, and must be done in large quantities for best results.

» The next two recipes are examples of how the Calcuttan eats. Punjabi dishes have been given a Bengali touch with delicious results.

Panir with a Touch of Bengal

Cottage Cheese with Mustard

Serves 6

Ingredients:
- **500 gms cottage cheese (cut in 1-inch cubes)**
- **6 green chillies (slit)**
- **1 tbsp yellow mustard seeds (ground to a paste)**
- **2 tbsp mustard oil**
- **½ tsp panch phoron**
- **½ tsp carom seeds**
- **¼ tsp turmeric**
- **1 tbsp ginger paste**
- **salt to taste**
- **juice of 1 lime**
- **1 tsp sugar**

Method:
Mix the mustard seeds in 1 cup water. Heat the mustard oil in a wok on a medium flame. Add the panch phoron, carom seeds and turmeric and stir fry until slightly browned. Add the ginger paste and stir fry for 2 minutes. Add the cottage cheese, green chillies, mustard paste in water and salt. Simmer gently until the water evaporates and the gravy is thick, with the oil on top. Add the lime juice mixed with the sugar. Cover and cook for 5 minutes. Serve hot with plain boiled rice.

Jeera Alu with Khoa

Potatoes with Cumin and Dehydrated Milk

Serves 6

Ingredients:
- 500 gms small potatoes (peeled)
- 1 tsp cumin seeds
- 2 tsp poppy seeds (ground to a paste)
- 1 tbsp water
- 50 gms dehydrated milk (khoa) (grated)
- 3 tbsp ghee or oil
- 2 tsp cumin powder (roasted)
- salt to taste
- freshly ground black pepper to taste

Method:
Heat the ghee or oil in a wok till medium hot. Add 1 teaspoon of cumin seeds and fry until just browned. Add the potatoes. Stir thoroughly. Add the cumin powder, salt and black pepper to taste. Lower heat, cover the wok and let it cook for 10 minutes, stirring occasionally. When the potatoes are three-quarters cooked, add the ground poppy seeds and dehydrated milk. Turn a few times, cover and cook for a further 10 minutes.

If the potatoes are too dry, sprinkle a little water before

covering. When the potatoes are ready, they will be coated
with the spices and the oil will appear on top of the spices.
Sprinkle the roasted cumin powder, mix well and cover the
pan. Remove from heat.

» We were very fortunate to get these recipes from
Amber restaurant, where people go to eat Tandoori
food in Calcutta. We present the recipes as they were
given to us. The quantities are for restaurant servings
and have to be cut down as required. The
measurements are in grams and may be converted to
cup and spoon measures.

Chicken Tangri Kebab

Barbecued Chicken Legs

Serves 10–12

Ingredients:
• **2 kgs chicken legs**

For marinade
• **30 gms salt**
• **30 gms chilli powder**
• **5 gms cumin powder**
• **3 gms coriander powder**
• **4 gms mixed large and small cardamoms and cinnamon
  powders**
• **2 gms mace**
• **½ nutmeg (powdered)**
• **30 gms cashew nuts (ground)**
• **30 gms tomato sauce**
• **5 beaten eggs**

For cooking
• **50 gms ghee**
• **80 gms gram flour (besan)**

- **80 gms wheat flour (atta)**
- **100 gms milk**
- **80 gms arrowroot mixed with a little flour**

Method:

Marinate the chicken legs in the salt, chilli powder, cumin powder, coriander powder, cardamom and cinnamon powder, mace and powdered nutmeg, cashew nuts, tomato sauce and beaten eggs. Set aside for an hour.

Heat the ghee in a wok and brown the gram flour and wheat flour in it. Remove from heat and add the milk and stir until the paste comes off the sides of the pan. Cool and knead the paste to make it soft. Rub over the chicken legs and roll them in a mixture of arrowroot and flour to hold the batter together and let them rest for 2 or 3 hours.

Heat oven to 350° F or 180° C and grill the chicken legs in a shallow roasting pan for 15 minutes. Baste with ghee and grill again till the legs are nicely browned but not dry.

Tandoori Prawns

Spicy Barbecued Prawns

Serves 4

Ingredients:
- **1 kg prawns (cleaned and de-veined)**

For marinade
- **5 gms salt**
- **5 gms chilli powder**
- **5 gms ajwain**
- **4 gms cumin powder**
- **2½ gms dried powdered fenugreek leaves**
- **3 gms powdered mace**
- **2 gms green cardamoms (powdered)**
- **a pinch of powdered nutmeg**
- **juice of 5 cloves of garlic**
- **1 tbsp lime juice**

Method:

Marinate the prawns in the salt, and all the spices and the garlic juice.

Pierce on a skewer and grill over charcoal for 5 minutes. Baste with ghee and grill for another 5-7 minutes. Add the lime juice just before serving.

» Mattar panir has become almost a standard item at Bengali weddings. The Amber recipe uses tinned peas, but we would suggest 6 cups shelled fresh peas.

Mattar Panir

Cottage Cheese and Green Pea Curry

Serves 8–10

Ingredients:

- **500 gms cottage cheese (cut in 1-inch cubes)**
- **750 gms fresh peas (shelled)**
- **200 gms ghee**
- **100 gms poppy seeds, 100 gms browned onions, 25 gms ginger, 20 gms garlic, 20 gms cumin - ground together**
- **4 bay leaves**
- **5 small cardamoms**
- **1 tsp turmeric**
- **1 tsp Kashmiri chilli powder**
- **250 gms tomato purée**
- **salt to taste**
- **paste of 100 gms cream, 2 tsp cornflour and 100 gms butter**
- **coriander leaves**

Method:

Fry the cottage cheese lightly in 2 tablespoons of ghee. Set aside.

Heat the ghee in a wok and add the bay leaves, small

cardamoms, turmeric and Kashmiri chilli powder. Cook over medium heat for some time and add the ground spices and tomato purée and cook until there is a thick gravy. Add salt to taste. Add the green peas, cottage cheese and the cream, cornflour and butter paste. Cook for 10 minutes. The gravy should be a rich reddish brown with the ghee on top. Add the coriander leaves before serving.

Nan Roti

Leavened Bread

Makes 10 nans

Ingredients:
- **150 gms milk**
- **125 gms yoghurt**
- **1 egg**
- **25 gms sugar**
- **50 gms baking powder**
- **½ tsp salt**
- **75 gms oil**
- **10 gms ghee**
- **1 kg flour**

Method:
Mix the milk, yoghurt, egg, sugar, baking powder, salt and oil and ghee. Add the flour and mix well. Knead and let the dough rest for an hour. Knead again for 5 minutes and make the dough into 10 portions. Roll out and pull to make it the shape of the sole of a shoe. Cook on a griddle for 10 minutes turning once, or in a moderate (350° F, 180° C) oven for 10 minutes.

Fish Tikka

Barbecued Fish Cubes

Ingredients:
- 1 kg bhetki (cleaned and cut in 2-inch cubes)

For marinade
- juice of 1 lime
- 10 gms ground ginger
- salt to taste
- 25 gms chilli powder
- 3 gms ajwain
- 4 gms cumin powder
- 2½ gms dried and powdered fenugreek leaves
- 3 gms mace
- a pinch of nutmeg (powdered)
- 3 tbsp oil

Method:
Marinate the bhetki and set it aside for 1 hour.

Pierce the fish on a skewer and turn over a fire or under the grill for 10 minutes.

Kulfi

Indian Ice-Cream

Makes 6 kulfis

Ingredients:
- 500 ml milk
- 100 gms sugar
- 10 gms chopped pistachios
- 3 gms saffron soaked in 1 tbsp milk
- 200 gms chopped raisins, almonds and cashew nuts

Method:
Reduce by boiling the milk in a pan to 300 millilitres. Add

the sugar. Add the pistachios, saffron, raisins, almonds and cashew nuts. Reduce further, cooking for another 10 minutes. Cool and fill into 6 kulfi moulds, screw on the covers and secure the tops with flour. Freeze till set.

» The Oriya cook has brought the weighing scale and measuring spoon into the Indian kitchen. A master cook will produce a shopping list for a party for 500, with meticulous calculations down to the last gram of salt. To meet demands he has mastered every cuisine in vogue from sukto to chilli chicken, from biriyani to mattar panir. From chingri maachher chiney kebab to the simple biuli dal he has at home his is the chef's touch.

Biuli Dal

Split Black Lentils

Serves 4

Ingredients:
- 1 cup biuli dal (split black lentils)
- 4 cups water
- ½ tsp turmeric
- ½ tsp chilli powder
- salt to taste
- 2 tbsp mustard oil
- 2 dry red chillies
- 1 tsp panch phoron
- 6 cloves of garlic (chopped fine)

Method:
Roast the biuli dal. Bring the water to the boil in a pan and add the dal with the turmeric and chilli powder. Remove scum and reduce heat. Add salt and cover and simmer until

the dal is soft and compounded with the water. Stir with a wooden spoon to break the grains. Heat the mustard oil in a small frying pan to smoking. Lower heat and add the dry red chillies. When they turn colour add the panch phoron. When it sputters, add the garlic. As soon as the garlic turns brown, pour the oil with the spices into the dal. Cover and simmer for 2 minutes. Serve with hot rice and crisply fried whitebait.

» Ananta is a mali by occupation, but spends much of his time over his bucket stove. He still follows his village practice of cooking on a cowdung fire and lovingly tends the arum in the vegetable patch because, as he says, back home in Orissa he eats that and not potatoes.

Anantar Kochur Tarkari

Ananta's Arum

Serves 4

Ingredients:
- root and stem of 1 arum plant (cut into 2-inch pieces)
- lime water
- 1 medium brinjal (cut into 2-inch pieces)
- salt to taste
- turmeric
- 1 tsp black mustard seeds
- 1 tsp cumin seeds
- 6 cloves garlic
- 100 gms any small freshwater fish (cut into 2-inch pieces)
- 3 tbsp mustard oil
- 2 red chillies
- 1 tsp panch phoron
- 1 cup water

Method:

Take the fibres off the arum stem. Soak the arum stem and root in lime water for half an hour. Sprinkle the brinjal with salt. Before cooking, lightly coat all the vegetables with turmeric. For the fish Ananta chooses the small rui fry.

Heat the mustard oil in a wok and fry the fish. Keep it aside. In the same oil fry the chillies till they turn colour. Add the panch phoron. When it sputters, add the prepared vegetables. Stir fry for 2 minutes and add the ground spices. Stir fry for another 3 minutes until the spices have turned colour. Add the water and cover. When the vegetables are nearly cooked, add the fish and salt to taste. Cook for a further 3-4 minutes and take off fire.

» When the hot April sun burns the skin, a glass of satua from a big mud pot on a roadside trolley is a welcome cooler. We like the drink so much, we serve it to our friends as a short starter before dinner.

Satua Pani

Gram Flour Drink

Makes 1 glass

Ingredients:
- **30 gms roasted gram flour (chana sattu)**
- **juice of ½ a lime**
- **½ tsp chilli powder**
- **½ tsp cumin powder, ½ tsp black pepper - roasted together**
- **a pinch of black rock salt (kala namak)**

Method:

Stir the roasted gram flour in a glass of cold water. Add all the other ingredients and mix well. The result is a thick lentil soup-like drink.

» The rivers of Sind are full of fish similar to those in
Bengal. Sindhis enjoy kok palla and methi palla with
hilsa and bhetki.

Two recipes from Chandra Lalwani.

Kok Palla

Fillet of Fish with a Green Sauce

Serves 6

Ingredients:
- 1½ kg hilsa or bhetki (cleaned and filleted in half)
- salt
- juice of ½ a lime
- 500 gms onions
- 2-inch piece ginger (chopped)
- 50 gms coriander leaves (chopped)
- 8 green chillies (chopped) mixed with 1 tbsp coriander
powder and ½ tsp turmeric
- 1 cup yoghurt mixed with juice of 1 lime or 1 tbsp thick
tamarind water
- 1 tbsp brandy
- 2 tbsp oil

Method:
Rub the hilsa or bhetki with salt and lime juice, and let it
rest for an hour.

Mix the yoghurt with the lime juice or thick tamarind
water, brandy and oil. Mix with all the other ingredients.

Place fish in an oven proof dish. Cook in a pre-heated
moderate (350° F, 180° C) oven for 20 minutes or till the fish
flakes easily when tested with a fork.

» Sindhis love the taste of fenugreek and much of their food is flavoured with it.

Methi Palla

Fish in Fenugreek

Serves 6

Ingredients:
- **500 gms bhetki (cut into thick fillets)**
- **salt**
- **turmeric**
- **1 medium onion (finely chopped)**
- **50 gms green coriander (finely chopped)**
- **50 gms fenugreek greens (finely chopped)**
- **1-inch piece green ginger (finely chopped)**
- **a few cloves garlic, preferably green garlic (finely chopped)**
- **2 tomatoes (finely chopped)**
- **¼ tsp turmeric**
- **2 tbsp oil**
- **salt to taste**
- **oil to fry fish**

Method:
Any white fish will do, but bhetki has the best taste and texture.

Rub the fish with salt and turmeric and set aside.

Add ¼ teaspoon turmeric, oil and salt to the fish. Heat oil in a frying pan and fry the fish and set aside. In the same oil, lightly cook the other ingredients. Spread the mixture evenly over the fish and place in a pre-heated moderate (350°F, 180°C) oven for 10 minutes.

Sayal Gosht

Mutton in Yoghurt

Serves 8

Ingredients:
- **1 kg mutton (cubed)**

For marinade
- **1-inch piece ginger, 4 cloves garlic - ground to a paste**
- **4 tomatoes (chopped)**
- **50 gms green coriander leaves (finely chopped)**
- **4 green chillies (finely chopped)**
- **1 cup yoghurt**
- **1 tsp coriander powder**
- **½ tsp chilli powder**
- **½ tsp turmeric**
- **2 tsp caraway seeds (shah jeera)**
- **2 tbsp oil**

- **4 tbsp oil**
- **4 onions (chopped)**
- **2 powdered green cardamoms**
- **½ tsp caraway seeds (shah jeera)**

Method:

Marinade

Mix in the yoghurt the garlic and ginger, tomatoes, coriander leaves and green chillies with the coriander powder, chilli powder, turmeric, caraway seeds and oil.

Marinate the mutton in the above ingredients. Let it rest for 6 hours in a glass or ceramic dish.

Heat the oil to smoking in a pressure cooker. Reduce heat and fry the chopped onions till golden. Add the mutton in the marinade. Stir a little and then pressure cook for 20 minutes, or cover and cook on slow fire till meat is tender. Uncover and stir fry the meat until all the liquid has been absorbed and the oil floats on top. Sprinkle a little powdered green cardamom and caraway seeds on top before serving.

Besan Curry

Vegetable and Gram Flour Soup

Serves 6–8

Ingredients:
- **200 gms carrots (scraped and cut in two)**
- **200 gms potatoes (peeled and cut in two)**
- **2 whole drumsticks (stringed and cut in two)**
- **200 gms peas in the pod**
- **2 tbsp oil**
- **1 tsp powdered cumin**
- **½ tsp fenugreek seeds**
- **6 tbsp gram flour (besan)**
- **water**
- **1 tsp chilli powder**
- **¼ tsp turmeric**
- **salt to taste**
- **1 tbsp sugar**
- **2 tbsp thick tamarind pulp**

Method:
Heat the oil to smoking in a pan. Turn down heat and fry the powdered cumin and fenugreek seeds for 1 minute. Add the gram flour and stir until it browns. Take the pan off the fire and slowly add ½ a cup of water to make a smooth paste. When it is quite smooth, add 5 more cups of water, mix and put it back on the fire. Simmer for half an hour. Add the vegetables, chilli powder, turmeric and salt. Cook until the vegetables are tender. Add the sugar and the thick tamarind pulp. Cook for another 5 minutes and take off fire. The soup may be served in cups and the vegetables separately with rice.

» China grass, the main ingredient of this dish is a kind of seaweed that grows on the shores of Malaysia and is known as agar agar. In the old days, this 'vegetable' gelatine arrived in India via China and hence the name.

China Grass Pudding

Serves 6–8

Ingredients:
- **100 gms china grass**
- **4 cups milk**
- **1 cup sugar**
- **½ tsp powdered green cardamom**
- **a sprinkling of rose water**
- **1 tbsp slivered almonds**
- **1 tsp chopped pistachios**

Method:
Soak the china grass in water until it is soft. Drain, put in a pan with the milk and cook until it is thick. Add sugar and cook till well mixed and creamy. Add green cardamom and a sprinkling of rose water for flavouring. Decorate with almonds and pistachios.

» This is a Gujarati recipe for moth, the dried bean much used in Rajasthan. Whole dried moong beans can also be cooked in this way. These recipes were given to us by Mrs Rupa Mitra, a Gujarati married to a Bengali.

Stir Fried Moth Beans

Stir Fried Dew Gram

Serves 4

Ingredients:
- **200 gms dew gram (moth beans)**

- 2 tbsp oil
- 1 tsp black mustard seeds
- ½ tsp cumin seeds
- a pinch of asafoetida
- salt to taste
- ¼ tsp turmeric
- 1 tsp coriander powder
- 1 tsp chilli powder
- juice of ½ a lime

Method:

Soak the dew gram overnight. Tie them in a piece of muslin and leave another night to sprout. Keep the muslin damp.

On the third day, heat the oil to smoking in a deep frying pan. Reduce heat and add the black mustard seeds, cumin seeds and asafoetida. When the mustard crackles, add the sprouted moat, salt and turmeric. Add a little water and cook till tender. Add the coriander powder and chilli powders and cook for another 3 minutes. Add the lime juice. Serve with rice and kadi.

Tomato Broth

Serves 4

Ingredients:

- 500 gms tomatoes
- water
- ½ tsp turmeric
- 1 tbsp molasses
- salt to taste
- 3 slit green chillies
- 1 tsp chopped ginger
- 10 curry leaves
- 1 tbsp oil
- 1 tsp black mustard seeds
- ½ tsp cumin seeds
- 2 dry red chillies (cut up)
- a pinch of asafoetida

- **chilli powder**
- **coriander leaves**

Method:
Boil the tomatoes in a pan till mushy and strain. Add enough water to make 4 cups. Put it on to boil and add the turmeric, molasses, salt, green chillies, ginger and curry leaves. Simmer for 10 minutes. Heat the oil to smoking in a small frying pan, reduce heat and add the black mustard seeds. When they sputter, add the cumin seeds. When they turn colour add the dry red chillies cut up and the asafoetida. Add the chilli powder and remove from the fire before the chilli powder burns.

Add the spices in oil to the tomato broth. Cover and simmer for 2 minutes. Garnish with coriander leaves.

To serve, remove curry leaves and pour into cups. This may be eaten with rice or as a light soup for dinner.

» Gujarati anytime foods are one of the conveniences in Calcutta today, and the sandwich concept has extended to the spongy dhokla 'bread' 'club sandwich' with a three-tiered filling of tomato ketchup, coriander chutney and processed cheese.

Dhokla

Lentil Sponge

Serves 6

Ingredients:
- **500 gms chana dal (split yellow Bengal gram)**
- **¼ teacup lukewarm water**
- **4 tbsp oil**
- **1-inch piece ginger**
- **a few green chillies (coarsely ground)**
- **1 tsp sugar**

- **1 tsp sodium bicarbonate**
- **salt to taste**
- **juice of 4 limes**
- **6–7 whole green chillies**
- **2 tsp whole black mustard seeds**
- **10–15 curry leaves**
- **¼ cup water**

Method:

Soak the dal overnight. Drain and grind to a soft consistency, dropping easily from a spoon. In the lukewarm water, add the oil, ginger and coarsely ground green chillies, sugar, sodium bicarbonate and salt. Add the lime juice. Mix well.

Pre-heat a steamer and grease the container. Pour in batter half filling the heated container. Cover with a cloth and put on the lid of the container. Steam for 5 minutes. Cut into squares while still warm.

Heat 2 tablespoons of oil to smoking, lower heat and add the whole green chillies split down the middle, whole black mustard seeds and curry leaves. When the spices sputter, pour over them ¼ cup water and sprinkle over the still warm dhoklas.

Dhoklas can also be made with rice or Semolina.

To Make Sandwiches:

Cut in half while still warm and spread a layer of tomato ketchup, a layer of coriander chutney and a layer of processed cheese. Put the halves together and add the tempering described above. Serve topped with freshly grated coconut and coriander leaves.

Green Chutney for Dhokla

Ingredients:

- **½ coconut (grated)**
- **25 gms mint leaves (picked and cleaned)**

- 25 gms green coriander (picked and cleaned)
- 5 cloves garlic
- ½ tsp cumin seeds (roasted and powdered)
- 3 tsp sugar
- 4 green chillies
- salt to taste
- ½ tsp oil

Method:
Grind all the ingredients together to a spreading consistency.

» To the average Calcuttan, South Indian food means idli, dosa, vada, rasam and sambhar. Not only have these become fast foods, but tiny idlis are served in many different ways at cocktail parties. We decided to give our readers a fleeting glance into the vast wealth of South Indian food that is cooked in Calcutta homes. Udith sannas are rice and lentil cakes from the Coromandel coast, similar to, and yet different from, idli. A recipe from Mrs Hazel Gupta.

Udith Sanna

Raised Rice Cakes

Makes 20

Ingredients:
- 3 cups parboiled rice
- ½ cup sun-dried rice
- ½ cup urad dal (split black lentils)
- ½ tsp yeast
- 1 cup hand hot (100° F, 36° C) water

Method:
Soak the 2 kinds of rice and dal separately in water

overnight.

Next morning, add salt to taste and grind them all together with the yeast dissolved in the hand hot water. Cover the batter with a damp cloth and leave to rise for 3 hours. Place in small containers and steam over hot water in a covered steamer. An idli steamer is ideal. These cakes should rise well and be light and fluffy. Serve with sambhar or any curry.

» The next recipe is from Radhika Neelakanthan. This is a Karnataka dosa, made of beaten rice.

Avil Dosa

Beaten Rice Cakes

Serves 8

Ingredients:
* 1 cup beaten rice (chura)
* 2 cups sun-dried rice
* salt to taste
* a pinch of bicarbonate of soda
* 1 coconut (grated)
* oil

Method:
Soak the beaten rice and sun-dried rice separately in water for 4–6 hours. Drain, add salt and the bicarbonate of soda and grind together to make a smooth batter. Cover and leave to ferment overnight.

Add the coconut to the batter in the morning.

Heat a griddle and grease it lightly. Spread 2 tablespoons of batter on it and turn the griddle to let the batter spread in an even circle. Lower heat and cover the griddle.

Flip the dosa after 3 minutes and brown the other side lightly. Use up all the batter in this way, pouring a few drops of oil on the pan between dosas to keep it greased.

Serve with chicken curry or fish curry.

» Nathu comes from Bihar, he works for Prasad Naidu an Andhraite who is married to Anisa, a Bengali Muslim. So Nathu's rasam is truly Calcuttan.

Rasam

Pepper Water

Serves 6

Ingredients:

Make rasam powder
- 1 tbsp arhar dal (split red peas), 2 tsp chana dal (split dried Bengal gram), 1 tsp urad dal (split dried black lentils), 2 tsp whole coriander, ¼ tsp fenugreek, 1 tsp cumin, 10 peppercorns, ¼ tsp asafoetida, 10 curry leaves - roasted and ground

Stage 1
- 4 cups water
- 2 chopped tomatoes
- 50 grams green coriander
- 1 lime-sized ball tamarind
- 10 curry leaves
- ½ tsp turmeric
- salt to taste

Stage 2
- 1 tbsp oil
- 3 dry red chillies
- 1 tsp black mustard seeds
- 10 curry leaves
- 1 whole pod of garlic

- **2 tsp whole coriander**

Method:

Stage 1
Bring the tomatoes, green coriander, tamarind pulp, curry leaves, turmeric and salt to the boil in the water in a pan.

Stage 2
Heat 1 tbsp oil to smoking in a small frying pan. Lower heat and put in the dry red chillies, black mustard seeds and ten curry leaves. Add the garlic and coriander. When the mixture sputters, pour it into the tomato mixture and boil for half an hour. Add the rasam powder, boil for 5 minutes and take off fire.

Pepper water is a popular accompaniment to jhal frazee (Chapter 5).

» The next recipe is from Mrs Ranjana Shivram.

Sambhar

Lentil and Vegetable Stew

Serves 6

Ingredients:

For Sambhar powder
- **3 tbsp coriander seeds, 1 tbsp chana dal (split Bengal gram), ½ tsp fenugreek, 6–8 red chillies, 1 very small piece of asafoetida, ¼ tsp oil - roasted in the oil and ground**

- **1 lime sized ball of tamarind pulp**
- **2 cups water**

- **1 cup arhar dal (split red lentils)**
- **3 cups water**

- ½ tsp turmeric
- salt to taste

- 3 tbsp oil
- 1½ tsp black mustard seeds
- 8 drumsticks (cut in 2½-inch pieces)
- 10 curry leaves
- salt to taste

Method:
Soak the ball of tamarind in water for 1 hour. Boil the arhar dal in 3 cups of water in a pan with turmeric and salt till well cooked. Reserve.

Heat the oil to smoking. Lower heat and add the black mustard seeds. When they sputter, add the drumsticks and curry leaves. Fry for 5 minutes and add the strained tamarind water, sambhar powder and salt. Cook till the drumsticks are done. Add the cooked dal to this mixture and cook for 10 minutes or until the dal is thick.

Variation:
- Cook masoor dal with turmeric, sambhar powder and tomatoes. Temper with black mustard seeds and green chillies.

» Puniya Devi whose home is in Uttar Pradesh learnt to make vadas by taste by sharing the snacks her employers brought back for tea.

Puniya's Vadas

Fried Rice and Lentil Cakes

Makes 10–12 vadas

Ingredients:
- 1 cup urad dal (split black lentils)

- **5 tbsp sun-dried rice**
- **2 onions (grated)**
- **1-inch piece ginger (minced fine)**
- **3 or 4 green chillies (minced fine)**
- **salt to taste**
- **2 cups oil**

Method:

Soak the urad dal and the sun-dried rice separately overnight. Drain and grind them in the morning and add the grated onions, minced ginger and minced green chillies. Allow to ferment for 6 hours. Add salt to taste before frying. Take a little of the mixture in the palm of the hand and make a soft ball. Press a hole into the middle with your thumb and drop gently into the hot oil in a wok. Deep fry to a crisp.

Coconut Chutney

Ingredients:
- **½ coconut**
- **4 green chillies**
- **2-inch piece ginger**
- **salt to taste**
- **1 tsp black mustard seeds**
- **a few curry leaves**
- **2 tsp oil**
- **1 tbsp urad dal (split black lentils) (optional)**

Method:

Grate the coconut with the green chillies, ginger and salt to make the chutney. Fry the black mustard seeds and curry leaves in the oil and add to the chutney. Soaked urad dal added to the coconut mixture add to the taste of the chutney.

» The next three recipes were given to us by Mr Zacharia, Executive Chef, Taj Bengal, Calcutta.

Porial

Stir Fried Vegetable from Tamil Nadu

Serves 8

Ingredients:
- 1 kg snake gourd (cut in small pieces)
- 2 tbsp onions (chopped)
- 1 tsp ginger (chopped)
- 1 tsp green chillies (chopped)
- ½ coconut (grated)
- 3 tbsp oil
- ½ tsp mustard seeds
- 1 sprig curry leaves
- 2 dry red chilli flakes
- 1 tsp chana dal (split Bengal gram)
- 1 tsp urad dal (split black lentils)

Method:
Boil the snake gourd in a pan with a little salt and drain.

Heat the oil to smoking in a wok and crackle the mustard. Add the curry leaves, dry red chilli flakes, dals, onion, ginger and green chillies and sauté to brown. Add the boiled snake gourd. Sauté. Correct the seasoning, finish with grated coconut.

» This curry from Kerala uses the Calcutta bhetki instead of the seer fish which is the Kerala fish. One of the ingredients is khumkhum tamarind, a Kerala speciality and available in the Lake Market or in South Indian groceries.

Travancore Fish Curry

Serves 4

Ingredients:
- 400 gms seer fish or bhetki (cleaned and cut in small pieces)

- **2½ tbsp khum khum or tamarind pulp**
- **¾ cup oil**
- **1 tsp black mustard seeds**
- **½ tsp fenugreek seeds**
- **1 tbsp ginger (finely sliced)**
- **6 green chillies (slit)**
- **1 pod garlic (chopped)**
- **100 gms onions (sliced)**
- **2 tbsp chilli powder**
- **1 tsp turmeric powder**
- **1 tbsp coriander powder**
- **200 gms tomatoes (chopped)**
- **1 sprig curry leaves**

Method:

Marinate the fish in 1½ tablespoons of tamarind pulp for half an hour, keeping the rest aside. Heat the oil in a pan. Crackle the black mustard seeds. Add the fenugreek seeds, ginger, slit green chillies, garlic and onions. Sauté. Add the chilli powder, turmeric powder and coriander powder and stir. Add the tomatoes and the remaining tamarind pulp. When the curry comes to the boil, add fish. Adjust seasoning. Add the curry leaves. Serve with rice, sannas or dosa.

Mutton Chettinad

Serves 4

Ingredients:
- **500 gms mutton (cut into pieces)**
- **100 gms onions (chopped)**
- **100 gms tomatoes (chopped)**
- **150 gms oil**
- **5 gms whole garam masala of cinnamon, green cardamoms and cloves**
- **2 tsp garlic and ginger paste**
- **2 tsp chilli powder**
- **2 tsp coriander powder**

- 1 tsp turmeric powder
- salt to taste
- 1 sprig curry leaves
- 3 tsp crushed pepper corn

Method:

Boil the mutton and keep aside.

Heat the oil. Add the whole garam masala. Add the onions and brown till glossy. Add the garlic and ginger paste, chilli powder, coriander powder and turmeric powder and sauté. Add the tomatoes and cook till the curry is thick. Add the boiled mutton and salt to taste. Simmer for 10 minutes until well blended with the spices. Finish with curry leaves and crushed peppercorns.

Correct seasoning. The curry should be a dark rich brown.

Chapter 8

Tables Turn

Buffet, Brunch and Baked Beans

A sea change swept through the second city of the British Empire in the early years of the twentieth century. Calcutta was a cauldron of bubbling nationalism. In 1912, the capital shifted to Delhi but Calcutta retained its leadership for another fifty years or so. Famine, war and communal riots, followed by the division of the subcontinent into two nations have left their marks in untold and never-to-be-forgotten ways.

Many of us remember India, Burma (Myanmar), and Ceylon (Sri Lanka) as one pink mass on political maps. It was after the Japanese attack on Pearl Harbour in 1942 that World War II came nearer home. The action moved to Eastern India. Bengali families settled in Burma, Anglo-Burmese and many other Indians joined the long trek along the Burma Road into India. They had lost their worldly possessions but retained the memories of happier days and the panthe khow sway. In Calcutta they shared the taste of this dish with their new friends—noodles, a bowl of coconut chicken curry and a half a dozen garnishes. A simple recipe for the busy and somewhat harassed Calcutta housewife, khow sway can be cooked at short notice when her husband brings home his colleagues from the Delhi office and allows her guests to flavour their meal-in-a-dish as they will from an array of garnishes on the table.

Wartime conditions were a new experience. The dimmed street gas lights made darkness more visible. Calcutta's monument, the Victoria Memorial, and the then brand new handsome cantilever Howrah Bridge were smothered in camouflage paint. To add to the wartime look on the main streets, convoys of olive green trucks snaked their way to the front lines. An invasion of British and American armed forces put the city into fourth gear. Those who returned as tourists after the war remembered Claire Ross, the American manager of Magnolia's, the first soda fountain on Park Street. Magnolia's, or Mags, for short, became synonymous with ice-cream popsicles in bright yellow handcarts with the name in blue. The sixty-plus recollect the thrill of ordering soda pops and multi-coloured milk shakes in their student days in institutions of learning within walking distance of Magnolia's.

New names from the new world changed forever the essentially European character of menus in hotels and restaurants—butter scotch pie, sundaes and chili con carne. Magnolia's fare is now more spirituous, but the blue logo is fraught with memories of those war years.

Night clubs mushroomed in and around Chowringhee with Las Vegas-like names such as Ace of Spades, King of Clubs, Puerto Rico and Club 60. Daddy Mazda's Golden Slipper remained one of the most popular night clubs till the 1960s. Mr Mookerjee, Chief Steward of the 300 Club moved to the Slipper and Boris's chicken à la Kiev and shashlik were exchanged for Chateaubriand steak with an

American addition of coleslaw. Calcutta cooks swear that a marinade of ground onions, ginger and garlic brings out the best in the best steaks in the country, available only in their city.

In those war years, tomato ketchup made its debut with a splash on most things edible and was really responsible for the big change in food flavourings. The base of the all-American prawn cocktail was the Mog bawarchee's four egg yolk creamy mayonnaise, hand-beaten to perfection with a generous helping of ketchup. Baked beans on toast smothered in tomato sauce was an eating-out breakfast treat for the vegetarian at Flury's Swiss Confectioners tea-room.

It is goodbye to wafer chips and French fried fingers served on saucers with a blob of tomato sauce as potato chips, often flavoured, in attractive foil sachets have become big business.

The city bade farewell to the 'propah' style of entertaining. The ladies of Calcutta donned aprons, doled out mugs of tea from stainless steel samovars for the troops and offered crisp pakoras made from off-the-ration commodities like gram flour, onions, brinjals and potatoes. And all on the doob grass tennis lawns of their Edwardian homes. The two hundred year old Galapagos tortoise was an added attraction at Sir David and Lady Ezra's open house tea parties at Kyd Street. The photograph of an elegant hostess pouring fragrant Darjeeling tea from a silver teapot while Butler Nanno Khan 'passed' paper-thin lettuce sandwiches and slices of Madeira cake took its place among the sepia prints in the family album.

The winds of war swept the Irish linen tablecloths and damask napkins, the Limoges, the 'cut glass' and the formidable array of Mappin & Webb cutlery into period cupboards and cabinets. In walked the informal stand-up dinner—the buffet—and paper napkins. The buffet table is as international as can be. Friday buffet lunch at the Bengal Club of cold collations, roasts, au gratin, polau, luchi and curries command full house.

Cocktail parties grew in number and in size. Hostesses competed with each other in the variety of canapés—which were often a substitute dinner. As waiters, carrying artistically arranged trays of small eats, dodged between groups of guests, the animated conversation froze momentarily as toothpicks speared Angels on Horseback, oysters replaced by chunks of pineapple or water chestnuts in season. Today, dips, pâtés and stuffed eggs are comfortable companions to bite-sized kebabs, samosas and Chinese spring rolls.

The merry marriage of breakfast and lunch produced a hearty brunch. Once again the ladies of Calcutta, renowned for their matchless tables, boldly planned a bohemian menu for a Sunday brunch. One such reads like a contemporary version of the eighteenth-century traveller, Eliza Faye and her description of breakfast after a morning ride. Sausages and mash have replaced sheep's head moulds and a clove-studded leg of ham, a dish of pickled hump. Parsee acuri has superceded kedgeree and to down it all, a Bloody Mary, in place of claret is the 'Loll Shrob'. Another menu was a collection of many family favourites like crumbed and fried brain cutlets, liver glacé (later discovered to be a Venetian speciality) sausages and bacon, an assortment of home baked crumpets, croissants, brioches and bagels. Milk for the babalog and freshly brewed coffee for the others.

A drastic change in the food habits of the man in the street was the result of rationing of rice and wheat.

Longevity is on the wane
Thanks to ration rice bane
Come join me then in hailing
The system we are all bewailing

is a translation of a song sung by the wistful Bengali as he collected his meagre quota of sub-standard rice supplemented by wheat. The 'one rice one roti' meal has come to stay in many Calcutta homes.

Besides new foods and flavours, a crop of wartime

English words entered the Bengali vocabulary which is best described as 'Benglish'. The rationing system was referred to as 'control' and the queue to collect ration, simply 'line'.

Meanwhile the women stepped out to fill the spaces when their men went marching off to war. The tradition in Bengali homes that men shopped and women cooked, though not quite reversed was revised. With new domestic technology from the West, the twenty-four-hour-on-call job at home has been gradually streamlined.

On the street, the original seller of pavement foods, the chhatuwala from Bihar sits with a basket of fine gram flour. His regular customers are the rickshaw and handcart pullers joined by the migrant construction workers from nearby skyscrapers. Each takes a platter and a water pot from the neat array of shining brass thalis and lotas propped against a wall. A measure of gram flour is kneaded with a little water into a stiff dough, rolled into balls and eaten between bites on a raw onion and a green chilli. A few yards away, another Bihari food, litti (whole wheat dumplings with a stuffing of gram flour, garlic and oregano) fries in a wok of boiling oil, a shortcut for the home-made litti baked on the embers of a cowdung fire in a Muzzafarpur village.

As new blocks burgeon on the site of demolished old and familiar buildings, blue plastic covered lean-tos cater to Bengali and Oriya workers who cannot do without their maachh bhaat (rice and fish).

At tiffin time in the office paras, boro and chhoto babus elbow their way out and make a beeline for the day's choice from the miscellany of pavement foods. To begin with, there is the cut fresh fruit salad handed out in cones of folded dried leaves. A crowd collects around the toasted bread and butter seller. He sprinkles salt and pepper on this otherwise spartan fare. Beside him, the andawala dips into his wire baskets of hard-boiled duck and chicken eggs. Hot puffed puris are served with a choice of alur dom or ghugni (curried chick peas). The more adventurous scramble for the cosmopolitan fare on wheelbarrows. These mobile kiosks

appear in their own territories, outstripping each other with
ingenious innovations. With catchy names like 'Wayfarer'
and 'Mona Lisa', each has its own local colour—rolls Nizam
style, cheap and filling masala dosa and chiney charchari,
a Bengalified spicy chow mein.

We meet her family at the acetylene-lamp-lit fairyland
on the Maidan in front of the Fountain of Joy. It is Sunday
and this office-going mother's evening off from the cooking
scene at home. The Maidan, described as Calcutta's Lung,
exhales smells from a gallimaufry of snack foods from all
over the country—phuchka from Bihar, Bombay bhelpuri
and pau bhaji, deep fried in a well-known brand of butter,
vada and dosa from the deeper south. The Gupta family
head for their favourite phuchkawala and the reason for
their preference is a family joke—a resemblance to a dear
departed relative! With alacrity, his prehensile thumb
punctures the phuchka and fills it with seasoned 'smashed'
potatoes one at a time scooping up tamarind water from a
large clay pot. The tamarind water spikes the phuchka and
is said to be a disinfectant for the entire process is by hand.
Chaat, that irresistible mix-up of sliced boiled potatoes,
whole Bengal gram soaked soft, sweet and sour tamarind
sauce and a sprinkling of green coriander leaves, is a taste
bud teaser and invariably a customer returns for more.

Tongues on fire have a choice of coolers on the Maidan.
We look for the man with the red cloth-wrapped pot of salted
factory ice turning between his hands. Time stands still as
he takes out a metal cone of custard apple flavoured kulfi
which would rival the cones at Murshid Kuli Khan's
banquet when ice came from the mountains.

Here comes the mooriwala. Jhal moori is the evergreen
snack of West Bengal. The omnipresent mooriwala
vigorously mixes with aplomb, quantities of puffed rice in
an old tin. He adds chopped onions, chillies, coconut slivers,
cucumber and boiled potato cubes from smaller tins,
chopped coriander leaves and a generous squeeze of lime,
shakes a few drops of pungent mustard oil from a hair oil
bottle and a secret formula of spices from an old talcum

powder tin. The jhal moori is ready and is measured into
newspaper bags in multiples of the rupee. Offered to a
stranger on journeys by train, tram or bus, it is a convivial
icebreaker and among good friends, a conversation
stimulator.

We invite you to accompany us to Nizam's behind the
New Market where we go to ferret out the recipe for
Calcutta's first fast food, the kathi roll. As we munched our
rolls, slowly unwinding its snug paper jacket, the young
supervisor rolled out the kathi ka kissa. Sheikh Reza was
the inventor of the kathi rolled in paper. His workshop was
his small eatery named after his son, Nizamuddin and
hence Nizam's. Kebab in its many variations was not new
to Calcutta. Whether it was Gurgin Khan's khalipha or Ali
Verdi Khan's favourite bawarchee, the kebab had
established itself in the Coolootola and Chitpur areas in the
city's youth. And all this while we have an ear for the story
and an eye on the strips of marinated meat, Bihari style,
skewered on bamboo sticks turning over a charcoal grill in
neat divisions of beef, mutton, chicken and kheeri (udders),
the speciality of the house. The marinade is a mystery but
not the give-away taste of the green papaya. Parathas are
rolled out with incredible dexterity, tossed between the
hands and cooked on a sizzling griddle. We are ready for
another as we watch the kathi unskewered on to the
paratha dressed with sliced onions, green chillies and a
squeeze of lime juice, rolled, packed in paper and presented
pronto!

Between interviews and recipe hunts, we stopped off at
one of the new fast food joints that pop up every month, for
a cold coffee and wedges of the 'Big Pizza Pie' which really
hits us in the eye like in Dean Martin's song. So many eager
cooks are now experimenting with their own brand of pizza.
Even the rotiwala brings pizza bases to the doorstep along
with the daily bread in his basket.

Fresh cheeses—Gouda, Edam and Brie—after the
European style are now made in farm houses in Bangalore,
Pune and Delhi.

Mushrooms in packets are prominent in the markets. An enterprising young lady takes orders for bakes. Her forte and our choice is her pizza with a topping of smoked Bandel cheese on Goa sausages to which have been added all the spices of the Orient! These are not substitutes but happy innovations. Pizza has become a household word and the Italian herbs have taken root in Calcutta to give the Neapolitan flavour.

The younger generation in Calcutta emulate international food habits. They snack off hamburgers and hot dogs ready-made and cellophane wrapped. The filling can be red meat, chicken, fish, cheese, vegetables or just potatoes and is loaded with chilli, garam masala and pepper instead of horse radish relish. The tomato ketchup is the common denominator.

It is indeed fitting that we leave our readers with a sweet taste in their mouths of misti doi, sandesh and rosogolla. We recall sometime in the nineteenth century, somewhere in Calcutta, someone mixed sugar before setting the traditional pot of unflavoured pristine doi. Like his other foibles and fancies, this innovation has been attributed to the refined palate of the Bengali babu.

Calcutta's undying and undenied contribution to the rest of the country are its Bengali sweet shops and the Bangla paan (a variety of the *Piper betle* leaf). The city may not qualify for a place in the sun but it does stake a claim in the Guiness Book of Records for the record breaking number of mishtir dokan selling Bengali sweets. These were the establishments that took to making mishti doi, commercially, which has become the standard dessert for a family meal or entertaining at home. Mishti doi is the most satisfying end to a good Bengali lunch or a Western meal for that matter. It is best served in the clay pot in which it was set either in its naked terracotta beauty or wrapped in a white napkin with just the rim peeping out of the folds.

The test of a good pot of doi is in its setting. Grandmothers used to warm the milk and their gauge was touch not the thermometer. Sugar was added and a teaspoon or so of a starter of leftover doi stirred in and put under a teacosy in a warm place in the kitchen to set undisturbed. Setting time was between six to twelve hours depending on the season.

Doi from shops comes in terracotta handis, though nowadays paper and plastic containers are used as well and it is whispered that china grass (agar agar) is sometimes used for an instant product.

We listened with attention to an expert's scientific treatise on doi. Naren Das of the K. C. Das family explained how the Lactobacillus Bulgaria and Streptococcus bacteria which have grown in yesterday's doi are mixed into the fresh milk boiled down to half its volume and then cooled to forty degrees centigrade. Sugar is added and the mixture is kept at a constant temperature until it sets.

Before the discovery of miracle drugs, Calcutta's allopathic physicians, among them Dr B. C. Roy, Col. Denham White and Sir Nilratan Sircar, prescribed misti doi for their patients with typhoid because the preparation is unadulteratable and has plenty of the vitamin Bs. Perhaps misti doi was initiated on its travels across the country by Dr B. C. Roy, West Bengal's first Chief Minister who used to send handifuls to the capital for his friend, Pandit Jawaharlal Nehru, India's first Prime Minister.

Bhapa doi is a Calcutta steamed pudding. Natural yoghurt, thickened milk and sugar blended together with a pinch of powdered or the essence of green cardamoms steamed and refrigerated can be cut in squares and garnished with raisins. Tinned sweetened condensed milk saves time and does wonders for the final product.

Jalajog, an enterprising chain of sweet shops of the 1930s, raised a delicious hybrid and called upon the Nobel Laureate, Tagore, to give their creation a very special name. He invented the name 'Payodhi' from the Bengali word payesh and the Sanskrit word dadhi (yoghurt). Jalajog set the trend and it has become the fashion for Calcutta's mishti doi to blush in varying shades of pink and therefore it is often also called lal doi (lal means red).

Identified by the rosogolla accent, the sweet-toothed Bengali's other obsession is sandesh, the acme of Bengali sweets. The sandesh saga is attributed by some to a thrifty milkman with a culinary flare who turned his curdled milk into a delightful confection cooked with gur and later sugar. He may have been influenced by the Portuguese fondness for cottage cheese introduced into Bengal in the sixteenth century, though we read about the sandesh in Bengali medieval literature, in the Chaitanya lyrics and in Kirtibas' *Ramayana* but its exact ingredients remain elusive.

The haute couture of the sandesh began with its appearance in Calcutta. The homely chhanar sandesh made from curds sweetened, rolled into a ball or flattened to a disc was cast in small wooden and stone carved moulds and patted out as custard apples, mangoes, conch shells and roses. Colour was added as demands became more daring. A model of Calcutta's Gothic High Court in pure sandesh presented to the bride by her barrister bridegroom as a wedding present was the talk of the town for a week!

Sandesh certainly continued to live it up, falling in line with political events in the city. Calcuttans celebrated Independence Day with a tri-coloured Jai Hind sandesh and the arrival of the erstwhile Soviet leader, Marshall Bulganin, was hailed with a creamy dreamy chhanar payesh christened Bulganiner Bishmoy (Bulganin's Wonder). The realm of satvic foods has been usurped by tamasic simulations in sandesh of a halved hard boiled egg, a slice of toast, chocolate cake, crumbed chop and a biscuit.

The rosogolla, that touch of genius, swims in bowls of syrup. The Belgians call the rosogolla, 'snowball' and so it was when Nobin Chandra, illustrious father of K. C. Das, invented it in 1868. Since then, it has become the test for those who claim culinary skills. To the milk-white rosogolla flavours and colours have also been added and we have kamala bhog (orange) and the pink kumkum. The historic swaraj bhog (freedom feast) was the breakfast food of freedom fighters travelling from Calcutta to Contai.

Fried variations on a chhana theme are the round

brown pantua, the bolster-shaped langcha, the square chitrakoot and the coiled chhanar jilepi. Lord Canning's Lady's preference for pantua coated with sugar enjoys proletariat patronage in independent India as Lady Kenny.

And so we end our tale amid the sizzling griddles on pavement bucket fires and the whistle of the pressure cooker in the highrises above as Calcutta's varied cooking pots bubble and boil. Wonderfully varied aromas, innumerable tempering of spices, flavourings and textures have mingled together over the centuries. Tastes, ways of eating, the enjoyment of a pot pourri of foods from the ordinary, meagre meal of sattu to the extraordinary banquets of yore have left a rich culinary legacy. Last, but not least, the most important ingredient which has made this unique city of ours is the Calcuttan's characteristic open-heartedness.

The major American contribution to Calcutta's table is tomato ketchup which is now added to the most conservative of dishes including kumror chhokka. And the Calcutta cook has turned out his version of 'all-American' dishes.

'Boston' Baked Beans

Serves 4

Ingredients:
- 250 gms white haricot beans or red beans (rajma)
- 50 gms dry molasses (gur)
- 1 tsp mustard
- 1 whole onion stuck with 2 cloves
- 3 tbsp tomato ketchup
- 1 tsp dry red chilli powder
- salt to taste

Method:
Soak the white haricot or red beans (rajma) overnight. Pressure cook the beans for 20 minutes and reserve the liquid. In a deep, covered oven-proof dish place the dry molasses (gur), mustard, onion stuck with cloves, tomato ketchup and dry red chilli powder. Put in the beans and add the liquid in which it was boiled to cover. Add salt to taste. Cook in a pre-heated moderate oven (350° F, 180° C) for 45 minutes. Uncover and cook for another 10 minutes until there is a crust on top of the beans.

A fat rasher of bacon is a good addition to this dish.

» Magnolia's served Chili Con Carne during the War.

Chili Con Carne

Serves 4

Ingredients:
- **500 gms beef or mutton (finely minced)**
- **2 medium onions (finely minced)**
- **5 cloves garlic (finely minced)**
- **500 gms tomatoes (finely minced)**
- **a handful (finely minced) mixed herbs including parsley, oregano and chives**
- **100 gms haricot beans or red beans (rajma)**
- **1 tsp chilli powder (roasted)**
- **1 tsp cumin powder (roasted)**
- **4 tbsp oil**
- **2 cups water**
- **2 tbsp tomato ketchup**
- **1 onion (cut in rings)**
- **salt to taste**
- **pepper to taste**

Method:
Soak the haricot or red beans (rajma) overnight, and pressure cook them for 20 minutes. Heat the oil in a pan and brown the onion and garlic. Add the tomatoes and cook until they are soft. Add the meat and brown. Add the water and tomato ketchup. Cook covered until the meat is almost done and the liquid has reduced to make a thick sauce. Add the beans, herbs and salt and pepper to taste. Cook until thick. Sprinkle with the powdered chilli and cumin and the onion cut in thin rings before serving.

Pia's Pizza

Serves 10

Ingredients:

For pizza base
- 30 gms yeast dissolved in ¼ cup hand hot water (100° F, 36° C) with ½ tsp sugar
- 2 cups flour
- 2 eggs
- 1 tbsp oil

For topping
- 1½ cups grated Kalimpong or any other cheddar cheese
- ½ cup chopped, smoked and white Bandel cheese
- 4 tbsp tomato ketchup
- 1 tsp salt
- 1 tsp chilli sauce
- 1 tbsp sugar
- 300 gms sliced tomatoes
- 500 gms pork sausages
- ½ tsp oregano or ajwain
- ½ cup sliced gherkins
- 1 tin sardines

Method:

For pizza base:
Measure the flour into a bowl, make a well in the centre and break the eggs into it and add the oil. Add the yeast when it is frothy and gradually mix in the flour from the sides of the bowl to the centre. Mix well and knead to a soft and pliable, but not sticky dough. Form into a ball and leave to rise in a large greased plastic bag for 1 hour or until the dough has doubled its bulk. Punch down dough and leave to prove (rise) for another half hour. Divide the dough in two and roll out each half into an 8-inch circle, one-fourth-inch thick. Pat a little oil on to the surface and top with recipe topping.

For topping:

Blend together the Kalimpong or any cheddar cheese and
the Bandel cheese. Reserve one-third for sprinkling on top.
Into the two-third cheese mixture mix in the tomato
ketchup, salt, chilli sauce and sugar. Spread this on the
pizza base. Arrange the sliced tomatoes over it. Spread the
meat from the pork sausages (we buy ours at Great Eastern
Pork Products in the New Market), and discard the skin.
Sprinkle with oregano or ajwain. Arrange sliced gherkins
and tinned sardines all around.

Cover with the remaining one-third cheese. Bake in a
pre-heated (425° F, 300° C) oven for 15 minutes and further
30 minutes at 350° F, 180° C.

Serve hot. Leave a rim around the edge of the pizza
when you spread the mixtures.

Variations:

- Leave out the sausage meat. Cook plain or add
  sliced mushrooms, cooked corn kernel, peas or any
  mixture of vegetables. Add sliced hard-boiled eggs,
  cooked shrimps or tinned fish. Do not use
  uncooked fish as it emits too much liquid while
  cooking.

Calcutta Prawn Cocktail

Serves 6

Ingredients:

- **500 gms shelled prawn tails or peeled shrimps**
- **a rind of lime or lemon**
- **a few peppercorns**
- **salt to taste**
- **1 cup canned tomato juice or canned undiluted tomato
  soup**
- **1 tbsp very finely minced spring onions**
- **2 tbsp tomato ketchup**

- **2 tbsp mayonnaise (see pp 213–214 or below)**
- **1 tsp freshly ground black pepper**
- **2 cups double cream**
- **salt to taste**
- **6–8 leaves of crisp lettuce**
- **Tabasco sauce**

Method:

Boil the shelled prawn tails if you are feeling extravagant, or the peeled shrimps which will do as well. Always add a rind of lime or lemon, a few peppercorns and salt to taste when boiling fish or shellfish.

Mix together the tomato juice or tomato soup, spring onions, tomato ketchup, mayonnaise, and black pepper. Mix in the shellfish. Add the double cream and salt to taste. Adjust the taste of the cocktail, adding more ketchup or mayonnaise if required. Refrigerate for several hours.

To serve, cut the lettuce leaves into thin strips.

Place at the bottom of 6 large cocktail or old-fashioned ice-cream glasses. Mix the cocktail well. Add a few drops of Tabasco sauce and spoon into cool glasses.

» We make our own style of Vinegar Chilli Sauce as Tabasco is not on the market.

Soak a handful of ripe, not dry, red chillies in white vinegar for a week. Drain and reserve the vinegar. Put the chillies in a blender and blend for 2 minutes or until they are quite liquid. Pour back into the reserved vinegar and bottle. This makes an excellent dressing for soups, salads and sauces.

» To make mayonnaise in a hurry, blend 1 egg with ½ teaspoon salt, 1 teaspoon white pepper, 1 teaspoon dry mustard, ½ teaspoon sugar, and ½ teaspoon chilli powder in a blender for 30 seconds. Add 1 cup oil in 6 blends, switching off the machine every 20 seconds. Add 2 tablespoons of vinegar to the thick emulsion.

» The American pie is one of the handiest desserts to make. A number of pie shells can be baked and stored and filled as and when required. Pureed green mangoes make a refreshing and unusual filling.

Green Mango Pie

Serves 8

Ingredients:

For pie shell
- **250 gms flour**
- **100 gms cold butter**
- **3 tbsp ice cold water**

For Mango filling
- **4 green mangoes (peeled, cut, seeded and sliced)**
- **½ cup sugar**
- **2 tbsp water**
- **1 tsp ginger (very finely sliced)**
- **50 gms raisins**

For the topping
- **200 gms flour**
- **100 gms powdered sugar**
- **75 gms butter**

For assembling
- **2 tbsp powdered sugar**

Method:

For a 9-inch pie shell

Sieve the flour. Cut into it the cold butter and mix with fingertips till the mixture resembles breadcrumbs. Mix the ice cold water and form the mixture into a stiff dough. A little more water may be required, but on no account must the dough be soggy. Knead into a ball and leave for an hour. Roll into a circle to fit a 9-inch pie plate, the pastry may overhang the rim. Trim the edges and push back with the tines of a fork. Prick the pastry all over with a fork. Leave in the refrigerator while you heat your oven to 375°F, 200°C. Bake the pie shell for 15 minutes or until it is golden and the pastry comes away from the edges of the pie plate.

Green Mango filling:

Boil the mangoes with the sugar and water. If the mangoes are very tart add ¼ teaspoon salt. Add the ginger, and put the mixture in the blender for 30 seconds. Add the raisins.

Make the topping:

Mix the flour with the powdered sugar and butter to resemble breadcrumbs.

To assemble:

Fill the pie shell with the green mango filling and sprinkle the powdered sugar over it and then sprinkle the flour/sugar mixture. Bake in a pre-heated 375°F, 200°C oven for 15 minutes or until the top is golden and crisp. Serve with whipped sweetened yoghurt or cream.

The basic tart is useful for sweet or savoury fillings.

» Brain Cutlets and Liver Glacé were two brunch favourites when brunch was a favourite way of entertaining in the swinging Sixties. A well-made Bloody Mary often added fire to the food.

Brain Cutlets

Makes 8 cutlets

Ingredients:
- **4 sheep's brains**
- **1 whole onion**
- **1-inch piece ginger**
- **1 bay leaf**
- **10 peppercorns**

For marinade
- **2 tbsp onion-ginger-garlic paste made with double the quantity of onion to ginger and garlic**

- **1 beaten egg**
- **browned breadcrumbs**
- **4 tbsp oil**
- **fried parsley**

Method:
Clean the sheep's brains and remove the thin membrane covering them. Boil them in salted water with the onion, ginger, bay leaf and peppercorns.

Drain, slice in half lengthwise and marinate for an hour in the onion, ginger and garlic paste. Dip the cutlets in the beaten egg and roll them lightly in browned breadcrumbs. Heat the oil in a frying pan and fry the cutlets over medium heat till they are golden. Serve at once, garnished with fried parsley.

» It is now possible to get a variety of fresh herbs in Calcutta and markets stock vegetables and fruit from other parts of the country. It is possible to have strawberry shortcake and asparagus rolls for tea. The flat leafed parsley is available round the year.

Asparagus Rolls

Makes 12 rolls

Ingredients:
* **12 asparagus spears (boiled or tinned)**
* **12 slices from a loaf of fresh sandwich bread**
* **12 pieces grease proof paper**

Method:
Drain the asparagus spears. Trim the crusts from the slices of bread. Cut the pieces of grease proof paper to fit the slices of bread. Butter each slice of bread well. On each piece of bread put 1 spear of asparagus. Place it on one side and place the bread buttered side up on grease proof paper. Roll the bread in the paper, and place on a plate.

Liver Glace

Serves 4

Ingredients:
* **250 gms liver**
* **3–4 onions (sliced)**
* **2 tbsp oil**
* **1 tsp sugar**
* **1 tbsp Worcestershire sauce**
* **salt to taste**

Method:
Clean the liver and slice thinly at an angle into 2-inch by 4-inch pieces. Coat the liver slices lightly with salt, pepper and Worcestershire sauce. Heat the oil in a frying pan and fry the onions until they just turn colour. Add the liver and fry for 4-5 minutes. Add the sugar and the Worcestershire sauce. Serve immediately with grilled tomatoes and fingers chips.

» There was a time when tinned pâté de foie gras was available at a price in Calcutta, and often appeared on menu cards of grand banquets as an hors d'oeuvres. The closing of Great Eastern Stores and later the resourceful Lagandeo's shop, put paid to the pâté. Some of us have improvised very good pâté de maison. Minakshie's effort is very worthwhile. In fact she specializes in pâtés and has concocted quite a few.

Liver Pâté

Makes 2 cups pâté

Ingredients:
- **16 large chicken livers (cleaned and halved)**
- **½ onion (finely sliced)**
- **6–8 cloves garlic (finely sliced)**
- **4 tbsp butter**
- **1 cup cream**
- **salt to taste**
- **finely ground black pepper**
- **1 tsp ground allspice (kebab chini)**
- **4 tbsp brandy**

Method:
Heat the butter and fry the onion, garlic and the chicken

livers until the livers are just done. They should not harden.
Take off the fire and grind or blend in a blender to a fine
paste Blend in the cream, salt, black pepper, and allspice
(kebab chini). Add the brandy and mix well.

Butter two medium-sized bowls and pour the mixture
into them. Leave overnight to set in refrigerator.

To unmould, wrap the outside of the bowls in a warm
dish cloth and turn out on a plate. Serve with toasted bread
or salted biscuits.

Shrimp Pâté

Makes 1½ cups

Ingredients:
- 250 gms cleaned shrimps
- ½ chopped onion
- 1-inch piece ginger (chopped)
- 4 cloves garlic (chopped)
- a rind of lemon (chopped)
- 3–4 tbsp mayonnaise (see pp. 213–214 or 358–359)
- 1 tbsp strong mustard
- 4 tbsp double cream
- 4–6 tbsp butter (melted)
- 1 tsp garlic paste
- freshly ground black pepper
- 2 tsp finely chopped chives
- chilli vinegar
- cucumber strings

Method:
Boil the cleaned shrimps in a pan with the onion, ginger,
garlic and rind of lemon. Drain and chop the shrimps
coarsely, reserving a few for later addition. To the chopped
shrimps, add the mayonnaise, strong mustard, double
cream, butter, garlic paste, black pepper, and chives. Mix
well with a wooden spoon, taste for salt and add more if
required. Add a few drops chilli vinegar.

Arrange the reserved shrimps at the bottom of the greased mould and turn the pâté into it. Unmould on to a plate and surround with cucumber strings.

Serve chilled with thin slices of toasted French bread or plain brown bread and butter.

Cheese Paté

Makes 1 cup

Ingredients:
- **100 gms Cheddar cheese**
- **100 gms processed cheese**
- **1 tbsp finely chopped chives**
- **8 cloves garlic**
- **1 tsp freshly ground black pepper**
- **4 tbsp double cream**
- **2 tbsp mayonnaise**
- **1 tbsp strong mustard**

Method:
Blend the Cheddar cheese, processed cheese, chives, garlic, black pepper, double cream, mayonnaise and strong mustard. Proceed as in previous recipes for pâté.

The basic pâté of the two cheeses and the cream can be dressed with finely chopped capsicum or pickled onions or gherkins.

With the appearance of Western herbs in the market, a handful of very finely chopped herbs makes a refreshing addition.

» The great demand for tomato ketchup led to home-bottling in a big way, and in season when the tomato prices are down, ladies get busy in the kitchen with mounds of tomatoes and rows of bottles. They have now learnt to use preservatives to give family recipes longer life.

Tomato Sauce

Makes 1¼ litres of sauce

Ingredients:
- **5 kg tomatoes**
- **1 pod garlic (peeled)**
- **3-inch piece ginger (sliced)**
- **10 dry red chillies**
- **2 green cardamoms**
- **4 cloves**
- **2-inch piece cinnamon**
- **2 crushed bay leaves**
- **10 peppercorns**
- **100 gms sugar**
- **3/4 cup vinegar**
- **salt to taste**
- **½ tsp sodium benzoate to preserve**
- **2 tsp water**

Method:
Cut up the tomatoes and pressure cook for 15 minutes until the fruit is pulpy. Put in a blender for 2 minutes and sieve through a nylon sieve getting as much pulp out as possible. Only the seeds and skin should be thrown away.

Tie the garlic and ginger up in a piece of muslin with the dry red chillies, green cardamoms, cloves, cinnamon, bay leaves and peppercorns. Cook with the sauce in a steel pan until it has reduced by one-third and is very thick.

Add the sugar, vinegar and salt to taste. Simmer for 15 minutes and remove from heat. Dissolve the sodium benzoate in the water and add to the sauce. Cool and bottle.

NB: Stir the sauce from time to time and scrape the sides during the last 10 minutes of cooking. Keep the heat low.

» Spiced vinegar is very useful for adding to salad dressings.

Spiced Vinegar

Ingredients:
- **2 blades mace (jaivitri)**
- **6 allspice berries (kebab chini)**
- **6 cloves**
- **1-inch stick cinnamom**
- **6 peppercorns**
- **1-inch piece ginger**
- **5 cups malt vinegar**

Method:
Tie up all the ingredients in a piece of muslin and bring to the boil in the malt vinegar. Take it off the fire and leave for 2 hours. Remove the spices and bottle.

» Khow swey or panthey khow swey to give it the correct name, is a perfect party dish especially when the guest list is mixed. The unobtrusive base of boiled noodles and bland chicken curry can be made pungent or mild according to the eater's taste from the choice of many garnishes which accompany it.

   This Burmese recipe was given to us by Mrs Beale. Visitors returning to the Andaman Islands nostalgically remember her late husband, Captain Beale, and his boats.

Panthey Khow Swey with Chicken - I

Noodles with Coconut Chicken Curry

Serves 8

Ingredients:
- **1 kg chicken**
- **milk and cream extracted from 1 coconut (see p. 66)**
- **2 medium onions (grated)**
- **1-inch piece ginger (grated)**
- **6 cloves garlic (grated)**
- **3 tbsp oil**
- **1 tsp turmeric**
- **1 tbsp gnappi (dried shrimp paste)**
- **salt to taste**
- **2 tbsp besan**

Garnishes
- **green coriander and spring onions (chopped together)**
- **chopped green chillies**
- **fried sliced onions**
- **fried sliced cloves of garlic**
- **grated hard boiled eggs**
- **crisp fried noodles broken up**
- **wedges of lemon**
- **a sauce made of gnappi and coarse chilli powder mixed with oil in which onions were fried**

Method:
Clean and boil the chicken in water to cover in a deep pan. Lift out of water, shred and make a stock of the bones. Add it to the water in which the chicken was boiled. Reserve the stock.

Heat the oil in a large pan and fry the grated spices with the turmeric and gnappi. (Gnappi may be substituted by any dried fish powder). Fry a little and add the chicken, the coconut milk stock and salt to taste. Allow the curry to cook for about 20 minutes on a slow fire before adding the gram flour (besan) to thicken. There should be a lot of soup in this dish. Serve with freshly boiled noodles and the garnishes.

» Another recipe for Khow Swey was given to us by the daughter-in-law of Mrs Parul Bose whose husband practiced law in Rangoon and lived there for many years.

Panthey Khow Swey - II

Noodles with Coconut Meat Curry

Serves 8

Ingredients:
- 1 kg boneless mutton or beef (cut into small pieces)
- 1 tsp coriander (roasted and ground)
- 1 tsp cumin (roasted and ground)
- 4 dry red chillies (roasted and ground)
- 1 tsp aniseed (roasted and ground)
- 1 tsp fenugreek (roasted and ground)
- 1 tsp powdered garam masala
- 2 medium onions (ground)
- 1-inch piece ginger (ground)
- 6 cloves garlic (ground)
- milk extracted from 1 coconut
- 4 tbsp oil
- 1 tsp turmeric
- 6 cups water
- ½ tsp powdered mace
- salt to taste

Garnishes
as in the previous recipe

Method:
Heat oil in a large pan and brown the meat. Lift it out and reserve. In the same oil in which you fried the meat, fry the

ground spices and the turmeric for 5 minutes. Add the meat and water and all but 1 teaspoon of the powdered spices. When the meat is cooked, add the coconut milk, mace and the reserved powdered spices. Add salt to taste, simmer for 5 minutes on a low fire and take it off the stove. Serve with freshly boiled noodles and the usual garnishes.

» Ghugni is a street food which has survived generations and still holds its own. We give two recipes, the first, we know by the ingredients, was probably cooked before the advent of the onion (see text Chapters I and II), and is therefore, completely vegetarian.

Ghugni - I

Savoury Chick Peas

Serves 6

Ingredients:
- 200 gms chick peas
- 1 tbsp thinly slivered ginger
- 2 tbsp fresh coconut (cubed)
- 1 tsp sugar
- 2 tbsp ghee
- 1 tbsp coarsely ground black pepper
- juice of 2 limes
- salt to taste

Method:
Soak the chick peas overnight. Drain and pressure cook with water to cover and with the addition of the ginger, fresh coconut, sugar and salt. Reduce pressure after 15 minutes. The peas should be soft but not mushy. Dry the liquid if the dish looks too watery. Heat the ghee and add the cooked

peas. Stir with a spoon, turning it over to mix well. Add the coarsely ground black pepper and cook for 5 minutes. Add the lime juice and mix thoroughly. Serve at room temperature.

» The ghugni which cooks on Calcutta's pavements for the office-goer's tiffin is like a chick pea curry and is often eaten with puris.

Ghugni - II

Chick Pea Curry

Serves 6

Ingredients:
- **200 gms chick peas**
- **2 tbsp mustard oil**
- **2 tbsp onion-ginger-garlic paste**
- **1 tsp chilli powder**
- **½ tsp turmeric**
- **2 green chillies**
- **roasted cumin powder**
- **chilli powder or tamarind sauce (see p. 372)**
- **salt to taste**

Method:
Soak and cook the chick peas as above. In the mustard oil fry the onion-ginger-garlic paste, chilli powder and turmeric for 5 minutes. Add the peas and green chillies and salt to taste. Cook for 5–7 minutes and take off the fire. To serve, sprinkle with roasted cumin and chilli powder or tamarind sauce.

You may also garnish the ghugni with tomatoes, chopped onions and chopped green coriander.

Both versions of ghugni may have small cubes of boiled potatoes added to them in the last 5 minutes of cooking.

Tamarind Sauce

Ingredients:
- 1 tbsp thick tamarind paste
- 1 cup water
- 2 tsp sugar or molasses
- 1 tsp roasted cumin
- red chilli powder
- a pinch of black rock salt
- salt to taste

Method:
Mix the thick tamarind paste with the water, sugar or molasses, cumin, red chilli powder, black rock salt, and salt to taste. Bring to the boil slowly in a small saucepan and cook until the sauce is a little thick and syrupy. The quantity of sweetening depends on taste.

This sauce is also good with dhoklas.

For alur chaat, omit the sugar and add pepper and pour on thickly sliced boiled potatoes.

» Nizam's kathi kebabs made of strips of skewered meat, are called Bihari Kebabs in some parts of the world and considered a delicacy.

Bihari Kebabs

Serves 3–4

Ingredients:
- 500 gms undercut of beef

For marinade
- 2 onions (ground)

- **5 cloves garlic (ground)**
- **2-inch piece ginger (ground)**
- **2-inch piece raw papaya (ground)**
- **2-inch piece cinnamon (powdered)**
- **2 green cardamoms (powdered)**
- **2 black cardamoms (powdered)**
- **6 peppercorns (powdered)**
- **6 allspice berries (kebab chini) (powdered)**
- **2 tbsp oil**
- **salt to taste**

Method:

Marinade:

Cut the undercut of beef in 1 x 3-inch strips. Mix the ground and powdered condiments and add the oil and salt to taste. Marinate the meat in this mixture for 6 hours.

Thread the pieces of meat through a skewer and pack them together. One long skewer should hold 5 strips of meat. Turn over glowing coals for 10–15 minutes, basting once to twice with oil. Do not overcook as the meat is very tender and will fall off the skewer. Slide the kebabs off the skewer on to a plate and serve with wedges of lime, onion rings and chopped green chillies.

» Calcutta's cooking pots would not be filled without a mention of sandesh and rosogolla. The two recipes we bring you are from the collection of Renuka Devi Choudharani.

Sandesh
_____

Makes 12–15 sandesh

Ingredients:
- **250 gms cottage cheese (chhana)**

- **2 tbsp water**
- **125 gms sugar**

Method:

Knead the cottage cheese (chhana) into a soft granular dough.

Put the water in a wok and place over moderate heat. Add the sugar and melt slowly. This is important as dissolving the sugar over high heat crystallizes it. Boil until syrup thickens, and add the cottage cheese gently, folding it in with a wooden spoon and stir until it begins to dry.

Remove wok, add the flavouring of your choice and continue pressing the now cooked sandesh against the side of the karai until it is cool. Shape the sandesh with your hands and press into clay or wooden moulds greased with ghee. Unmould and place on plate.

Rosogolla

Makes 12–15 rosogollas

Ingredients:

- **500 gms sugar**
- **2 cups water**
- **250 gms cottage cheese (chhana)**

Method:

Bring the sugar to the boil in the water in a pressure cooker. Stir the sugar until it dissolves and then let the syrup boil.

Strain the syrup. Put back in the pressure cooker. Knead the cottage cheese (chhana) into a soft dough and shape into balls of desired size. Remember that the cottage cheese will expand with cooking.

Drop carefully into the boiling syrup. Place lid on cooker and cook under pressure for 5–6 minutes. For light sponge rosogolla remove pressure cooker from heat after 5 minutes and cool the cooker with the lid on under running water. This ensures roundness. When the cooker is cool, remove lid and gently remove rosogolla. Serve hot and fresh.

Table of Foods

VEGETABLES

thor muri ghonto 55
mocha paturi 81
neem begoon 12
shada tarkari 16
palang saag, dhoney pata aur methisaag bhaja 50
pata bhaja 52
suktoni or sukto 45
lal saager sukto 46
sambole 23
palang chhanar kofta 74
sheem aur dhoney saag 58
kamala phulkopi 59
beet hingi 60
khagina 61
gota siddho 20
baigan bharta 141
boiled peas with mint 221
kashmiri alu dom 64
alur dom 65
khosha charchari 47
enchorer korma 141
chhanar chop 241
mochar chop 242
sarson saag 341

EGG & CHEESE

FISH & CRUSTACEANS

BREADS & PIZZAS

SOUPS AND SAUCES

RICE, RICE DISHES & CEREALS

Glossary

Abbreviations used for other languages:

S Sanskrit   P Persian   G Gujarati   C Chinese
R Rajasthani T Tibetan   Ta Tamil   Sin Sindhi
U Urdu

ENGLISH	HINDI	BENGALI/OTHER LANGUAGES
MILK PRODUCTS		
clarified butter	ghee	ghee
cottage cheese, casien,	panir	chhana, T chhurpi
dehydrated milk	khoa	khoa
milk	dudh	dudh
thickened milk	kheer	kheer
yoghurt drink	lassi	ghole
yoghurt	dahi	doi
CEREALS		
cooked rice	chawal	bhaat
cooked rice soaked overnight in water	—	panta bhaat
dried, beaten rice	chura	chirey
Indian corn flour	makai atta	—
millet	bajra	bajra

parboiled rice	ushna chawal	siddha chaal
popped rice coated with molasses	mudki	mudki
puffed rice	moori	moori
semolina	sooji	sooji
sun-dried paddy	aatap chawal	aatap chaal
vermicelli	sewai	sewai
wheat flour	maida	moida
whole meal flour	atta	atta

LENTILS AND PULSES : GENERIC INDIAN NAME : DAL

Dals used in the recipes are whole, unwashed (H sabut) and split, washed (H dhuli).

aconite beans, dew gram	moth	R moth
chick peas	kabuli chana	kabuli chhola
dried red beans	rajma	—
glass noodles	faluda	T phing
gram flour	besan	besan
poppadum	papad	papər
red gram	toor, toovar	arhar
roasted finely ground gram/barley flour	sattu, satua	chhatu
split dried Bengal gram	kala chana	chhola
split dried lentil paste fried in strips	ganthia	G ganthia
sun-dried cooked lentil paste	—	G khandvi
sun-dried lentil paste in small cones	bori	bori
whole or split dried red lentil	masoor	masoor
whole/split dried moong beans	moong	moong
whole/split dried peas	matar	matar
whole/split dried black lentil	urad	kalai, biuli

VEGETABLES

—	kundri	—
astringent dried green berry	ker	R keria

banana flower	kele ka phool	mocha
bitter gourd	karela	korela, ucchhey
bitter margosa leaves	neem patti	neem pata
bottle gourd	lauki	lau
broad bean	seem	sheem
cabbage	bund gobi	bandha kopi
carrot	gajar	gajar
cauliflower	gobi	phulkopi
Citrullus cucurnitaceae	tinda	tinda
cluster beans	gawarphali	—
colocasia	arbi, ghuiyan	kochu
cucumber	kheera	shasha
dried bean (Rajasthan)	—	R sangar
dried lotus stem	kamal gatta	R bhey
elephant apple	—	chalta
elephant yam	ole	ole
green banana, plantain	kacha kela	kanch kala
green jackfruit	kacha kathal	enchor
green peas	hara matar	matarshuti
horse radish	mooli	moolo
Indian fig	anjeer	dumur
leaf of the *Piper betle*	paan	paan
leafy vegetables	saag	saag
leaves of the wax gourd	parval saag	palta pata
mustard greens	sarso ki saag	sorshey saag
onion	piaz	piaj
peels, scrapings	chhilke	khosha
potato	alu	alu
red pumpkin	kaddu	kumro
red spinach	lal saag	lal saag
ridged gourd	torai	jhingey
small dried fruit (Rajasthan)	—	R fogla
spinach	palak	palang saag
spring onion shoots	piaz patti	piaj koli
sweet potato	shakarkand	ranga alu
turnip	salgam	salgam
vegetables	sabzi	sabji, tarkari
water spinach/fern	katha saag	kalmi saag
wax gourd	parval	potol
white pith of banana stem	kele-ka-tana	thor

yam	zimikhand —	

FRUIT & NUTS

almond	badam	badam
banana	kela	kala
cape gooseberry	rasbari	tepari
Carissa caranda	karonda	karamcha
fruit	phal	phal
Garcina indica Substitute: khum khum	—	kodampoli (Kerala)
guava	amrood	piara
hog plum	—	amra
Indian plum	ber	topa kool, narkeley kool
Indian plum (Eugenia jambolana)	kala jamun	kalo jaam
jackfruit	kathal	kanthal
lemon	nimbu	gandharaj lebu
lime	nimbu	pati lebu
mango	aam	aam
orange	santra	kamala lebu
papaya	papita	pepey
peanut	mungphali	chine badam
pineapple	ananas	anaras
pistachio	pista	pesta
raisin, sultana	kismis, munaqqa	kishmish
sour citrus	jamila	jamila
tamarind	imli	tentul
unripe/green mango	keri, kacha aam	kancha aam
water chestnut	singara	pani phal

FISH AND CRUSTACEANS

beckti, beckty, becktee, cock-up (Substitute: any flaky white fish)	bhetki machchi	bhetki
carp	rohu, mirgel, katla	rui, mrigel, katla
cat fish	magur, singhi, tangra	magur, shinghi, tangra
climbing perch	—	koi

crab	kakkra	kankra
fish	machchi	maachh
fresh water cray fish	burra jhinga,	golda chingri
(Substitute: small lobster)	gorara	
hilsa	hilsa machchi	ilish, G palla
(Substitute: shad)		Ta oolum
Indian butter fish	pupta	pabda
Indian salmon	ravas	gurjali
mango fish	topsi	topshey
mandarin fish	—	—
(Substitute: red snapper, sea bhetki, salmon, mullet)		
mullet	boi	parshey
murrel	shole	shole
pomfret	pomfret	pomfret chanda maachh
prawns	jhinga	chingri
roe	machchi ka anda	maachher dim, Sin ani
seer	surmai	nameen
(Substitute: Indian mackerel)		
shrimps	jhinga	kucho chingri
turtle	kachhua	ketho
tiger prawns	—	bagda chingri
white bait	morolla	morolla

MEAT AND POULTRY

beef	gai ka gosht	gorur mangsho
brain	magaz	magoj
country chicken	chota murghi	chhoto murghi
duck	batak	hansh
egg	anda	dim
fattened castrated goat	khashi	khashi
goat	bakri	pantha
large fowl	murgh	murghi
leg of mutton	raan	raan
meat	gosht	mangsho
mince	keema	keema
mutton	bheri	bherar mangsho
mutton shin bone and hooves	paya, tangri	paya, tangri

pork	suwar ka gosht	suwarer mangho
rib chop	chaap	chaap
shin bone	soorwa ka haddi	souper haar

BREADS

bread	roti	roti
fried wheat bread rolled out with lentils flavoured with asafoetida	—	radhaballabi
fried wheat pastry with a seasoned filling	kachori	kochuri
gram flour bread	besan roti	—
Indian corn flour bread	makai ki roti	—
layered crispy paratha	lachcha paratha	Daccai paratha
layered paratha with cloves	laong paratha	lobongo paratha
leavened fried bread	bhatura	—
leavened handmade bread	naan	—
light, unleavened handmade wholemeal flour bread griddled on a hot plate	chapatti	chapatti
loaf of bread	pau roti	pau roti
puffed fried flour bread	luchi	luchi
paratha coated in beaten egg sometimes stuffed with minced meat	Moghlai paratha	Moghlai paratha
potato filled paratha	alu ka paratha	alur paratha
puffed fried wholemeal bread	puri	puri
small thin chapatti	phulka	phulka
thick crispy bread grilled in clarified butter	paratha	paratha

SPICES AND SEASONING

ajinomoto, monosodium glutanate	—	chiney noon
allspice	kebab chini	kebab chini
aniseed	saunf	mauri
asafoetida	hing	hing
bay leaf	tej patta	tej pata
black caraway	shah jeera	shah jeera
black cardamom	bara elaichi	boro elach

black pepper	kala mirch,	gol marich
carom seeds	ajwain	jowan, randhuni
chilli, green	hara mirich	kancha lanka
chilli, red dried	sukha lal mirich	sukno lanka
chilli, tiny pungent	—	dhani lanka
curry leaves, sweet margosa	kari patta	kari pata Ta karvaypillai
cinnamon	dalchini	dalchini
cloves	laong	labongo
cloves, cinnamon & green cardamoms	—	garam masala
cloves, cinnamon, green cardamoms, black cardamoms & black peppercorns	garam masala	—
coriander leaves	dhania patta	dhoney pata
coriander seeds	sabut dhania	dhoney
cumin	sada jeera	sada jeera
dill greens	soya saag	sowa saag
dried ground ginger	sont	shoont
fenugreek greens	hari methi	methi saag
fenugreek seeds	methi dana	methi
five spice: aniseed, cumin, fenugreek, mustard & nigella	panch phoron	panch phoron
galingale	—	aam ada
garlic	lasoon	rasoon
ginger	adrak	ada
green cardamom	elaichi	chhoto elach
mace	javitri	jaitri
mint leaves	pudina patti	pudina pata
mustard seed	rai sarso	sorsey
nigella	kalonji	kala jeera
nutmeg	jaiphal	jaiphal
oregano	substitute: ajwain	substitute: jowan
poppy seeds	khus khus	posto
saffron	zaffran, kesar	jaffran
salt	namak	noon, laban
sesame seeds	til	til
spices	masale	mashla
turmeric	haldi	halud

UTENSILS & STIRRERS

cooking pot, deep, round bottomed	handi	handi
curved blade mounted on a wooden stand	—	bonti
griddle	tawa	tawa, P tasst
grinding stones	sil butta, lodhi sil lodha	sil nora
hand mixer for dals, wooden/metal	ghuntni, madani	ghuntni
knife	chakku	chhuri, P karad
ladle	hatha	hatha
pan, deep, round, rimmed & flat bottomed	dekchi	dekchi
pastry board & rolling pin	chakla belan	chakibelon
perforated flat spoon	jhanjri	jhanjri
pincers to turn breads on the griddle	chimta	chimtey
platter	thali	thala
skewer	seekh	sheek
small bowl	katori	bati
spatula	khurpi	khunti
spoon	chammach	chamoch, P qashaq
steamer for momos	—	T moktu
tongs to remove vessel from the fire	pakkar	sarashi
utensils	basan, bartan	bashan G patilla, lagan
wok	karai	kara, karai

INDIAN TERMS

achar H,B	vegetable or fruit pickle in oil or vinegar
adaab qaidas U	manners and mores
anna	old Indian coin, one-sixteenth of a rupee
Annada B	giver of food, another name for Goddess Durga
Annapurna B	another name for goddess Durga
babalog H	children
Baisakhi H	north Indian harvest festival in mid-April
bandar P	wharf

bania H,	trader
banian B	comprador to English trading agencies
baraha S	boar
Basmati	a particularly fragrant long-grained rice
bawarchee H	cook
bawarcheekhana H	kitchen
bazarer tholi B	shopping bag
begum U	title of respect for a Muslim lady
bhandar ghar B	store room, larder
bhien ghar	makeshift kitchen
bhog B	offering
bibikhana H	room for women only
Bijoya B	last day of Durga Puja in West Bengal
bikriwala H	rag-and-bone man
Bohag Bihu (Assamese)	spring festival in Assam
bottlekhana H	pantry
burra H	big, senior
Burra Din H	Christmas day
Burra Khana H	banquet
burruf H	ice
Charak Mela B	Hook-Swinging festival in mid-April
chhota H chhoto B	small
chiney B	chinese
chitties H	letters of reference
chop, chop	quickly, fast
churan H	digestive sweet and sour mixture of pomegranate seeds
cowrie H,B	small shell once used as currency in India
dalmot H,B	snack, mixture of fried lentils, pressed rice and peanuts
dastar khwan P	tablecloth
dastoors U	rules and regulations
dhabas H	open air motels on the highway, eating houses
dighis B	lakes
doob H	kind of fine grass
doolie H	meat safe
dumpoke H	bake

Durga Puja	Calcutta's biggest celebration, autumnal advent of Goddess Durga for four days
farṣan G	generic name for breakfast foods and snacks
firinghee P	old term for Europeans in Asia, later used derogatively
firman P	permission, order
gandhabaniks B	spice merchants
ginni B	housewife, chatelaine
gharries H,B	horse drawn carriages
ghat H,B	river landing stage
gosul wasoo U	bath and ablutions
gunas S	qualities
gur H,B	molasses
haat H,B	weekly village market
hajmi H	a digestive mixture
hakim P	doctor of the Unani system of medicine
handi H,B	metal, terracotta cooking pot
henshel B	hearth
hissab H	accounts
homa S	Hindu sacrificial fire
hundi H,B	indigenous banking system
huo buo C	literally, fire time, cooking time
huzoor (Arabic)	address of respect
Ids U	Muslim festivals of Id-ul-Fitr and Id-uz-Zoha
Ihudi B	a Jew
ishtu B	stew
kancha B	raw, unripe
kari Ta	curry
kathi ka kissa H	story of the kebab
kathi roll	ready to eat kebab rolled in paratha
kshatriya H,B	one of the castes, warrior
Kabuliwala H	man from Kabul
khansama U	house steward
khawasses P	ladies-in-waiting
kheeri H	udders
khitmatgar U	waiter
khubburdar U	beware
kingkhab P	brocade

koi hai H	literally, anybody there? summons for a retainer
laddus H	gram flour based round shaped sweets
lal H,B	red
langar H	community eating
lap chok C	red candle
lohar kalai B	lentils made of iron
loll shrob	red wine
lota kambal H	water vessel and blanket
makhmul U	velvet
malis H,B	gardeners
masalchi H	scullion
mela H,B	fair
mishtanna bhandar B	sweetmeat store
mishtir dokan B	Bengali sweetmeat shop
mistri H,B	technician
Mog B	tribe in the Chittagong Hill Tracts
Mohurram U	festival commemorating the Battle of Karbala
muluk H	place of origin, village
murabba P	fruit conserve
nagar H,B	town
namaz P	prayer
neel kuthi B	indigo plantation owner's residence
pak saf U	pure and clean
paka B	ripe.
palkies B	palanquin
paramanna S	first among foods, rice pudding
petha H	crystallized white pumpkin
pindo B	cereals, fruits and vegetables offered for ancestors
puja H,B	worship
rajasic S	rich foods, kingly
rakabdar U	master cook
Ramzan U	month of fasting before Id-ul-Fitr
ranna B	cooking
ranna bari B	cookhouse
ranna ghar B	room for cooking, kitchen
Sadamada S	hymn in the Rig Veda
saklee	saddle of mutton

samavalkaran Ta	cook
Saraswati Puja H,B	festival of the Goddess of Learning
satvic S	milk, fruit and vegetable foods, ascetic
shakkar H	unrefined sugar
sherbat P	rose flavoured or sweetened fruit drink
soma S	nectar of immortality in Vedic times
Sonar Bangla B	the Golden Land of Bengal
subah H	provincial courts
surma P	sulphide of antimony powder used for darkening the eyes, kohl
tabac	edible silver leaf
tamasha H	fun and games
thumri U	light classical music
topee H	hat lined with shola pith
torans G	flower garlands
wala H	suffix, belonging to or seller of
zenana P	women's quarters where only kinsmen were permitted to enter

Index